Mainstreaming
Microfinance

Mainstreaming Microfinance

How Lending to the Poor Began, Grew, and Came of Age in Bolivia

ELISABETH RHYNE

KUMARIAN
PRESS

Mainstreaming Microfinance: How Lending Began, Grew, and Came of Age in Bolivia

Published 2001 in the United States of America by Kumarian Press, Inc.,
1294 Blue Hills Avenue, Bloomfield, Connecticut 06002 USA.

*Design by Nicholas A. Kosar. Copyedited by Joan Weber LaFlamme.
Proofread by Beth Richards. Indexed by Robert Swanson.
The text of this book is set in Adobe Caslon 11/14.*

Printed in Canada on acid-free paper by
Transcontinental Printing and Graphics, Inc.
Text printed with vegetable oil-based ink.

∞ The paper used in this publication meets the minimum requirements
of the American National Standard for Information Sciences—Permanence of
Paper for Printed Library Materials, ANSI Z39.48–1984.

Library of Congress Cataloging-in-Publication Data
Mainstreaming microfinance : how lending to the poor began, grew, and came of age in
Bolivia / Elisabeth Rhyne.
    p.   cm.
Includes bibliographical references and index.
ISBN 1-56549-127-0 (cloth : alk. paper). — ISBN 1-56549-126-2
(pbk. : alk. paper)
    1. Microfinance—Bolivia.
HG178.33.B5 R49 2001
332.2—dc21   00–054453

10 09 08 07 06 05 04 03 02 01   10 9 8 7 6 5 4 3 2 1

First Printing 2001

CONTENTS

ILLUSTRATIONS

ACKNOWLEDGMENTS

THIS BOOK WOULD NOT HAVE HAPPENED without the support and active participation of Maria Otero and Martin Connell. Together, they conceived of the project, sought me out to write it, and took care of the associated business and logistical requirements. They both contributed to the final product in substance and spirit, and they provided steadfast moral support throughout. It has been wonderful to work with them. It was possible for me to write this book because of the generosity of the Tinker Foundation, and in particular the support of its representative Nancy Truitt.

This book came to life through the many interviews I carried out in Bolivia in March 1999 and March 2000 and a few interviews outside Bolivia at various times. Any quotation or paraphrase from individuals listed below that appears in this book without an endnote was taken from these personal interviews with the author. Some of the conversations stand out in my mind as especially enlightening, memorable or fun, including a storm-tossed talk in the dark with Prodem chairman Fernando Romero, a chance to talk with the truly impressive former president of Bolivia, Gonzalez Sánchez de Lozada, an impromptu lecture on rural development from Eduardo Bazoberry, and a wander through the past with Jeff Ashe.

The following people were kind enough to share their facts, memories, and opinions through interviews. They are listed with affiliations current at the time of the interviews. Gloria Almeyda, WOCCU; Fernando Anker A., Committee to Create Prodem FFP; Fernando Archondo, independent; Pedro Arriola Bonjour, Caja Los Andes; Jeffrey Ashe, Working Capital; Jorge Baldivieso, Mutual Guapay; Amparo Ballivian, Minister of Housing and Basic Services; Eduardo Bazoberry, Prodem; David Blanco Z., Banco Boliviano

Americano; Liliana Bottega Bortolini, Caja Los Andes; Roberto Casanovas Sainz, Idepro; Félix Choque, Prodem; Michael Chu, BancoSol and Acción International; Jorge Crespo, minister of Commerce and Industry; Manuel Cuevas, AFP Futuro; Juan Domingo Fabbri, BancoSol; Marisol Fernández Capriles, Ministry of Finance; Mary Elena Flores J., Cooperativa Jesús Nazareno; Matías Franco Viruez, Agrocapital; Juan Carlos García Zapata, Cooperativa Jesús Nazareno; Horst Grebe López, economist; Percy Jiménez Cabrera, vice-minister for Microenterprise, Ministry of Labor; John Hatch, Finca; Miguel Hoyos B., Funda-Pro; José Hurtado Duabyakosky, Fassil; Peter Kooi, independent consultant; Hermann Krützfeldt S., BancoSol; André La Faye B., Acceso; Magda Lahore Uriarte, Bolivia Central Bank; Hernado Larrazábal, CEDLA; Marcelo Mallea Castillo, Prodem; Reynaldo Marconi, Finrural; José Abel Martinez, FONDESIF; Elizabeth Naba, FIE; Claudia Ordoñez Cuellar, Fassil; Alfredo J. Otero Montero, Fassil; Pancho Otero, IPM; Eliana Otondo, COBOCE; John V. Owens, USAID/Bolivia; Francisco S. Pérez Tono, WOCCU; Gonzalo Puente I., EcoFuturo; María Elena Querejazu, Prodem Foundation; M. Pilar Ramírez, FIE; Mario Requena Pinto, vice-minister for Financial Affairs, Ministry of Finance; Robert Ridgely, Freedom from Hunger; Jorge Rodríguez Aguilo, NAFIBO; Fernando Romero, Prodem Foundation; Richard Rosenberg, CGAP; German Sánchez, BancoSol; Gonzalo Sánchez de Lozada, former president of Bolivia; Gabriella Santa Cruz, USAID/Bolivia; Gabriel Schor, IPC; Jean Steege, Acción International; Jorge L. Tipisman Nogales, Sartawi; Jacques Trigo Loubière, Superintendent of Banks and Financial Entities; Mario Usnayo, BancoSol; Mauricio Vasquez Guzman, Asociación Departemental de la Pequena Industria de La Paz; Victor Vego, Illimani Radio Taxi; Carmen Velasco, ProMujer; Monica Velasco, Idepro; Martina M. Wiedmaier, GTZ-FONDESIF; Justo Yépez Kakuda, Banco Económico; and Edgar Zurita, Fades.

Many of the things I learned in working on this book came from informal interviews with microentrepreneurs, particularly clients of the microfinance institutions, and from conversations while walking up hills or riding on bumpy roads with the loan officers who took me to see them. Unfortunately, I do not have the names of the microentrepreneurs I spoke with or the field staff who accompanied me, but I am most appreciative nonetheless. These two groups of people are the bedrock of the story.

I would like to thank the people who were kind enough to read and comment on parts of the book as it was being written. Charles Oberdorf and Megan Rhyne tried to show me how to give more life to the writing. Martin Connell, Hannes Manndorff, Maria Otero, Pancho Otero, and Nancy Truitt all offered important substantive advice. Most important, Marguerite Robinson, with the care and patience that characterize all her work, reviewed the first draft. She suggested ways to improve it that make the book both more balanced in its treatment of several issues and more useful for readers. I am also grateful to Kumarian Press for the enthusiasm it has shown for the book and its professional advice in preparing it.

Finally, several people were invaluable in helping with the process of gathering information. Foremost among these was Cheryl Frankiewicz, who organized the initial interviews and accompanied me on most of them. Cheryl gave much more than her skills as a translator and logistical organizer. Because of her knowledge about and commitment to microfinance, she was an excellent sounding board, turning the interviews into a joint process of discovery. Cecilia Campero played the same role, equally enthusiastically, on my brief update visit in 2000.

In Bolivia, Tania Landler and Marcela Montero helped cheerfully with logistics and appointments. In Mozambique, where I wrote the book, Isabel Machava made it possible for the writing to proceed by keeping my little one occupied while his mom was working.

WHY BOLIVIA?
WHY MICROFINANCE?

AS RECENTLY AS THE LATE 1980s, the banks and financial institutions of Bolivia regarded the country's majority low-income and indigenous people with disdain, if they thought of them at all. They offered them few services and discouraged them from entering their banking halls. A decade later, hundreds of thousands of these same people were the hotly contested customers of banks, financial institutions, and credit programs, all vying for shares of this new market. In cities and larger towns across the country virtually anyone with an ongoing economic activity could get a loan.

Through this dramatic transformation Bolivia has largely solved one of the most stubborn challenges in the field of development finance, a challenge that stumped development professionals for decades: access to finance, primarily credit, for people and activities at the bottom end of the economic spectrum. This new participation in finance by an enormous segment of Bolivia's population constitutes a structural change with potentially momentous consequences for Bolivia's society and economy. This book tells the story of how the transformation came about and examines why it matters.

At one level this story is worth telling simply as a fascinating development drama, peopled by a cast of activists, politicians, technicians, donors, businessmen, and the clients themselves. The characters make and break alliances as they feel their way toward increasingly ambitious goals. Each chapter in this book chronicles a new installment in an unfolding plot.

For the most part the story shows development at its best, with lessons about how the keepers of the development mandate—governments, donors, and do-gooders—can work effectively. It points out that, contrary to widespread belief, the fundamental contribution of development assistance has not been the transfer of funds but the creation of institutions.

The tale also illustrates the unpredictability of progress, its dependence on individual leaders, and its continued vulnerability to setbacks and shocks. Today, despite heroic past accomplishments, the Bolivian microfinance institutions are facing fearful challenges from competition, brought on in part by their very success. Some of the pioneers feel estranged from the future they themselves have created.

Before launching into the story itself, I would like to invite the reader to consider why the evolution of Bolivian microfinance merits his or her attention, speaking first to development-finance professionals and friends of microfinance.

Most readers who know something of microfinance already realize that Bolivia is one of the countries in which microfinance has advanced farthest within a short time, but they may not know what to look for in the Bolivian experience. That experience illuminates three of the most important topics within microfinance. In its struggle with these issues, Bolivia has been a stage dramatizing some of the central conflicts in the field.

The first and probably most obvious of these topics concerns how to create successful microfinance institutions and a vibrant microfinance industry. Bolivia not only has premier institutions, it has a sufficient number of competitors to make microfinance a genuine industry. How did this small, poor, landlocked country not widely known as an innovator provide an environment that allowed microfinance to blossom? Does Bolivia have hidden commonalities with other countries that also nurtured microfinance, like Bangladesh and Indonesia? Given that in most countries the majority of low-income clients still cannot get loans, it is important to sort out the accidents of time and place that made microfinance take off in Bolivia and to assess which factors can be replicated elsewhere.

Some of those factors, like cultural traditions and demographics, are part of a country's endowment, and Bolivia's endowment was exceptionally positive for microcredit. But other factors, such as economic policies, also influenced the outcome. Policy differences help explain why microcredit grew faster in Bolivia than in Peru or Ecuador, Bolivia's nearest neighbors, which share some aspects of its culture and demography. But to understand fully why Bolivian microfinance became an industry, one must examine the lending institutions themselves, get to know the people behind them, and understand how those people built their institutions. The lessons Bolivia provides about institution building are highly relevant to the supporters and promoters of microfinance institutions around the world.

A second topic of major importance for microfinance professionals is Bolivia's evolution as a textbook case of the financial systems approach to microfinance.[1] This line of thinking within the broader microfinance field sees the aim of the microfinance movement as developing the ability and willingness of the financial system to serve the poor on a fully commercial basis. The financial systems approach views donor and government subsidies as temporary phenomena, recognizing that the scale necessary to reach the vast potential market can be reached only if microfinance connects to the mainstream financial system. Thus, the financial systems approach is concerned with finding pathways to bring microfinance into the financial system. One widely applied pathway evolved in Bolivia, involving the transformation of microcredit non-governmental organizations (NGOs) into formal financial institutions. We will call this the Bolivia Model of microfinance transformation and examine in detail how it works. More generally, Bolivian microfinance illustrates what microfinance can accomplish when led by a strong orientation toward commercialization. For example, Bolivia's experience demonstrates the value of a positive working relationship with competent supervisory and regulatory authorities.

The commercialization of microfinance has advanced to such a point in Bolivia that it is no longer primarily a donor-driven movement but an industry, and this is the third topic of major interest to development-finance professionals. Commercialization has proceeded farther in Bolivia than perhaps any other country, but observers in many countries see the same trends at work. In that sense Bolivia's current microfinance scene offers a prophecy about the future under conditions of commercialization and competition. That scene is more complicated than most supporters of the financial systems approach originally envisioned. Fierce competition requires institutions accustomed to a sheltered quasi-monopoly to fight for their survival. In this setting it is much harder to achieve the unique blend of profit and social objectives around which some microfinance institutions have built their operations. Microfinance professionals throughout the world need to understand more about the effects of competition in order to prepare themselves in advance, and Bolivia's recent experience offers plentiful lessons.

These three topics explain in part why microfinance professionals should understand the story of Bolivia, but this book will show that the story is important for a broader audience as well.

The most important development questions are broad and deep: What factors influence economic growth? How does growth affect the poor? How does a country build the institutions that underpin future progress? How does economic progress relate to social and cultural change? Few writings on microfinance address such fundamental questions. Although some writing discusses the enabling environment for microfinance, the purpose is usually narrow: to point out factors that are either especially conducive or prohibitive for the development of microfinance institutions.[2] Another set of writings attempts to assess the contribution of microfinance by examining the impact of loans on individual clients.[3] This book takes a different approach. It identifies the most important development questions facing Bolivia and then examines how microfinance might relate to them, tracing the multifaceted interactions between events and trends.

During the decade in which microfinance developed, Bolivia was involved in an experiment to see whether liberal economic policies and a return to democracy could lift it out of the economic morass it had reached by the mid-1980s; and more, whether this approach could solve fundamental development problems that kept Bolivia the poorest country on its continent. Today, it appears that these liberal policies have helped provide a framework in which growth can occur, but the rate of growth has been disappointing, and no one has a really compelling vision about where the impetus will come from to pull Bolivia's living standards up to those of its neighbors.

Bolivia has also faced a longstanding problem of wide disparities in income, education, and political power between its major social groupings. The elites are overwhelmingly of European descent and Spanish-speaking, while the poor come mainly from mixed or native extraction, many still speaking the traditional languages—Aymara, Quechua, and others. Despite progress during recent decades, the latter group is often still excluded from the opportunities society provides to those better off.

Bolivia's struggle with these central problems, growth and social equity, provides the context in which microfinance grew. If over time microfinance did not contribute materially to progress in these areas, it would be only a development sideshow. Certainly the promoters of microfinance aimed to make such differences. Through the process of examining the interconnections between microfinance and the broader Bolivian scene, this book considers three propositions: first, that over the course of a generation microfinance will help spark a transformation in which the informal sector households and businesses it serves will prove to be significant sources of economic progress; second, that microfinance will contribute to fuller integration of the majority population into society; and third, that the institution-building process of the microfinance institutions themselves will influence other Bolivian institutions in finance, government, and development. The book can only pose these statements as propositions, in part because data are not available (and in some cases never could be) to establish a causal link from microfinance to such sweeping national changes, and in part because such changes require a longer time frame to become apparent.

The plausibility of the propositions is suggested if one considers the nature and scale of what has occurred. An enormous share of Bolivia's households—to date perhaps as many as a third, with more likely—have for the first time gained access to reliable sources of finance for their businesses through microcredit. In fact, Bolivia is one of the few places where microfinance has grown to such a scale that its value as part of the overall economic development picture can be considered. The collective result of this kind of sector-wide opening of access could be dramatic.

An analogy may be found in the creation in the United States of the 30-year home mortgage. In the middle of the twentieth century this new financial instrument provided first-time access to housing finance to a major segment of the American population, perhaps the majority. As a direct result the United States has become a nation of homeowners, and homeownership is today a pillar of American life, part of the country's physical, political, and cultural landscape.[4] Though the analogy is merely speculative, it serves to point out that the opening of microcredit to Bolivia's population constitutes a sectoral change of a similar potential magnitude in its own context as the home mortgage in America.

The value of the change will depend on how Bolivia's microentrepreneurs use their resources. The 1990s witnessed tremendous dynamism in the sector microfinance institutions serve. Unfortunately, empirical evidence linking that dynamism directly to microfinance is scant. But who knows what may happen when masses of previously ignored people suddenly gain access to the means to accomplish some of their most cherished goals?

BOLIVIA'S PLACE IN THE INTERNATIONAL MICROFINANCE MOVEMENT

For those unfamiliar with the international microfinance field, a quick overview will show how Bolivian institutions fit within this rapidly growing movement. Although the entire movement shares some common views, several strands within microfinance emphasize quite different—and at times opposing—core values and approaches. As stated above, Bolivia's experience as a whole exemplifies the financial systems approach, which contrasts along several dimensions with the public image of microfinance created by Mohammad Yunus, founder of Grameen Bank in Bangladesh. At the same time, the various institutions within Bolivia's industry reflect the influence of several strands of international microfinance, and it is interesting to see how they play out in the Bolivian context.

In microfinance, as in most fields, terminology carries ideological messages that may not be apparent to a casual observer. The term *microfinance* is used in a broad sense to refer to the provision of financial services to the low-income segment of the population. This definition encompasses any institution engaged in this pursuit, whether or not it identifies itself as part of microfinance. A narrower definition refers to the global movement to expand financial services for the poor that resulted from a body of technical innovations which emerged around the world in the late 1970s and early 1980s. This is the self-identified microfinance movement, and this book is a history of that movement as it has unfolded in Bolivia. We recognize the broader definition, however, in acknowledging the participation of other providers.

Microfinance replaced the earlier terms *microcredit* and *microenterprise finance* at about the time the movement began to notice the importance of savings. In fact, the change of terms indicated several shifts in perspective, including not only the value of savings but also a broadening of scope from microenterprises to low-income clients generally (households, farms, individuals), and a concern with building financial institutions free of donor dependence. The term *microcredit* has since become associated with the Microcredit Summit and the Grameen Bank philosophy, while the term *microfinance* is more closely associated with the financial systems approach.

Thus, although strictly speaking the story in Bolivia is mainly about credit for microenterprises, this book often uses the term *microfinance*. In using the term *microfinance* this book asserts Bolivia's identification with the financial systems approach and recognizes the unfinished agenda on the saving side. As chapter 7 discusses, Bolivia has contributed very little to knowledge about savings. The terms *microfinance, microenterprise finance* and *microcredit* are often used here interchangeably, though generally *microfinance* is used to refer to the field as a whole and to the development of financial institutions, while the other terms refer more narrowly to the provision of credit.

Only a few brave studies have attempted to develop a quantitative portrait of the worldwide microfinance movement. The World Bank's Sustainable Banking with the Poor project compared this task to counting grains of sand on the beach—you never know when to leave off.[5] That study found over 1,000 microfinance institutions meeting its criteria (founded before 1992 and serving more than 1,000 clients), with new institutions appearing at an increasing rate. Among the 206 institutions from which the study collected data, the total number of loans outstanding was 13 million, valued at $7 billion, with savings accounts totaling $13 billion. The Microcredit Summit, a campaign to raise international commitment to microcredit, reports data from 1,065 microfinance institutions, serving a total of 24 million clients, 13 million of whom it considers among its "poorest families" target group.[6] *The MicroBanking Bulletin* publishes data from the small set of microfinance institutions that can—and are willing to—provide rigorous financial performance information. The 102 institutions it included in February 2000 held $4.4 billion in loans to 8.9 million borrowers, with an average loan balance of $755. Among this select group of institutions, 58 were fully financially viable—that is, genuinely profitable.[7] *Bulletin* staff believe that this data captures most of the world's financially viable microfinance programs. These numbers give a general impression of the proliferation of institutions, the relative paucity of really viable institutions, and the fact that the total numbers of clients and amounts of money involved have become significant.

Greater insight comes from looking at the major approaches various institutions take. Microfinance first emerged on the international scene in the early 1980s, when experiments in several places, including Bangladesh, Indonesia, and Latin America, began demonstrating techniques for lending to the poor that were more effective than previous methodologies at reaching large scale and covering costs. These achievements of scale and sustainability put microfinance on the map. The early microcredit programs used different methodologies (some lent individually, others in groups) but similar principles. Among the principles: character rather than collateral as the primary loan security, streamlining of administrative processes to lower costs, rapid response to late payments, positive incentives for repayment, interest rates that approached or covered costs, and emphasis on the long-term sustainability of the lending institution. These sturdy principles have guided the development of microcredit ever since.

Despite several common principles the early microfinance programs set off in slightly different directions, creating what have become distinct strands within the movement. We can identify five strands that bear on the Bolivian experience.

The Grameen Bank Model

The most widely known strand, often synonymous with microcredit in the public's eye, is the Grameen Bank approach. Grameen Bank developed a group-lending methodology suited to the conditions in Bangladesh: the poverty of landless agricultural laborers densely distributed across the country, the subjugation of women in a highly conservative culture, and the dominance of large, non-governmental organizations (NGOs) as development powerhouses. On the strength of its methodology and capacity to organize, Grameen Bank grew to serve more than two million borrowers, overwhelmingly women. Grameen's methodology appears in several other Bangladeshi institutions and in replication programs linked to Grameen Trust (a subsidiary) and Cashpor (an independent network). Grameen's website lists 223 replications in 58 countries, particularly in Asia.

Grameen is perhaps even more influential as an ideology. Its views are the driving force behind the Microcredit Summit and are shared by many organizations that use other methodologies. The message of Grameen overwhelmingly centers on microcredit as a poverty alleviation tool, particularly for women. Grameen Bank makes optimistic claims about the ability of microloans to lift women out of poverty, judging microfinance programs on the basis of whether they reach the poorest segments of society and move their clients above the poverty line. By implication, programs that serve those who are only moderately poor are not doing the most important work of microcredit. A salient feature of this philosophy is the subordination of sustainability to poverty alleviation. While Grameen Bank's ideological colleagues acknowledge the goal of becoming sustainable, they are content to allow long, often receding, time horizons. By choice, they have not been at the forefront in moving microfinance from a donor-dependent phenomenon to a commercially underwritten one.

Village Banking

The Grameen Bank ideology is relevant to the Bolivian experience mainly as a foil, because most of the Bolivian organizations represent the other end of the microfinance spectrum, viewing commercial-level operation as a means to achieve sustainable outreach to the excluded. However, a significant strand of microfinance that does appear in Bolivia is philosophically linked to the Grameen outlook: village banking. Village banking is a methodology that John Hatch and the American NGO Finca developed; it has become the method of choice for most American NGOs promoting microfinance. Finca, Save the Children, Catholic Relief Services, Freedom from Hunger, Opportunity International, World Relief, World Vision, and others all use this methodology, which involves lending to groups of (mainly) women, organized into "banks" that in turn lend to their members. Together, the North American NGOs sponsor 237 programs around the world, and there are numerous other independent programs.[8] Most village banking programs are small; only a fraction serve more than 10,000 borrowers. Although the method differs from Grameen's, the two approaches share the commitment to targeting the poorest women. Two prominent microfinance institutions in Bolivia, ProMujer and Crecer, are village banking programs, and as we will see in chapter 3, Bolivia has some claim to be the birthplace of this methodology, through Hatch's earliest experiments.

More recently it is interesting to observe in Bolivia how the village banking organizations have adapted to a setting in which the dominant paradigm is the financial systems approach. They feel the influence of the financial rigor demanded of microfinance programs in Bolivia and have become more efficient and professional as a result. But they steadfastly maintain the primacy of their social and poverty-alleviation objectives, often finding themselves swimming against the tide.

The BRI Model and Credit Unions

The Bank Rakyat Indonesia's (BRI's) unit banking division embodies another important strand in microfinance. BRI, a large, state-owned commercial bank, implemented a nationwide microfinance system in the mid-1980s. Only two years after its network of several thousand village-based units began offering a package of individual loans and savings products based on microfinance principles, BRI's unit banking system turned a profit. Since then many microfinance institutions and policy makers, including several in Bolivia, have studied and applied the straightforward techniques that make the BRI units work. No other institution, however, has come close to duplicating BRI's achievement of scale and profitability. At the end of 1999 the BRI Unit Banking System had 2.5 million borrowers, with a portfolio worth $848 million, and savings deposits of over $2 billion. The latter figure reveals the area of BRI's most important success: savings mobilization.

Most of the microfinance movement, including Grameen, village banking, and the leading Bolivian institutions, has been about credit. BRI, initially almost alone, raised the issue of savings. It showed that savings is an important financial service for the poor, that the poor can save and will save in a bank, and that savings mobilization from a micro level can be an excellent funding source for a financial institution. These lessons began penetrating the microfinance movement a decade ago. In fact, the name microfinance emerged—rather than microcredit or the earlier microenterprise finance—because of the general recognition that finance involves savings and eventually other financial services as well as credit. However, few microfinance institutions, particularly NGOs, have been in a legal position to mobilize savings, and progress in this area has therefore been slow.

In its emphasis on savings, BRI shares a position with the credit union movement, which spread throughout developing countries a couple of decades before microfinance. Credit unions have always been savings-based institutions. They occupy a somewhat awkward position, not quite within microfinance. When microfinance began to emerge, the credit union movement was partly discredited as a provider of financial service to the poor. In many countries it had suffered from capture by elites, political interference, policies tilted against depositors, and a bias toward middle-class clients rather than the poor. The weakened credit unions were slow to pick up the method-ological innovations of microfinance that would have allowed them to go downmarket on the credit side. Today many credit union systems have re-stored themselves, and because they have always been savings based, they are proving to be better positioned to develop this side of microfinance than most NGOs. Such is the case in Bolivia.

Acción and IPC

Two leading microfinance promotion organizations represent the final strand in Bolivia's microfinance skein: Acción International and IPC (Internationale Projekt Consult). These organizations have been the driving forces behind many of the large, sustainable microfinance institutions in Latin America, in-cluding the most successful Bolivian ones, BancoSol, Prodem, and Caja Los Andes. The affiliates of these organizations, and others that follow their ap-proach, account for most of the microcredit delivered in the region. Acción's network had a total of 455,000 active clients in 1999 and a combined loan portfolio of $268 million in 15 countries.[9]

The most salient feature of both Acción and IPC is the drive for the insti-tutions they sponsor to become commercial so as to participate in the financial systems of their countries. The institutions in this strand—like BRI and the credit unions—are willing to serve a somewhat broad spectrum of clients, rang-ing from the near poor to the very poor, as the basis for profitable operations. They aim to provide high-quality financial services to previously excluded seg-ments. Thus, while they do aim to serve the poor, they do not engage in pov-erty targeting. This strand of microfinance has been very influential in raising the standards for microfinance, pushing toward greater rigor in measuring fi-nancial performance and innovation in ways to link to the private sector. Their moves in this direction penetrate the field as a whole, resulting in more sus-tainable microfinance institutions even among the other strands.

That quick summary of the main currents in microfinance places the Bo-livian story in the context of a set of debates going on within the field about poverty targeting, savings, financial performance, commercialization, and other issues. It shows Bolivia has been involved with most of the main strands of microfinance, but that its predominant role is to illustrate the financial sys-tems approach, particularly as it appears in Latin America.

A GUIDE TO THE BOOK

This book tells the story of microfinance in Bolivia from its origins in the mid-1980s to the present, reflecting, as much as possible, the voices of the people who helped create the industry. It attempts to show how microfinance interacted with the political and economic events of its time. Most of the book is based on interviews conducted in Bolivia during February and March 1999 and March 2000. It is intended both for the microfinance professional and for readers interested in economic development who may know little about microfinance, although the two groups may be interested in different aspects of the book. It is presented as a story rather than an academic work. However, it is also an analytic work that interprets events and draws out important lessons.

The author's own bias undoubtedly shows through. I am, it will be plain to see, a supporter of the microfinance movement and especially of the Bolivian approach to that movement. I have great admiration for those who helped create the industry, though I intend to show them as fallible people who have both accomplished a great deal and made mistakes. This is not a promotional book. It attempts to be critical where criticism is due and to represent both sides of arguments.

Chapter 1. Bolivia Today

Chapter 1 describes microfinance as it appears in Bolivia today. It aims to give the reader the flavor of the setting, the clients, and the institutions, laying the groundwork for the story that follows.

Chapter 2. The Historical Context

In the mid-1980s Bolivia suffered a crisis of hyperinflation and overcame it through a new president and new economic policy. Improved policies, economic stability, and financial-sector reforms created the conditions that made the supply of microcredit possible, while massive public-sector layoffs and accelerating migration to the cities created the huge informal sector, and thus the demand for microcredit. This chapter recounts that time and also pauses to examine the Bolivian informal sector, discussing various perceptions of the role and value of the sector.

Chapter 3. The Origins of Prodem

Chapter 3 begins the story of the creation of microfinance, focusing on the first really successful microfinance institution, Prodem. It introduces the key players, especially the formerly radical activists and elite businessmen who allied themselves to create Prodem. This chapter examines the secrets of Prodem's success, both in relating to clients and in building an extraordinary institution.

Chapter 4. Other Microlenders Arise

This phase of the story continues with a look at other pioneering institutions—Procredito, FIE, ProMujer, Crecer, Idepro, and Fades. Each of these institutions has a different perspective on microfinance, and thus a tour of the institutions is also a tour of some of the main debates within the microfinance field. Chapters 4 and 5 will be relevant to the general reader who wants to understand what makes microcredit work. For microfinance professionals the chapters are, in effect, essays on how to create strong institutions.

Chapter 5. Transformation

Chapter 5 describes the Bolivia Model of microfinance transformation. This is the story of how a group of NGOs became formal financial institutions, beginning in 1992 with the transformation of Prodem into BancoSol, a licensed commercial bank dedicated exclusively to microfinance. Much of the story revolves around the quest for an effective ownership structure for the new organizations that would combine commitment to the original mission with an eye for the bottom line. Another theme concerns the interplay between institutions and the Bolivian Superintendency of Banks to ensure that the Superintendency would have confidence in the safety and soundness of any strange new institutions it licensed. NGOs around the world are contemplating similar transformations as a logical next step toward sustainability and freedom from donor dependence. The principles of these transformations are often poorly understood, however, and there is surprisingly little writing on the subject.[10] This chapter may stand alone as an essay on the Bolivia Model of microfinance transformation.

Chapter 6. Commercialization and Competition

By the end of the 1990s microfinance institutions had produced such impressive returns to investors that purely private organizations began to enter the market. At the same time the transformed institutions grew in scale, and consumer lending entered the country in a big way. Thus, for the first time, the microfinance institutions face serious competition, while microfinance clients find themselves in a buyer's market. Competition has fundamentally altered the relationship between borrower and lender. As a result, loan delinquencies have surged, creating a general panic in the microfinance community that remains unresolved. Commercial entry and competition arrived in Bolivia sooner than in other countries, so a look at the situation there should allow those in other countries to anticipate what the future may hold for them.

Chapter 7. New Frontiers

This chapter looks at the reassessments taking place as mission-driven organizations search for new frontiers in the face of competition. They have turned in two main directions: to the rural areas, still sadly underserved; and to the savings side of microfinance, which most Bolivian microcredit organizations had ignored until recently. In both of these areas the search is still on for the kind of financial innovations that originally sparked the rise of microcredit—ways to convince Bolivians to put their money into banks and ways to overcome the logistical and risk factors associated with rural areas.

This chapter also examines the reassessments going on within donor and government organizations. At a time when the need for their support is disappearing, donors and governments are sorely tempted to remain associated with success.

Chapter 8. Development Accomplishments

Chapter 8 explores the significance of microfinance for Bolivia, asking whether it has all been worthwhile. It picks up the thread of Bolivia's economic development from chapter 2. It airs debates over whether the informal sector can be an important contributor to the country's growth and whether microfinance can spark significant growth in that sector. The informal sector made important productivity gains throughout the 1990s. However, only anecdotal and circumstantial data link those gains directly to microfinance. The chapter also examines the possible effects of microfinance on poverty alleviation, finding an important message about microfinance as a risk-protection mechanism. Finally, it looks at the changing social and political status of the informal sector and microfinance clients. Readers interested in the broader development context could read chapters 3 and 8 together.

Chapter 9. International Relevance

The last chapter applies lessons from Bolivia to microfinance and development in other countries. The discussion proceeds through five of the principal questions facing microfinance today, arguing that the Bolivian experience is relevant both as a model for emulation and as a harbinger of the future of microfinance.

NOTES

1. One of the earliest discussions of the financial systems approach is found in chapter 1 of Maria Otero and Elisabeth Rhyne, eds. *The New World of Microenterprise Finance: Building Healthy Financial Institutions for the Poor* (West Hartford, Conn.:

Kumarian Press, 1994).

2. For example, see Joanna Ledgerwood, *Microfinance Handbook: An Institutional and Financial Perspective* Sustainable Banking with the Poor (Washington, D.C.: World Bank, 1999).

3. The most extensive writings on impact have come recently from the AIMS (Assessing the Impact of Microfinance Services) project, which may be located through the Microenterprise Innovation Project website, www.mip.org, or through MSI, Washington, D.C.

4. There are surprising parallels between the creation of the Bolivian microfinance industry and the development of the home-mortgage market in the United States. Before 1930 most American families could only buy homes with cash. During the 1930s the Federal Housing Administration (FHA) began giving guarantees to cover the risk of bank mortgages for up to 30 years, a risk not previously considered bankable. The new mortgage instrument made house payments affordable, and the mortgages turned out to be good investments, backed by valuable real estate and the interest of families in keeping in their homes. Private insurers began offering a similar mortgage insurance product, and a new industry appeared. The story of microfinance in Bolivia has a similar plot. It begins with a national economic crisis, Bolivia's hyperinflation of 1985, and attempts by social reformers to pull the country out of crisis. It also begins with a genuine financial innovation—new techniques for lending to poor entrepreneurs without traditional collateral. Conventional bankers scorned these techniques, but they have proved to be effective ways of managing risk for this clientele. In both stories the private sector was unwilling to experiment with what it viewed as a high-risk, low-return product, overlooking vast potential market. Only government (in Bolivia through international donor agencies) was willing to finance the risks of experimentation, but refrained from actual implementation. These stories both provide models of appropriate forms of government intervention in financial markets to widen outreach.

5. Julia Paxton, "A Worldwide Inventory of Microfinance Institutions," Sustainable Banking with the Poor (Washington, D.C.: World Bank, 1996), 1.

6. Microcredit Summit, "Empowering Women with Microcredit: 2000 Microcredit Summit Campaign Report," www.microcreditsummit.org.

7. "Bulletin Highlights and Tables," *The MicroBanking Bulletin*, no. 4 (February 2000): 48–49.

8. SEEP (Small Enterprise Education and Promotion Network) Poverty Lending Working Group, private communication.

9. Acción International, *Annual Report 1999* (Somerville, Mass.: Acción International, 2000).

10. An important reference is Anita Campion and Victoria White, *Institutional Metamorphosis: Transformation of Microfinance NGOs into Regulated Financial Institutions,* Occasional Paper No. 4 (Washington, D.C.: MicroFinance Network, 1999).

CHAPTER ONE

A SKETCH OF BOLIVIAN
MICROFINANCE IN 1999

IN EARLY 1999 THE BOLIVIAN microfinance industry was flying high. During the years since its origins in the mid-1980s, the early players saw their experiments flourish and become vibrant institutions, spawn imitators, and eventually create a full-fledged industry. Every trend line pointed up, and horizons seemed at times limitless. Bolivia itself was enjoying its most prosperous and stable decade for generations.

The optimism of this period ended in 1999 as Bolivia experienced its first recession in years, brought on by economic shocks throughout Latin America. The recession hit microfinance especially hard because it was already undergoing momentous change. A new breed of commercial consumer lenders had begun flooding the market with credit, and the microlenders themselves had grown to a large scale, creating market saturation and a debt crisis among clients.

By way of introducing the Bolivian microfinance sector, this chapter sketches the industry in early 1999, a point that marks the transition from the optimism of its first phase into a more mature and complex future. At the time described in this sketch the early efforts had borne fruit, and although the factors of complexity were already at work, their effects were not yet obvious. Through this portrait readers will gain an overview of Bolivia's microfinance sector and its institutions, together with something of its local flavor in the cities of La Paz and Santa Cruz and in two rural centers. This overview sets the stage for chapters 3 through 6 which describe the birth and development of the industry. We will return in chapters 7 through 9 to look at how recession, consumer lending, and increased competition are reshaping the microfinance industry as it enters a second, more sober era.

LA PAZ AND EL ALTO

We begin with La Paz, where Bolivia's microfinance movement originated. La Paz is surely one of the most peculiarly situated cities in the world. Just below the rim of the altiplano, the high Andean plateau, the city spreads dramatically across the steeply descending hillsides and plunges into the valley. It clings precariously to its perch. The sandstone base on which the city is built crumbles into dirt at a touch. A good rain can turn these stalagmites of sandstone into mud, wash away roads, or undermine the foundations of buildings.

At every step in La Paz one must either struggle against gravity or yield to its unrelenting downward pull. Perhaps it is the altitude that makes visitors unusually conscious of gravity's strength. One wants to descend, even a little, to breathe deeply. This struggle also affects cars, whose oxygen-deprived engines contend with La Paz's vertical spaces while operating on half their normal power. Every turn provides glimpses of mountain peaks and a luminous sky whose clouds are barely out of reach.

The Aymaras, the main indigenous ethnic group of Bolivia's altiplano, settled in this seemingly unlikely place because the valley offered shelter from cold, fierce winds, and that element of protection remains important today. La Paz inverts the usual relationship between elevation and social status. The rich of most cities escape to the hills to find cooler temperatures, while in La Paz, they flee to the lowlands. To reach the poorer neighborhoods, one must climb and climb, finally emerging onto the altiplano itself at El Alto, the fast-growing city of the informal sector.

From a microfinance point of view, La Paz offers a scene just as dramatic as the city's geography. Microfinance is everywhere. On the dizzying taxi ride from the El Alto airport over the edge of the altiplano into La Paz, the taxi driver named the major microfinance institutions—BancoSol, Caja Los Andes, FIE—with a guided tour past their offices. Another taxi driver opened his glove compartment and pulled out his BancoSol payment coupon book, launching into an analysis of the relative merits of BancoSol and its rural counterpart, Prodem. It seems that everyone in La Paz has an opinion about microfinance.

To see why microfinance has become ubiquitous in La Paz and El Alto, we first take a look at the informal markets it serves. From the earliest times La Paz was a trading center where the people of the altiplano exchanged their potatoes and wool for the fruits of the warmer foothills. Life on the altiplano has long depended on the exchange of such complementary products.[1] This kind of commerce continues today.

The amount of economic activity conducted on the streets of these two cities can seem overwhelming. A 1993 InterAmerican Development Bank

(IDB) estimate placed the number of microenterprises in La Paz and El Alto at 190,000.[2] The sector has grown significantly since then. To understand just how many microenterprises there are, consider that the total population of the two cities is figured to be 1.1 million.[3] If households average five people, these estimates would mean that there are nearly as many enterprises as households. While this may be something of an overestimate, it is clear that the number of people engaged in microenterprise is an extraordinarily large percentage of the total population.

In parts of the city it is easy to believe that there is an enterprise per household. The streets of whole neighborhoods teem with vendors of vegetables, fruit, meat, flowers, school supplies, shoes, clothing, toiletries, festival decorations, and hardware. Potatoes from the altiplano crowd alongside bananas from Santa Cruz and grapes from Tarija. Many of the goods on offer are contraband—ordinary items smuggled into Bolivia without duty. Two lines of vendors occupy the streets, selling from platforms covered by blue plastic tarpaulins, from metal containers they can padlock at the end of the day, or from cold seats on the pavement. Behind them, shopkeepers in permanent premises sell somewhat more formally but still cater mainly to the low-income clientele that frequents the informal markets. These shops are on the borderline—some may be informal, while others have obtained the employer's tax number that places them on the first rung of the formal sector. The feeling in the markets is one of plenty. Women surround themselves with bulging sacks of merchandise. Most have far more than they can carry on their backs. A BancoSol loan officer points out that many vegetable vendors on the street have a better income stream than some of the formal shops behind them.

Market vendors are the most numerous and visible members of the informal sector, but manufacturers also operate, often behind doors that give no hint that they lead to anything other than a simple residence. This is particularly true for textiles and clothing, sectors with strong growth prospects in La Paz. At the top of a long, steep climb from the El Tejar branch through a quiet neighborhood in the heights of the city, the BancoSol loan officer knocked at the door of a brick house, as dilapidated as most of the neighboring houses. After a long pause a woman in traditional dress cracked the door, her daughter peeping out below. The BancoSol officer explained who he was and asked to see his client, her husband. She shut the door. BancoSol loan officers are undoubtedly used to standing outside on the pavement while the family inside discusses whether to trust them. In this case the owner soon appeared. The house contained a thriving knitwear factory with at least half a million dollars worth of machinery. In the basement, at the bottom of a pitch dark stairwell, sophisticated German knitting machines tended by six or seven men were wedged into corners, while in rooms on the second floor women put finishing touches on wool/acrylic blend sweaters for export to Paraguay. The owner claimed to know 40 or 50 other automated textile/clothing businesses operating in this neighborhood. The view from the street offered no evidence of any of these businesses.

The knitwear manufacturer represents the upper end of the sector that microfinance serves. His loan of $15,000 places him among the 1 percent of BancoSol clients in early 1999 with loans over $6,000. The vendors seated directly on the pavement represent the opposite end of the spectrum. They have few products to sell, and many wear a dazed, suffering look. Babies lie passively beside their mothers in cardboard boxes, swaddled so tightly one almost mistakes them for parcels.

The clients of microfinance institutions in La Paz are the people who give Bolivia its unique Andean flavor. Most of them descend directly from the Inca (now Quechua) and Aymara empires. They still speak Quechua or Aymara, though now nearly all also speak Spanish. The traditional dress of the market vendors—long black braids, full skirts and bowler hats—conceals from outsiders the existence of significant differences in economic status. Official statistics confirm that most of the members of the informal sector and their families live below the poverty line, but there is wide variation ranging well above and well below the line.

A 1993 World Bank poverty study based on minimum consumption levels found 60 percent of the population of La Paz to live below the poverty line, and 73 percent of the population of El Alto. Approximately half of those people in each city had such low consumption that they were considered extremely poor.[4] This study used the most widely practiced method for measuring poverty, consumption of a minimum basket of food and other necessities. *Extreme poverty* means having too little income to purchase a minimum adequate food basket; *poverty* allows purchase of a few items in addition to basic food. Using a different methodology, a 1992 study by the Bolivian Ministry of Human Development put the percentage of poor in La Paz/El Alto at 56 percent and the extremely poor at 17 percent.[5] This study defined *poverty* as failure to achieve minimum acceptable levels of four basic needs—housing, water and sanitation, schooling, and health services. These studies found that the incidence of poverty was significantly higher for indigenous people and for the informal sector. Figures are not yet available to show whether these rates of poverty have changed significantly since 1992–93.

One thing that *has* clearly changed, however, is the access of these informal sector enterprises to credit. In the La Paz of 1999, nearly anyone operating a microenterprise who wants to borrow money from a formal financial institution or microcredit program can do so, provided he or she can find a couple of friends to form a solidarity group or pledge a personal guarantee.

By mid-1999 there were 39 branch offices in La Paz and El Alto offering microenterprise credit. Of those, 13 belonged to BancoSol; 18 to *fondos financieros privados* (FFPs, private financial funds) (Caja Los Andes, FIE, EcoFuturo, and Acesso); and 5 to NGOs (ProMujer, Idepro, and Diaconia).[6] Combined, these institutions had a La Paz/El Alto loan portfolio of $91 million lent out to 112,000 borrowers (including consumer loans by Acesso). This number of active clients is 60 percent of the 1993 estimated total number of microenterprises. Allowing for growth in the number of enterprises since 1993, and allowing for multiple loans by the same enterprise, a rough estimate is that between a quarter and a third of all enterprises are active borrowers. Market penetration numbers like these are very high for microcredit, even in Indonesia or Bangladesh. Microfinance market analysts recognize that many microentrepreneurs avoid borrowing altogether, while others borrow at some times but not at others.

The access barriers to microcredit have fallen to unprecedented lows. Daily routines bring most potential clients within a few blocks of at least one microfinance institution, so physical access is no longer an issue. Nor is availability of funds, for most of the institutions are now part of the formal financial system and can obtain funding to meet demand. Eligibility requirements are within reach of most potential borrowers, if not at one institution, then at another. BancoSol solidarity group borrowers must have an ongoing enterprise, no outstanding bad debts, and at least two other people willing to form a group. At Caja Los Andes individual borrowers must have an ongoing enterprise, a clean credit history, and two personal guarantors. In addition, they must be willing to provide *prendarias* or liens on movable property. Although Caja Los Andes does not generally disqualify borrowers whose assets are not valuable enough, microentrepreneurs lacking household or business assets probably begin borrowing through a solidarity group institution like BancoSol. For those without an ongoing microenterprise activity, especially very poor women, ProMujer has positioned itself to serve as an entry point into microcredit. Women must be willing to join a communal bank and attend weekly meetings. FIE and Idepro make special efforts to reach manufacturing enterprises. There is a service for nearly everyone.

These services are of high quality, although the product range is limited. All the microcredit programs start with small loans and gradually build loan size on the basis of good repayment history. BancoSol, FIE, and Los Andes all cite $50 as their minimum loan size, though in practice, most first loans are significantly larger. BancoSol solidarity group loans usually start about $200–

$250 and rise eventually to the range of $1,000–$3,000, sometimes more. All the programs pride themselves on quick response. Some promise to disburse loans within three days of application. The maximum wait is said to be two weeks. These figures are probably somewhat idealized. They do not include the time it might take a client to learn about the program, gather group members, and assemble required documents, because the timing of these preliminary steps is up to clients. Interest rates range from 24 to 30 percent for dollar loans and from 36 to 48 percent for loans in bolivianos. These quoted rates are not far below annual effective rates, as most interest is charged on the declining balance with few up-front fees. These prices, although not the lowest among microfinance programs around the world, are within the lower range of such prices and have been gradually decreasing. Loan terms range from four months to two years; in general, longer terms are only available to experienced customers.

The microfinance lenders in La Paz provide few other services. Only BancoSol provides a significant amount of savings services. Idepro and FIE offer some nonfinancial training and consulting services. Lines of credit are not available, nor are loans for special purposes, such housing or automobile purchase. Insurance is not widely available. Some of these other services can be obtained through standard commercial banks or mutual societies, but those institutions aim primarily at higher income residents who work in the formal sector.

The microentrepreneurs of La Paz and El Alto, however, are attracting the attention of a different breed of financial service providers—consumer lenders. Consumer lending entered the Bolivian market in the late 1990s, using lending methodologies that have been wildly successful in Chile. The largest consumer lender, Acceso FFP, is in fact a Chilean import. Most of the main commercial banks have established consumer lending departments, giving them names like CrediAgil, Solucion, Presto, and Fassil. A big billboard for Acceso in El Alto shows a hand snapping its fingers and the words *fast* and *easy*. The Chilean consumer-credit methodology was designed for salaried workers in the formal sector, whose wages can be garnished if loans are not repaid. In Bolivia, however, the prime formal sector is relatively small, so consumer lenders have expanded to serve small enterprises and microenterprises. Clients' credit histories at established microfinance lenders such as BancoSol and Los Andes become tickets to qualify for consumer credit. The consumer lenders attempt to make loans even faster than the microcredit lenders—within 24 to 48 hours—and offer larger loans sooner. Their entry has heightened the competition that was already strong among microlenders, and many customers are becoming dangerously over-indebted.

BATALLAS

On the *altiplano* between El Alto and Lake Titicaca, Batallas is a market town that provides a glimpse of the penetration of microfinance into rural areas. Saturday mornings are market days in Batallas. People from neighboring communities board buses early in the morning, arriving in Batallas by first light. The central plaza soon fills with vendors, each section devoted to a different product. By 8:00 a.m. hundreds of vendors are working, their wares spread on blankets on the ground. Urban and rural meet at Batallas, with vendors from La Paz selling alongside producers from the neighboring areas. The market features many of the same products seen in La Paz—the toiletries, boom boxes, clothes, and school supplies. But other sections reveal a distinctly rural flavor. In one area children hold burlap bags containing shivering baby animals—chicks, puppies, and rabbits. In another, vendors sell hand tools for farming. The vegetables are not clean and shiny as in La Paz; they look like they've just been pulled from the earth. And in the livestock market people stand on cold muddy ground holding their cattle on ropes while potential customers wander around inspecting. A nearby area is devoted to used bicycles.

The market in Batallas is a movable feast, occurring on different days of the week in different locations throughout the province. For Prodem, the largest microfinance lender in the area, Saturdays in Batallas are intense workdays. Prodem schedules as many of its transactions as possible to coincide with market days. It accepts loan repayments, makes disbursements, answers inquiries, and gives client-orientation talks. Other microlending NGOs also operate in Batallas: Sartawi and Crecer. Prodem's clients include both vendors and farmers, while Sartawi is focused more exclusively on farmers. Crecer, a village banking program, seeks out very poor women with young children and provides health and nutrition messages along with loans. Because Batallas is only a short hour's drive from El Alto, the urban microlenders sometimes appear. Loan officers from BancoSol or Caja Los Andes occasionally drive out to Batallas to visit clients who have applied for loans at in-town branches.

The microfinance programs operating here have developed a deep understanding of the rural economy and have adapted their products to fit the rhythms of rural life. They follow market days and agricultural calendars. The seasonal patterns of farmers in the Batallas area reflect their many mechanisms for protection against risk. Most families grow several different crops in different locations, including potatoes, quinoa (a traditional grain), and vegetables. Many raise cattle, and the women produce cheese. The women in many families also become vendors, particularly in an accessible area like Batallas. Some family

members contribute by becoming seasonal migrant laborers. Even playing traditional Andean music can be a source of income. Prodem and Sartawi look at
the whole family picture in defining loan size and repayment schedules for
their customers. Crecer, with its more rigid village banking methodology, is
less able to make these adaptations, though its clients may respond to seasonal
opportunities by using their group savings to lend to one another.

The clients of microfinance in rural areas are generally poorer than those
in the cities. The World Bank and government poverty studies show that nearly
everyone in rural areas is poor, whether measured by lack of adequate income
for food or access to basic needs. The 1995 figures for the rural areas of La Paz
Department, where Batallas is located, showed 95 percent of the people as
poor, with nearly all (94 percent) qualifying as extremely poor.[7]

Batallas, only a short drive from La Paz, is one of the most accessible of
rural locations, and yet there is already a large difference in the availability of
microfinance. Services are still provided primarily by NGOs, though both
Prodem and Sartawi are in the process of becoming formal FFPs. The commercial banks and consumer lenders have no more than a shadow presence.
Microfinance in rural areas still huddles around the secondary towns. There is
no doubt that it serves a population dominated by agriculture, which is very
different from the urban population, but its penetration into remote areas remains limited. The Banzer government has taken up the issue of extending
microfinance services—and in fact banking services of any type—into more
remote areas. Government statements frequently cite the statistic that out of
the 311 municipalities in Bolivia, 227 have no banking or microfinance outlets
at all.[8]

SANTA CRUZ

It is sometimes hard to believe that Santa Cruz and La Paz are part of the
same country. La Paz is cold, arid, and traditional; Santa Cruz is flat, green,
steamy, and on the make. It's the Dallas of Bolivia. A generation ago it was a
sleepy farming town, largely isolated from the mainstream of Bolivian economic life, which was centered on the highlands. The development of commercial agriculture—soybeans, rice, and sugar cane—as well as oil and natural
gas have since transformed the region into the most economically dynamic
part of the country. On the roads in and out of the city, big, new corporate
logos advertise the outlets for Ford trucks, Caterpillar tractors, and agricultural chemicals. At the popular restaurants shiny sport-utility vehicles drop off
the teenage daughters of the newly rich, who sit outside in skintight clothes
and perfect make up, sipping milkshakes, watching and being watched.

The economic growth around Santa Cruz has drawn migrants from all over the country. In 1950 it had 42,000 people, while today more than 700,000 live there.[9] The immigrants include the rural residents from the surrounding Department of Santa Cruz, as well as people from the highlands—Potosi, Oruro, La Paz, and Cochabamba. In the process some traditions are brought and others left behind. A small-scale melting pot emerges.

Despite the booming farm sector, rural migration into the cities has created an informal sector nearly as large as that in La Paz. Many of the market vendors occupy dedicated market structures built by the municipal government or by an association of market vendors. These are typically large metal hangars with rows of stalls built inside. The women vendors at each market all wear the same color apron and the men the same color baseball cap, signifying their membership in that market's association or trade union.

Just as in La Paz, the informal sector spans a wide range. In La Mutualista, a new market structure built to move vendors away from the center of the city, one corner of the market was devoted to the vendors of bananas. These vendors represent one of the lowest rungs, with few items of paltry value. They sell bananas for two cents each. One tiny young woman, whose sweet smile was marred by rotten teeth, would have sold her entire stock for less than four dollars. She was clearly one of the 45 percent of Santa Cruz residents below the poverty line, and probably one of the 12 percent considered extremely poor. On the other side of La Mutualista, a large shop with a gleaming white tile floor, high ceiling, and shelves lined with attractively arranged groceries represented the other end of the spectrum. Middle-class people pulled up in their cars and came inside to buy. This shop was the result of a generation of effort. It belonged to the mother but was tended by the daughter. It had grown from a stall outside, where the inventory got soaked every time it rained, into beautiful new premises with the help of the vendors' association and a microenterprise loan from a cooperative. In the residential neighborhoods of Santa Cruz, just as in La Paz, unlikely looking doors opened to reveal production: a bakery with 14 employees or a kitchen producing 700 *empanadas* (meat pastries) a day.

Microfinance is just as vibrant in Santa Cruz as in La Paz, with a slightly different cast of characters. BancoSol is less dominant here, though it still remains the largest provider, with nine branches. However, it faces different competition. The farm economy and earlier geographic isolation of Santa Cruz, together with the devoted efforts of local Catholic priests, resulted in a history of strong agriculture and credit cooperatives. A few credit cooperatives, left nearly without assets by the hyperinflation of 1985, have since built themselves into financial institutions with large memberships and a range of services. Their names—Cooperativa Jesús Nazareno, San Martin de Porres, Fatima, La Merced, and others—carry strong "brand" recognition in the Santa Cruz area. These cooperatives are deservedly proud to have grown on the basis of member savings, not donor contributions. They all serve microenterprises to some degree, some using the solidarity group model adapted directly from BancoSol.

A private finance company, Fassil FFP, also offers solidarity group credit. Private entrepreneur Alfredo Otero founded Fassil after observation of the microfinance NGOs convinced him that microenterprise offered an opportunity for profit. Several of the microcredit staff of Fassil—and of the cooperatives—are former BancoSol staff, lured away by offers of higher salary and greater responsibilities. Another important player, Banco Económico, is headquartered in Santa Cruz. This highly profitable small commercial bank has a market strategy focused on the small and medium enterprise sectors, reaching downward toward microenterprises. Finally, as in La Paz, consumer lending is here in force. With such strong competition, the main microfinance markets show signs of saturation.

MINEROS

Mineros is a farm town in the Department of Santa Cruz, a satellite of one of the main secondary cities in the department, Montero. It is not far from the city of Santa Cruz, only an hour and a half by car on a good, flat road. In the town's markets, women sell basic groceries—pasta, oil, and other staples. These women straddle the worlds of the town and the farm. Their families all have fields planted in crops. Land is plentiful, and some Prodem clients have as many as 50 hectares or more planted in sugar cane, rice, or soybeans. The women's market stalls only bring in a fraction of the overall household income. One woman said that she maintains the business to provide the extra income to send her children to good schools. Her son was studying engineering at the university in Santa Cruz. Another woman winked as she said that life on the farm was too hard for a woman. Her shop provided a good excuse for her to live in town.

One of the poorer clients was a single woman selling vice: coca leaves, tobacco, and grain alcohol. Her sweet, grandmotherly care for the little girl on her lap was a far cry from the North American image of a drug dealer. Moreover, her business was entirely legal. She had a license to sell coca leaves, which she traveled to La Paz to buy. On the journey back with eight enormous sacks of leaves, she paid sin taxes to the police at every checkpoint. With the help of her business and a Prodem loan she had managed to buy 15 hectares of land, a relatively small plot in this region, but she did not know how she would get the help to plow, plant, and tend it.

For these families vending provides a steady source of income throughout the year and a buffer against the bad years in which droughts or low commodity prices reduce farm income. Opportunities for diversification are relatively limited in Mineros because of the strong dependence of the economy on a limited number of field crops and the lack of variation in agro-climatic zones, unlike the altiplano, where conditions vary within short distances. Some better-off clients rent out farm machinery. Another client provides a machinery maintenance service. Despite the abundance of land, most people in the rural sections of Santa Cruz remain poor.

Prodem has an office here, as does a small Montero-based cooperative, but there are no other banking outlets. Occasionally, lenders from the big city have penetrated as far as Mineros. Loan officers from BancoSol or Jesús Nazareno, the largest Santa Cruz cooperative, sometimes show up in Mineros. And customers report buying farm machinery on credit from urban machinery dealers, with installments due every harvest time. Mineros is an example of Bolivian microfinance at its edges, where town and farm interact.

THE MICROFINANCE INSTITUTIONS

The institutions operating in Bolivia make a more complex microfinance market than comparable markets in any other country, with the possible exception of Indonesia. Services are provided by NGOs, commercial banks, cooperatives, mutuals (a type of savings and loan aimed at housing), and a special category of institutions, *fondos financieros privados* (FFPs), as shown in Table 1.1.[10] It is characteristic of the Bolivian industry that private, formal financial institutions provide the majority of services. Government wisely decided in the late 1980s not to provide financial services or own institutions that provide them, and this decision proved to be an enabling factor from the early days of microfinance. The dominance of formal financial institutions is a relatively recent development, however, as microfinance in Bolivia originated mainly among NGOs. The story of the transition from NGOs to financial institutions is a central theme in the development of the industry and in this book (chapter 5).

BancoSol

Any sketch of the institutional players active in 1999 must begin with the single largest provider of microfinance services, Banco Solidario, S.A. (BancoSol), a licensed commercial bank. For most of its life this extraordinary

Table 1.1   Microfinance Loans by Institution, June 1999

Institution	Type of Lending	Microfinance Borrowers	Microfinance Portfolio (US$ million)	Average Loan Balance	Number of Branches
NGOs:					
ProMujer	VB	17,641	1.82	103	4
Crecer*	VB	15,584	2.41	155	6
Sartawi*	SG, In	6,149	2.56	143	11
Diaconia	n/a	8,581	4.26	497	13
FUNBODEM	In	1,306	1.45	1,108	1
FONDECO*	SG, In	5,239	2.60	496	3
Total, NGOs		**54,499**	**15.07**	**277**	**38**
NGOs becoming FFPs:					
Prodem*	SG, In	42,205	16.70	396	50
Idepro (EcoFuturo)	SG, In, As	14,626	7.07	483	11
Fades (EcoFuturo)*	SG, As, In	23,253	9.17	394	21
ANED (EcoFuturo)*	As, SG, In	45,359	6.08	134	20
CIDRE (EcoFuturo)[a]	In, As	656	3.10	4,727	1
Agrocapital[a] *	In, As	4,410	10.75	2,438	10
Total, NGO/FFP		**130,509**	**52.87**	**405**	**113**
FFPs					
Caja Los Andes	In	33,852	27.64	817	14
FIE	In	23,522	15.16	645	15
EcoFuturo[b]	n/a	263	0.26	987	4
Fassil[c]	SG, In, As	30,101	18.03	599	6
Total, FFPs		**87,738**	**61.10**	**696**	**39**
BancoSol	SG, In	74,679	59.84	801	46
TOTAL		**347,425**	**188.88**	**544**	**236**

Source: Asofin, Cipame, and Finrural, *Microfinanzas: Boletin Financero*, no. 4 (June 1999).
Notes: VB = village banking; As = associations; SG = solidarity groups; In = individual. Listed in order of emphasis in the program. * = primarily rural lenders. n/a = not available
[a] Small business lenders with no microloans.
[b] Just starting as FFP. Will absorb much of the portfolio of Idepro, Fades, ANED, and CIDRE.
[c] Includes both consumer and microloans.

institution has offered one basic loan product—the solidarity group loan for microenterprises. On the strength of that sole product, it generated performance indicators that placed it at the top of the Bolivian banking industry during the mid-1990s. Every March the Superintendency of Banks publishes data on the banking system's performance during the previous year, numbers the press seizes and reports with fanfare. In 1999, as in each of the previous three years, the newspaper headlines stated, "BancoSol was the best local financial entity."[11]

BancoSol consistently tops the list on three of the five key performance indicators the analysts cite: return on assets (5.2 percent in 1998), asset quality (0 percent arrears), and capital adequacy (16.3 percent).[12] These are unusual and outstanding figures for a bank in any country. Most banks would be happy with return on assets at or above 1 percent and arrears of less than 2 or 3 percent. The minimum standard for capital adequacy in Bolivia is 12 percent, and most banks struggle to maintain it. Although BancoSol is never the leader in return to shareholders' equity, not being as highly leveraged as other banks, its 29 percent return on equity in 1998 placed it among the top-performing banks. Only in administrative efficiency does BancoSol score below the norm, reflecting the high cost of microfinance relative to volume.

These numbers changed the course of microfinance in Bolivia. When a microfinance bank put everything together to produce a bank both safe and profitable, people began to notice. Mary Elena Flores of Cooperativa Jesús Nazareno believes that the publication of the BancoSol statistics was the turning point that moved microfinance from its development period into its current competitive phase. The numbers convinced other institutions that there was money to be made in lending to the poor.

Despite the growth of competition BancoSol retains its leading market position. At the end of 1998, BancoSol was serving 82,000 clients through 41 branches, located mainly in urban areas. Its loan portfolio was $74 million.[13] The majority of the portfolio consisted of solidarity group loans, though BancoSol increasingly offered individual loans as well. The average size of loans was $908 (outstanding balances). BancoSol also provides savings services through savings accounts and time deposits. The story of BancoSol's creation, and that of its predecessor, Prodem, will be considered in detail in chapter 3.

Other Commercial Banks

Mainstream banks make some loans to microenterprises and supply savings services for some micro-level clients. Large banks, such as the Bank of Santa Cruz and Banco Boliviano Americana, lend to microenterprises through their consumer credit divisions. However, to date, only one other bank, Banco Económico, a relatively young bank whose main focus is small and medium enterprise, has moved into microfinance as a significant aspect of its business strategy. Its Presto division offers both microenterprise and consumer loans.

Fondos Financieros Privados (FFPs)

The next tier of microfinance providers are the FFPs, as well as several NGOs in advanced stages of converting into FFPs. FFPs are formal financial institutions whose minimum capital requirements are lower than those for commercial banks and who are not allowed to provide certain services banks provide. The government created this category in 1994 especially to accommodate the emerging microfinance industry. Much of the work to create the regulations for FFPs revolved around a specific case, Procredito, an NGO which spawned the first FFP, Caja Los Andes. Another microfinance FFP, FIE, also evolved as an NGO before converting. This pattern has become so much the norm that most of the established microfinance NGOs are at some stage in the process of becoming FFPs, including rural lenders Prodem, Sartawi, and Agrocapital, and a group of four NGOs (Fades, Idepro, ANED, and CIDRE) joining to form one FFP, EcoFuturo. The process of transformation has been one of the major contributions of Bolivian microfinance to international experience, and we will consider it in depth in chapter 5.

Although these institutions share the same regulatory category, each institution exudes a unique personality. Caja Los Andes is a no-nonsense, focused financial institution that makes individual loans to a total of 34,000 clients, with an active loan portfolio of $25.2 million.[14] Its strong individual loan methodology makes it a formidable competitor in the urban areas where it operates. It has achieved excellent profitability, with returns to equity of 36 percent in 1997 and 27 percent in 1998.[15] FIE, the other La Paz-based individual lender, has a somewhat softer image and aims to support the broader development of the enterprises it serves. Two other institutions, Agrocapital and CIDRE, are primarily small-enterprise lenders, with average loan balances above $2,000.

The largest organization in this group is Prodem, the original NGO from which BancoSol was born. After it spawned BancoSol, Prodem turned its attention to the still unserved rural population. Prodem's macho corporate personality is epitomized by its hard-charging, chain-smoking group of four senior managers; they see Prodem as a brash innovator not afraid of getting its hands dirty. Prodem has the best nationwide outreach in rural areas, which gives it a strong market position as other institutions begin pushing out from the major cities. With 50 branches, it has more outlets than BancoSol, and 42,000 clients.[16]

The FPP category also includes some institutions who began as financial institutions with purely commercial backgrounds, rather than converting from donor-supported NGOs. Fassil and Acceso specialize in consumer lending, while also conducting a significant microenterprise lending business. Fassil reflects the homegrown entrepreneurship of a single businessman and his backers. Its portfolio includes some 35,000 loans, split between consumer and microenterprise loans. Acceso, a subsidiary of a Chilean holding group, comes across slick and professional, as the multinational corporation it is. With 90,000 consumer-loan clients, Acceso led the entire financial sector in numbers of loans in 1999, which is particularly striking since it only began operating in 1995.

None of the FFPs are primarily savings based, although they are licensed to offer savings accounts and time deposits. In general, this bias reflects their histories as NGOs not authorized to take savings and as consumer lenders.

Non-Governmental Organizations

Mainstream microfinance in Bolivia has been handed over to the formal financial sector. Most NGOs aspire to become FFPs "when they grow up," in part because they expect to compete more effectively as FFPs. However, at least two NGOs have no intention of converting. ProMujer and Crecer are village banking programs whose aim is to reach the poorest possible clients, particularly women. This focus is reflected in their low average loan balances, around $160. They represent a type of microfinance institution prevailing throughout the world, with strong social and poverty-alleviation goals. However, they are not the norm in Bolivia. ProMujer emphasizes training and empowerment, while Crecer emphasizes nutrition and health education. Both deliver educational messages on these subjects and provide referrals to other service providers during their regular meetings with clients. They will not become FFPs partly because they believe the Superintendency would force them to abandon their broader missions. Nevertheless, the performance standards associated with FFPs spur them to make their operations as much like professional financial institutions as possible. ProMujer numbers 18,000 women among its clients, and Crecer 16,000. Most other NGOs are new and still small.

Cooperatives and Mutuals

Credit cooperatives (credit unions) in Bolivia include tiny localized institutions throughout the country, as well as a handful of large, sophisticated organizations based mainly in Santa Cruz. The vast majority of the members belong to the large cooperatives, which offer services little different from those available in a bank. They boast large, impressive corporate headquarters. Inside, only the discreetly placed Catholic statues hint at the difference between the cooperative and a commercial bank. The cooperatives and the mutual societies, which specialize in housing finance, have successfully cultivated images as places to save. They attract depositors by linking savings in clients' minds with meeting the qualifications for loans or home mortgages. A typical microentrepreneur said she saved at the mutual because she hoped to buy a house someday. Unfortunately for her, the mutuals serve a more middle-class market segment, especially salaried workers, and it is unlikely that she will ever qualify for a housing loan. The cooperatives also serve the middle class, though they do reach down market. Several cooperatives have established explicit microenterprise lending divisions. Among the 20 largest cooperatives affiliated with the World Council of Credit Unions, about 100,000 of their 226,000 members can be classified as micro and small enterprises.[17]

Aggregate Size

Taken together, the microfinance institutions number roughly 350,000 loans outstanding (excluding consumer loans and loans from cooperatives, which would probably double the number). This coverage reaches a large share of the estimated national market of 600,000 to 1,000,000. There is no way of knowing how many separate clients are represented in the number, because of the popularity among borrowers of borrowing from several institutions at once. The total active loan portfolio associated with microenterprise loans is $189 million. While this is a substantial sum in the microfinance context, it still represents less than 5 percent of the overall financial sector, which has an aggregate loan portfolio of $4.3 billion.[18] Nevertheless, in terms of numbers of clients, microcredit exceeds the rest of the financial sector. Thus, depending on whether one is concerned with magnitudes of financial flows or with delivery of financial services to people, the microfinance industry is either the least or the most prominent part of the financial system. This dichotomy must pose an ongoing dilemma for the superintendent of banks in allocating his scarce supervisory resources.

SIGNS OF CHANGE

Although the microfinance industry in Bolivia has never been static, in 1999 it was in the throes of change. The issues that people talk about, have conferences on, and worry over differ from those of 1992 or even 1996. The emergence of competition and commercialization as represented by Acceso, Fassil, and other new entrants is poised to have a major impact on the industry as a whole. Many people forecast an industry shakeout because the market cannot accommodate the growth goals of all current players.

The most pervasive immediate concern of everyone from front-line loan officers to industry analysts is market saturation in the urban areas and the closely linked problem of "over-indebtedness." The older microfinance institutions with NGO origins argue that the new commercial players, particularly the consumer lenders, seduce clients into borrowing more than their repayment capacity allows. They complain of irresponsible lending practices that encourage borrowers to move from provider to provider, taking out multiple loans. The solidarity group lenders are particularly concerned that these practices undermine the foundations of their methodology. They have always believed that the methodology rests on the concept of long-term partnership. But borrowers have less stake in a long-term relationship when they have their pick of several lenders.

The superintendent is reacting to the emerging risks with tougher regulations regarding loan documentation, analysis of repayment capacity, and limits on indebtedness. These changes carry their own costs. They trouble certain members of BancoSol's field staff who see the bank becoming more bureaucratic. Even clients notice the difference. One long-time BancoSol customer in Santa Cruz complained, "BancoSol doesn't trust us as much as it used to." His loan officer responded that the Superintendency, not the bank, required the signatures and certificates.

The formalization of the lending process accompanies increasing formalization of the sector as a whole as NGOs become FFPs with obligations to shareholders and banking authorities. Some observers believe that formalized organizations are already starting to shun risky innovations and less attractive markets in favor of immediate profitability and a safer portfolio. One concern is that more competitive, formalized microfinance lenders will move upmarket to larger, wealthier clients. Table 1.1 shows that in general the more formal the institution the larger the average loan. Other data show that the top loans are getting larger as institutions continue serving their fastest-growing customers. The question is whether this increase at the upper end implies abandonment of the lower end. Opinions here are strongly divided, as we will examine in chapter 7.

While fears of oversupply dominate the urban scene, traditional promoters of microfinance rush to tackle the unfinished agenda. Rural lending leads this agenda, particularly because of the prevalence of poverty outside the cities. Savings mobilization comes second. Some organizations with enterprise-development goals are turning, after a long hiatus, to small-enterprise lending and business-development services (nonfinancial assistance). A few experimenters contemplate new financial products, such as payment services and insurance. Government and donors are shifting their support programs into these newer areas.

Meanwhile, on a day-to-day basis, the front-line staffs of microfinance institutions concentrate on their clients. The Prodem loan officer in Batallas spends his Saturday sitting across a desk from clients who come in from the market with muddy shoes to inquire about the rules of the program, request to prepay their loans, or ask for a reference to Prodem's office in another city. BancoSol loan officers in Santa Cruz hold their weekly credit committee meetings over sandwiches and cups of thick coffee, arguing about how much money a group qualifies to receive, how to treat a good borrower in a bad group, and other problems at the heart of microfinance. They rarely have a chance to reflect on how much the birth and rapid growth of this industry have contributed to their clients and to the country as a whole (as we will in chapter 8). Instead, they look to the future with worried expressions, recognizing the forces propelling them into a new, more complex time.

NOTES

1. Herbert S. Klein, *Bolivia: The Evolution of a Multi-Ethnic Society.* 2nd ed. (New York: Oxford University Press, 1992), 11.
2. Olivier Berthoud and Walter Milligan, *Sector Informal Urbano y Crédito: Bolivia 1995* (La Paz: CEDLA and COTESU-NOGUB, 1995), 55.
3. Bolivia's Instituto Nacional de Estadísticas, website: www.ine.gov.bo
4. World Bank, "Bolivia: Poverty, Equity, and Income: Selected Policies for Expanding Earning Opportunities for the Poor," Report No. 15272-BO (Washington, D.C.: World Bank, 1996), 1:10.
5. Sergio Navajas, et al., "Poverty and Microfinance in Bolivia," Economics and Sociology Occasional Paper No. 2347 (Columbus, Ohio: Ohio State University, Department of Agricultural, Environmental, and Development Economics, 1996).
6. Asofin, Cipame, and Finrural, *Microfinanzas: Boletin Financiero*, no. 4 (June 1999).
7. World Bank, "Bolivia: Poverty, Equity, and Income," vol. 2 (1996), 10.
8. Ministry of Finance (FONDESIF), "Microcredit, the Pillar of Opportunities" (La Paz: Government of Bolivia, 1998), 11.
9. Klein, *Bolivia*, 319; Instituto Nacional de Estadísticas website.
10. The informal sector also provides its own services through informal finance, but these services are largely beyond our scope of concern.
11. *La Razon*, 3.21.99 (La Paz), B1.
12. *La Razon*, 3.21.99 (La Paz), B5.
13. Banco Solidario, "Memoria 1998" (La Paz, 1999), 112–14.
14. Asofin et al., *Microfinanzas*.

15. Caja Los Andes, "Presentacion" (La Paz, 1998).

16. Asofin et al., *Microfinanzas.*

17. World Council of Credit Union statistics (unpublished). Number of loans outstanding is not available, which makes comparisons to microfinance institutions difficult.

18. Superintendencia de Bancos y Entidades Financieras, *Boletin Informativo*, no. 125 (December 1999).

CHAPTER TWO

MICROFINANCE IN
THE TIME OF ADJUSTMENT

THE EVOLUTION OF MICROFINANCE in Bolivia is a story within a story. The broader story is about Bolivia's entry from 1985 into an era of stable democracy and economic liberalization. The question at the heart of this story is whether Bolivia's embrace of a market-led economy and stable democracy is succeeding in creating prosperity for Bolivia's citizens. Microfinance, which began at the start of the new era, is part of the answer to that question.

The events of 1985 marked a turning point for Bolivia more profound than any since the country's celebrated national revolution in 1952. A new government took charge in 1985 with an economic program that dismantled the state capitalism on which the national consensus had rested since the 1952 revolution. This new government stanched hyperinflation and began outlining an economy based on liberal principles. If not deep enough to be considered a revolution, the change in 1985 was at least a major course correction. The principles introduced at that time have continued through three presidential elections, giving Bolivia a period of unprecedented political and economic stability. Since 1985, World Bank and other experts have held Bolivia up as a model of economic reform. Its privatization/capitalization program, its financial-sector reforms, and its Popular Participation (a decentralization program) are all viewed as models for international emulation. And although microfinance was never a government initiative, it too earns Bolivia a place as a prominent international example.

The emergence of microfinance is intimately connected with these political and economic changes. Like these other initiatives, microfinance has been a handmaiden of Bolivia's economic adjustment, in the sense that it both served and was served by the adjustment. It is no coincidence that the microfinance story begins immediately after 1985. The adjustment created the conditions that allowed microfinance to flourish, both by increasing demand and by facilitating supply. Microfinance even helped reinforce the new governing consensus by offering the economically disenfranchised a taste of the fruits of economic liberalization, partially mitigating the social costs of adjustment. Although the government did not plan it, microfinance complemented the government's program beautifully.

This chapter explores the relationship between microfinance and the social and economic forces transforming Bolivia at the end of the twentieth century. In addition, it examines the growth of the informal sector, the customers of microfinance. It describes how the informal sector explosion of the 1980s related to the economic crisis and the adjustment that followed. A look at the economic and (briefly) the political role of the informal sector at the start of microfinance will lay the groundwork for chapter 8, when we try to understand how significant microfinance has been, and may yet be, for Bolivia's social and economic development.

THE HYPERINFLATION CRISIS

During the 1980s, inflation was a way of life for most South Americans. Ordinary people became as expert as macroeconomists at calculating inflated prices and anticipating inflation's effects on their lives. But in 1984 and 1985, Bolivians surpassed them all with eighteen months of true hyperinflation (defined as inflation above 50 percent per month). At the peak of the crisis, in February 1985, prices nearly tripled within a month, and the annual inflation rate reached 24,000 percent.[1] A pair of shoes that had cost 300 Bolivian pesos in 1982 (about $10) would sell in May 1985 for nearly 700,000 pesos.[2] The government became so desperate that it began issuing "bearer notes," flimsy IOUs issued because the government had no more authority to print money.

Hyperinflation quickly made a pauper of anyone unlucky enough to hold savings in Bolivian currency. Everyone who could fled the money economy. The rich took their wealth out of Bolivia, while the poor put theirs into tangible things and even reverted to barter. People postponed their economic plans, hunkering down to await a return to normality, or engaged in unproductive speculative activities such as black market trading or hoarding goods for subsequent sale. Although many people profited from hyperinflation, it was devastating for the economy at large. The value of the assets of the banking sector evaporated into thin La Paz air.

Students of macroeconomics have examined the specific events that triggered the hyperinflation crisis: the debt crisis, the overvalued exchange rate, the printing of money. However, for our purposes it is more important to understand that these macroeconomic events sprang from long-term political and economic problems. In essence, the crisis demonstrated that the revolution of 1952 had not provided Bolivia with a basis for long-run economic growth. Although it took 33 years for the system established in 1952 to reveal itself as bankrupt, Bolivia had long been living on borrowed time.

THE NATIONAL REVOLUTION, 1952

The populist revolution of 1952 had been a great step forward, transforming the power structure that had dominated Bolivia since the earliest colonial times. From the Spanish discovery of silver, Bolivia's economy centered on the extraction of wealth from her mountains, wealth that was invested anywhere but in Bolivia. Aside from mining and large-scale *hacienda* farming, the Bolivian economy consisted almost entirely of peasant agriculture. The tiny stratum of elites—people in charge of the mining companies and *haciendas*—controlled the government and used it to serve their interests. It is not too gross an oversimplification to say that in mid-century, despite over 100 years of independence, Bolivia was still a colonial society run by a small group of people for extractive purposes.

The populist coalition that took power in 1952 sought to open the Bolivian economy and political power to the broader population, primarily the emerging urban middle class and to a lesser extent the peasants. The movement did not so much envision a new kind of economy as a change in control of the existing economy. Its leaders vowed that government would take control of the mines and put them to the service of the Bolivian people. The Nationalist Revolutionary Movement (MNR), the party of the revolution, quickly nationalized the three largest tin-mining companies. The other big nationalization, creating Bolivia's state oil company, had been carried out fifteen years earlier. Among the most revolutionary changes the MNR made were an agrarian reform to distribute the land of the *haciendas* among small farmers and enfranchisement of the overwhelming majority of the population.

Throughout the next three decades successive governments pursued state capitalism, in which government owned or controlled the country's main strategic industries, while allowing the private sector to operate. Ultimately, however, government-as-producer could not provide Bolivia with a sound basis for economic growth.

The problem arose from a factor beyond government control. The tin industry slowly declined as international prices fell and Bolivia depleted its easily reached deposits. Bolivia desperately needed new sources of economic dynamism, but most of its key players devoted their energies to getting a bigger cut of the declining mining industry. Sachs and Morales, writing in the late 1980s, identified deep flaws in the country's political economy.

Various sectors in Bolivian society are highly mobilized to do battle over their respective shares of a highly unequal distribution of income and wealth. Since the Revolution, each social faction has looked to the central government to satisfy its particular distributional agenda. Consequently, the battle for political power has also been a battle over the sharing of the "national pie."[3]

Whether in the hands of civilians or military men, state capitalism effectively became a means of distributing the pie, rather than a means of enlarging it.

In politics, these battles led to frequent changes in government, splintering of parties, and violence between government and militant labor unions.[4] Writing in 1985, a World Bank team stated, "Since 1979 there have been no less than three elections, six presidents, three coups that succeeded and twice as many that failed."[5] In the economy the results were predictable. Foreign investors found Bolivia too unstable. Even Bolivians sent their money to safer places. The World Bank noted that private participation in Bolivia's industry was among the lowest of any non-socialist countries.[6] The only bright spots, the beginnings of export-oriented agriculture in Santa Cruz and investment in newly discovered hydrocarbon fields, were not enough.

The political leaders gradually bankrupted the government by attempting to satisfy demands for the prosperity the economy was not producing. Government gave out wage benefits it could not afford during populist phases and corporate subsidies it could not afford during conservative ones, printing money as necessary. It borrowed freely from foreign banks until the bankers finally decided in the early 1980s that Bolivia was no longer creditworthy. The emerging debt crisis marked a beginning of the slide into hyperinflation. The democratically elected Siles government attempted a series of flawed stabilization programs, but each left the situation worse than before, until in 1984, with hyperinflation taking off, Siles could continue no longer. He moved the election timetable forward one year, and a new government took office in August 1985.

THE NEW ECONOMIC POLICY

It is a great irony in Bolivian history that the party and president of 1985 were the same as in 1952: the MNR and Paz Estenssoro. However, the ideas behind Estenssoro's New Economic Policy differed dramatically from the MNR platform from the National Revolution. The new team listened to neo-liberal economists and included senior members educated at the University of Chicago and Yale. According to Jeffrey Sachs, who advised the new government, "The so-called 'New Economic Policy' was nothing less than a call to dismantle the system of state capitalism that had prevailed over the previous thirty years."[7] In fact, it was more than that; it was the start of an agreement among most of the key actors (though in some cases a grudging agreement) to spend less energy worrying about dividing the pie and more energy creating a bigger one.

The new government took immediate, credible measures to extinguish the hyperinflation, including, among other things, unifying the exchange rate and implementing tight monetary and fiscal policies. Klein calls the package "a textbook model of conservative economic policy."[8] Astonishingly, prices stopped rising almost overnight. By 1986, annual inflation had fallen below 12 percent, where it has remained ever since. In addition to short-term stabilization, the Paz Estenssoro program called for deeper structural changes, moving away from state-owned enterprises and focusing the state instead on providing a supportive environment for private-sector growth. These structural adjustment policies continued through three MNR administrations and even survived a change of party to the ADN (*Acción Democrática Nationalista*). They represent a fundamental economic consensus accepted—or at least tolerated—by the majority of Bolivians.

Observers of economic development note that periods of sound economic policies often follow periods of cataclysm, such as war or, in this case, hyperinflation.[9] The chaos and desperation of 1984–85 frightened Bolivians deeply enough to accept bitter medicine they refused in ordinary times, including the need for a new economic consensus. The majority accepted the recession that the stabilization program triggered, understanding, perhaps, that it was the inevitable hangover after a long binge. And, grateful for the end of hyperinflation, they gave the new government time to demonstrate that its more fundamental adjustments would put the country on a growth path. The government needed that time; although hyperinflation ended immediately, the return to economic growth was slower. The economy climbed out of recession by 1987, but growth remained weak and the slide in per capita income only stopped in 1991.

At the broadest level the new leaders had to show that their liberal approach would solve Bolivia's ultimate development problem, namely, the lack of sources of economic dynamism beyond the extractive sectors. The liberal creed said that failure to develop such sources resulted from a history of poor economic and political policies, and that good policies would convince Bolivians and foreigners to begin investing. Yet Bolivia faced serious geographic disadvantages, and it was not obvious where growth could arise. Microfinance, as an aspect of the liberal approach to development, was challenged to show that the economy's low end could become a source of growth. We will return in a later chapter to see how it has performed.

THE NEW ECONOMIC POLICY SETS
THE STAGE FOR MICROFINANCE

The fresh memory of the 1985 crisis and the new government's bold changes in national policy provided the setting for microfinance. In fact, microfinance could only start in earnest once the hyperinflation monster was back in its box. Although there had been a few earlier experiments in lending to the poor, these had not led to anything substantial or lasting. The real starting point for today's microfinance industry was the launching of Prodem in 1986 and of several other initiatives at roughly the same time.

Both the successes and the difficulties of adjustment contributed to the growth of microfinance. Potential demand for microfinance was booming in the form of a fast-growing informal sector. The previous economic chaos had contributed to the swelling of the informal sector, but the layoffs associated with adjustment made it even larger. Adjustment facilitated on the supply side, too, through favorable economic and financial policies under which microlenders could operate successfully. Finally, the adjustment provided a motivation for microfinance: concern over the effects of adjustment spurred the founders of microfinance into action.

Supply Conditions for the Emergence of Microfinance:
Financial Reforms

The events of 1985 transformed the environment for the financial sector from prohibitive to strongly favorable. During the first half of the 1980s, Bolivia's economic environment choked off the development of sound financial institutions in general, not just institutions serving the poor. Hyperinflation sucks value from the financial system. Depositors frantically pull their money out of local currency and local banks, while borrowers repay loans with money worth a fraction of its original value. In order to survive Bolivia's hyperinflation, banks made investments abroad and put their equity into real estate and other tangible assets that would not devalue. Some of the banks privileged to obtain foreign exchange at the low official rate made astonishing profits selling it at the sky-high black-market rate. Credit unions, which had few links outside the country, bought real estate or opened nonfinancial enterprises to maintain their incomes. One credit cooperative in La Paz survived for several years by running a sauna and health spa.

The hyperinflation came on top of a weak financial system of a kind all too common in the developing world. The commercial banks were essentially the financial arms of private corporate groups owned by families or close-knit groups of wealthy men. They offered few services to the public at large. Banking supervision was ineffective, and government controlled interest rates. Service to middle and lower-end customers was left to development banks, which operated at a loss. The credit programs of NGOs and government development banks lent their money at interest rates that did not come close to adjusting for inflation, effectively turning them into grant programs, even when borrowers repaid in full. Looking at this environment in 1984, Acción International concluded that it would be self-defeating to launch any microcredit work until economic conditions improved.

With the arrival of the New Economic Policy the government began to lay the foundation for a modern financial sector, simultaneously creating favorable conditions for the growth of microfinance institutions. Full-scale reform has taken years and continues today, but in the beginning the government took two steps particularly important for microfinance.

First, it set good macroeconomic policies, specifically, control of inflation and liberalization of interest rates. Low inflation meant that lenders could maintain the value of their assets over time, and liberalized interest rates meant that they could charge microfinance clients the higher rates necessary to cover the higher operating costs of small loans. Low inflation and interest rate de-control were the policy prerequisites for creating a microfinance program with some hope of becoming sustainable. Without them, nothing would have changed.

Second, also relatively early on, the government decided to close its money-losing state development banks. This move, coupled with the debilitating effects of the hyperinflation on nearly all financial institutions, left a gaping vacuum in delivery of financial services, especially for the low-income population. Microfinance faced an empty field.

Those enabling policies began the financial-sector recovery, but painful steps continued. Through a series of banking crises and reforms, culminating in new banking legislation in 1993, Bolivia has gradually transformed the oligopolistic club that was its financial system into the beginnings of a sound, modern banking sector. Among the most important aspects of the new system is a capable and independent Superintendency of Banks, which has played a crucial role in microfinance development. The Superintendency upholds high prudential standards and at the same time supports developments that provide financial services to more Bolivians. As microfinance progressed, so did the Bolivian financial sector: individual banking institutions matured, and the capital markets developed new financial instruments. By the time microfinance was ready to join the mainstream financial sector, the mainstream offered a framework that permitted microfinance to be welcomed. We will discuss these financial reforms at greater length in chapter 5, describing the transformation of microfinance programs into formal financial institutions.

Demand Conditions for Microfinance: The Informal Sector

The adjustment program introduced in 1985 increased demand for microfinance by creating a situation in which growing numbers of workers became self-employed. Massive layoffs affected the now unprofitable state mining company, COMIBOL. Coincidentally, the international tin market collapsed. During the first three years of adjustment, COMIBOL dismissed a total of 23,000 miners, and the state-owned oil company YPFB laid off 4,000 workers.[10] Over the course of the next ten years, government closed, sold, or shrank a variety of state enterprises, large and small, generating more displaced workers. In 1985, the public sector had employed 24 percent of the labor force in the three main cities of La Paz, Cochabamba, and Santa Cruz. By 1989, its share had fallen to 17 percent.[11] Most of these workers found their way into the informal sector.

The link between microfinance and the shrinking public sector was largely indirect. Although a few microenterprise development programs tried helping unemployed miners start businesses, including small mines, they were not very successful. One pioneering organization, Fades, is still trying to recover loans to miners from those early days. Apparently an outside program could not turn a miner into an entrepreneur. Rather, the link between layoffs and microfinance took place at the macro level, in that the public sector was no longer a source of employment growth. The informal sector took the burden of providing jobs.

We will now examine the informal sector, a portion of the economy that many people saw as the evidence of economic failure, but which a few mavericks saw as a potential source of economic development.

THE NATURE OF THE INFORMAL SECTOR

On first acquaintance it is easy to mistake Bolivia's informal sector for a remnant of the past. It looks like the antithesis of the modern world, nowhere more than in La Paz. After all, commerce between highlands and lowlands first created the city and caused it to grow. Artisans in the informal sector often work with hand tools, using technologies that have changed little for decades or even centuries. The colorful traditional costumes and displays of fruits, flowers, and vegetables make the city's open-air markets a picturesque window into earlier times. The tourist who seeks out vendors of traditional remedies and magic is rewarded by gruesome displays of preserved llama fetuses. He thinks, "What could be more deliciously primitive?" Such impressions are misleading, however, for the urban informal sector is a fairly recent, and in some ways very modern, phenomenon. Its numbers, the diversity of goods sold, and its relationships to government and the economy are all products of the late-twentieth century.

Several decades ago informal sector vendors did not crowd city streets. The cities were small, and the poor stayed at home in the rural areas, where they continued a life of traditional agriculture. At mid-twentieth century, most people worked on farms, with mining also employing large numbers in the altiplano near Oruro, Potosi, and Chuquisaca. Bolivia's urban axis (La Paz, Cochabamba, and Santa Cruz) accounted for only 15 percent of the country's population.

The urban informal sector grew as the poor migrated into cities throughout the twentieth century, particularly after 1950. Among other factors the 1952 land reforms disrupted traditional relationships between rural residents and their lands. Improvements in health brought faster population growth, increasing pressure on the land. Many people went in search of new opportunities. By 1988, 30 percent of the population lived in the three axis cities.[12] Yet Bolivia's cities did not produce enough formal jobs to absorb the newcomers. Moreover, most of the new arrivals were unschooled and unskilled. Many spoke only Quechua or Aymara. They were ill-suited for formal employment. Bolivia's informal sector grew until it reached unanticipated proportions.

The informal sector in Bolivia is larger, relative to the formal sector, than in other Latin American countries. Its magnitude stems from the underdevelopment of the Bolivian economy generally, particularly its reliance on extractive industries that generate relatively little employment. Beginning in the late 1970s, the poor performance and slide into crisis of Bolivia's economy accelerated informal sector growth. Between 1976 and 1983, informal employment in La Paz grew at nearly 8 percent per year, while formal employment only grew at 2 percent.[13] By 1983, a household survey showed that 57 percent of the La Paz labor force was involved in the informal sector. Nearly all the city's retailers (89 percent) were informal.[14]

At first no one paid much attention to the informal sector, in Bolivia or in the other countries experiencing rapid urban growth. Only in the 1970s did economic analysts start to consider the informal sector worth examining as a distinct phenomenon, and it was then that the International Labor Organization first coined the term. It was difficult for economists to "see" the informal sector through the familiar lenses used in labor economics: employment and wages. Labor economists measure economic health in labor markets by tracking wages and employment. These indicators make sense in developed economies where the vast majority of people are formal employees. But the informal sector does not offer work normally recognized as a job, nor is it easy to determine earnings—especially as they vary from month to month. These features rendered the informal sector largely invisible in statistics on the work force. Government often developed policies and plans as if the informal sector did not exist.

It was also hard at first for Latin American activists to "see" the informal sector. Nurtured on Marxist ideas, they focused on the plight of the proletariat of employed laborers. Microfinance expert Gloria Almeyda recalls that in the 1960s the issue driving activists all over Latin America was equity for workers. In Bolivia this concern focused on the miners. Activists helped organize mine and public employee unions, which were significant political forces in Bolivia from the 1950s through the 1970s. As the informal sector continued to grow, it became clear that not only would economists require new tools for understanding the informal sector, but activists would also need a new agenda to improve the lot of the people in it.

The first serious attempt to study the informal sector in Bolivia came from the Center for the Study of the Development of Labor and Agriculture (CEDLA), a think tank combining activism and labor economics. CEDLA published its first empirical study of the informal sector in 1988, calling it a new departure. Since then CEDLA has maintained a strong focus on this sector in research, advocacy, and action.

Before describing CEDLA's findings about the effect of adjustment on the informal sector, it will be helpful to digress for a moment to review how different schools of thought regard the informal sector. Among analysts of the informal sector, three basic perspectives predominate. One group, particularly macroeconomists, see the sector as residual, a source of pseudo-employment that reflects the failure of the formal sector to provide enough jobs. It swells when times are bad and shrinks when the economy is growing. It offers a social safety net but little else. These analysts assume that most participants in the informal sector would prefer formal wage employment if they could get it. Economists with this viewpoint are joined by social critics who see the formal sector playing a sinister role in exploiting the informal sector for its own convenience—for example, using it as a disguised source of workers not subject to labor regulations or as a pacification strategy against social unrest.[15]

A second perspective predominates among organizations that work actively with the informal sector, including microfinance institutions. They are more apt to use the term *microenterprise* rather than *informal sector*, though in this book the terms are used interchangeably. This perspective emphasizes the positive role the sector plays in providing employment and incomes, without discounting its safety-net functions. It sees a source of dynamism in the informal sector, a huge body of people who are surviving and improving their lives by their own efforts. The informal sector is a seed bed for enterprise growth, as some microenterprises grow to become small and even medium-sized businesses. Over a generation the informal sector provides the income families use to keep their children in school and serves as a training ground for entrepreneurial skills, so that even if a particular business does not grow, an important process of human development may be taking place.

A third perspective, whose leading proponent is Hernando de Soto, views the informal sector primarily in relation to the legal framework affecting business operations. The informal sector becomes the prime exhibit in the case for reform of commercial codes and regulations. Regulations and red tape impose huge barriers to becoming formal, particularly at the municipal level. De Soto is famous for documenting that in Peru, if a businessman wanted to fulfill all the requirements to become formal without paying bribes or using personal connections, he would need more than a year of consistent effort.[16] This perspective focuses on the continuing skirmishes that take place between the informal sector and the authorities over licensing, taxes, and operating space. Some of its proponents are particularly concerned with the links between informality and illegality, such as a 1989 study describing the role of Bolivia's informal sector in plowing cocaine revenues into the economy.[17]

Clearly these three perspectives are not mutually exclusive. In fact, all three are correct portrayals of important aspects of the sector. Microcredit, which serves microenterprises within their own milieu, is strongly linked to the second perspective. Explicit in microcredit is the belief that better access to finance will generate significant improvements in the well-being of participants in the sector. Those who hold the first perspective tend to ignore the sector, focusing instead on promoting formal sector growth, while those who hold the de Soto perspective concentrate on legal changes to integrate informals into the mainstream.

This book is written largely from the second perspective, recognizing both the safety-net function and the productive ones. The question for the present context is how the crisis and subsequent adjustment affected the balance between these two functions in Bolivia as microfinance began. We will see that in the crisis period of the late 1980s, the informal sector acted largely as a safety net, but that later, as economic stability returned and microcredit became available, the balance moved toward growth.

A simple framework assumes that the informal sector is both a cushion and a seed bed, but at different times one or the other of these functions may predominate. CEDLA's empirical observations of the changes between 1985 and 1989 offer a basis to organize the framework. CEDLA provides numbers that distinguish among key segments of the sector and allow for estimation of some of the flows within it. First, CEDLA divides the informal sector into two distinct segments: the semi-entrepreneurial and the family sector. A semi-entrepreneurial enterprise has some paid employees, while a family enterprise is either one person or involves unpaid family labor. Semi-entrepreneurial businesses are more likely than family enterprises to use more advanced techniques, to have fixed premises, and to sell to a more specialized market. In effect, semi-entrepreneurial businesses represent the growth dynamic within the informal sector. These are the businesses most likely to become larger formal businesses.

Second, CEDLA looks at the proportion of commerce and service businesses in the informal sector vs. manufacturing. Its not-so-implicit view is that manufacturing is more productive than commerce and services, and therefore increases in the share of manufacturing are a sign of forward movement. One does not have to subscribe to the view that commerce and services are unproductive, however, in order to recognize that small-scale vending is the easiest point of entry into the informal sector, and that when the informal sector plays its safety-net role, flows into street vending probably increase.

A simple flow diagram of the informal sector, one that distinguishes between the positive dynamics of the sector and its passive safety-net effects, shows three types of flows or movements of people and businesses: those constituting positive economic development, those constituting negative development (worsening conditions), and underlying demographic trends. The first flows that constitute positive economic dynamism include (see Figure 2.1):

- family enterprises becoming semi-entrepreneurial (Business Growth)
- an increase in the share of manufacturing businesses in the sector as a whole (shown by the placement of the dotted line across each box)
- semi-entrepreneurial businesses becoming formal (To Formal Sector)
- informal sector participants getting formal jobs (To Wage Employment)

Only in the last case is the source of the growth outside the informal sector. Conversely, the negative flows are:

- semi-entrepreneurial businesses sliding back to the family sector (Business Contraction)

Figure 2.1 Informal Sector Flows

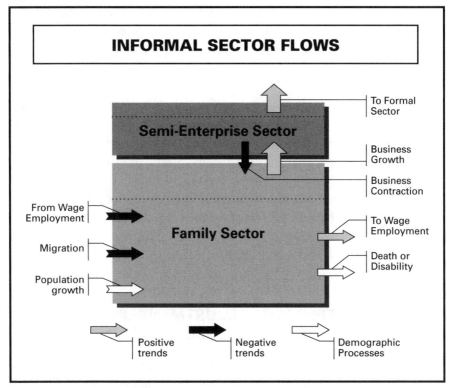

Note: The dotted horizontal line inside each box shows the division among commerce and services (the largest portion) and manufacturing.

- increase in the share of commerce and services in the sector as a whole (upward movement of the dotted line)
- formal businesses moving back to the informal sector (rare, not shown)
- redundant formal employees joining the informal sector (From Wage Employment).

Underlying these flows is a more neutral set of trends caused by demographics, including population growth and the urban migration that has always fed the informal sector. Urban migration would actually be a mixed flow, as it reflects a long-term demographic trend but would also fluctuate with economic conditions, rising during hard times. Figure 2.1 displays these flows.

The active role of the informal sector is represented by the arrows showing movement of the enterprises from the family to semi-entrepreneurial segments and of participants into wage employment. It also appears when the proportion of manufacturing businesses in each segment increases. The role of the sector as a place of refuge is represented by the arrows showing movement into the family sector from the semi-entrepreneurial sector, wage employment, and increased urban migration (though to some extent, urban migration is a long-term demographic trend). It would also appear in increased proportions of commercial businesses.

Incomes also pose critical questions for analyzing the role of the informal sector over time. One of the strongest reasons for the negative image of the informal sector is the paltry income it provides to owners and workers. When the informal sector acts as a safety net, incomes would be expected to go down. When it acts as a positive force, the expectation would be of gradually increasing incomes, after taking into account the effects of demographics. Unfortunately, incomes are hard to track reliably, even with expensive surveys, and a good map of incomes over time is not available. We must learn as much as possible from the information gleaned from changes in sectoral composition, which is at least indicative of the basic processes at work.

THE EFFECTS OF ADJUSTMENT ON THE INFORMAL SECTOR

With this framework we can examine what CEDLA's data reveal about the effects of Bolivia's 1985 adjustment program on the informal sector. CEDLA analyzed changes in the distribution of employment in the three axis cities between 1985 and 1989. Unfortunately, it is not possible to measure the actual flows shown in Figure 2.1. Data is only available on the net effects, making it hard to distinguish between the flows that bear on the response of the sector to current economic conditions and those that represent demographics. For example, an increase in the number of one-person vendors may reveal the safety-net effect, but only after correction for the long-run rate of entry from rural-urban migration.

During the late 1980s the total urban labor force was growing at 6.1 percent annually, not quite as fast as in the late 1970s and early 1980s. More important, the shares of the sectors absorbing that labor force changed significantly. As a direct result of the adjustment policies, employment in the state sector fell from 24 to 17 percent. The overall share of the informal sector changed hardly at all, but within the sector the family segment rose from 38 percent to 43 percent of all employment, while the semi-enterprise segment shrank from 19 to 14 percent. At the same time that the semi-enterprise segment was losing ground to the family segment, manufacturing was losing ground to commerce and services in the informal sector as a whole. The changes were particularly

Table 2.1   Informal Sector in Three Cities: Shares of Employment by Type of Activity (percent)

Activity	Semi-Enterprise Sector		Family Sector	
	1985	**1989**	**1985**	**1989**
Manufacturing	31.4	17.7	18.3	12.9
Commerce/Service	34.9	56.3	65.1	72.8
Other	33.7	26.0	16.6	14.3
TOTAL	**100**	**100**	**100**	**100**

Source: Silvia Escobar de Pabón, *Crisis, Política Económica y Dinámica de los Sectores Semiempresarial y Familiar: La Paz—Cochabamba—Santa Cruz, 1985–1989* (La Paz: CEDLA, 1990), table 8.

dramatic in the semi-enterprise segment, as Table 2.1 shows.

The small semi-enterprise manufacturing businesses were particularly hard hit, falling from nearly a third of the enterprises to less than a fifth. The informal sector was increasingly concentrated in one kind of business, single-person commerce and services.

The story told in these numbers can be summarized, if somewhat over-simplified, as the replacement of the small, male-run workshop with the female market vendor. The most dramatic trends of all involve the rapid entry of women into the labor force. While the total urban labor force was growing at 6.1 percent, the female urban labor force was growing twice as fast, at 12.1 percent, so that in five years women rose from 36 percent to 45 percent of the work force. By 1989, female work-force participation was concentrated in the family sector (employing 55 percent of all women vs. 34 percent of all men), and within the family sector, in commerce.[18]

Looking at these trends, CEDLA concluded that the sector was sliding backward, that the strong growth of female, family-sector commerce and service businesses reflected a coping strategy by thousands of people whose economic aspirations were thwarted—refugees from state employment, from manufacturing and slightly larger businesses, and from the poverty of rural areas. Women took a more active part in the labor force because their husbands could not support their families alone. This development can be seen as a step forward for women into greater economic independence or as simply another form of exploitation, given that women's enterprises tend to offer very low returns. CEDLA found evidence that incomes within the sector were dropping, and that employees of informal businesses were forced back into increasingly insecure arrangements—from salary, to hourly wages or piece rate work, or to unpaid family labor. In short, the safety-net function of the informal sector dominated.

It was in this setting that microcredit began, not surprisingly, with women selling in the marketplace. These women were the bread and butter of microcredit from the start, and even today female market vendors probably outnumber any other group of clients. In the decade since microfinance began, it has reached beyond these origins to a somewhat broader spectrum of clients and range of services. We will return in chapter 8 to ask whether market vendors and the informal sector have been sources of economic progress during the past decade, and we will see evidence that throughout the 1990s strong progressive forces worked in the sector, with the backing of microcredit.

THE INFORMAL SECTOR AND POLITICAL CHANGE

Microcredit grew in a time of important political changes for Bolivia as well as economic changes. Here, too, the role of the informal sector has posed fundamental questions. As the informal sector emerged into numerical importance, its political significance lagged behind.

The 1970s and early 1980s saw intensive political strife with heavy military intervention in government. Until 1982, power changed hands more often through coups than elections. By the late 1970s most influential Bolivians had become convinced that Bolivia could and should return to democracy, and in 1982 President Siles Suazo was elected; but only with the return of Paz Estenssoro and a revamped MNR in 1985 did the political scene gain real stability. The MNR led the government through three administrations—Paz Estenssoro, Paz Zamora, and Sánchez de Lozada. Finally, in 1997, the electorate asked for a break from the steady diet of economic reform and voted for General Hugo Banzer (who had been president during the only relatively calm and prosperous years of military rule in the 1970s). The Banzer government did not dramatically alter the MNR course, and the political scene throughout most of the 1990s involved healthy interchange, with general agreement on fundamentals.

Nevertheless, the great political question for Bolivia remains open. That question, which is highly relevant for our purposes, concerns the political integration of the mass of poor Bolivians. When will it happen and how? How much progress has taken place? This question unavoidably contains an ethnic dimension, though political correctness prevents many people from speaking of it openly. It is plain to see that most of the population of Bolivia is poor and of Native American origin, descendants of the Inca (Quechua), the Aymara, and other groups, while nearly all the political and economic leaders continue to come from the traditional, elite descendants of the Spanish. Friends of former President Gonzalo Sánchez de Lozada jokingly call him a Hong Kong governor—a foreigner at the end of a long line of colonial overseers like the British rulers of Hong Kong. Though exaggerated, this image has a grain of truth.

Until the National Revolution of 1952, the mass of Bolivian rural peasants lived under semi-feudal arrangements or in small free communities (indigenous groupings, recognized by the authorities). Only in 1952 did they gain the right to vote, and, as supporters of the MNR, some measure of political influence. It was progress, but real power remained elusive. Later, as the informal sector emerged, it was essentially a new force, even though it was made up of these same people, now living in the cities and developing different interests from their rural relatives. To have a complete understanding of the origins and development of microfinance, it is important to see how the political role of this group evolved.

The informal sector began as a disorganized body of people lacking political clout or even effective means of representing their interests. In the 1980s, when members of the informal sector took some first steps toward organizing, with the help of activists, they drew from the existing tradition of labor-union militancy that had so dominated Bolivia in previous decades. Each local market developed its own syndicate, modeled on labor unions. Members paid dues to the syndicate, which was run by a few elected leaders. The syndicates used time-tested protest tactics, such as street marches, which even today routinely tie up traffic in the cities. However, as Roberto Casanovas, a long-time observer of the informal sector, points out, informal-sector syndicates are rarely as well funded or disciplined as labor unions. Unlike informal sector syndicates, labor unions can force dues-paying membership as a condition of employment. Moreover, it is characteristic of Bolivian politics of all kinds—parties, unions, and interest groups—that political groups remain localized and that frequent fissures among factions hinder collective action at higher levels.[19] The informal sector illustrates this point in force. Its syndicates focused almost exclusively on immediate concerns of the most practical and local variety—market space and amenities, and keeping license taxes low—the de Soto issues. Although activist groups such as CEDLA encouraged them to organize for higher-level collective action and published how-to manuals, the syndicates failed to build effective higher-level coalitions or federations at the city or national levels.

It is clearly only a matter of time until the mass of people of Native American origin and the growing mixed population come to dominate political life in Bolivia. But it is not yet clear whether this will come about through direct action of specific power groups or through assimilation as the middle class absorbs people from lower economic levels. Indirectly, microfinance supports the assimilation strategy. Its operative model is not collective political action but individual economic action, a fundamentally nonmilitant approach. In chapter 8 we will see that the informal sector has made some gains over the past decade but still lags in access to power. At that point we will describe in more detail how microfinance, despite being a basically apolitical movement, has had political side effects.

REACTIONS TO THE SOCIAL COSTS OF ADJUSTMENT

Even though full political integration of the informal sector remains years away, there were nevertheless in 1985 important political forces concerned with the well-being of the country's low-income population. These forces, particularly activists on the left, used the plight of the poor as a major plank in their critique of the government. The crisis and New Economic Policy had dealt a stunning defeat to the left, most visibly in the evisceration of labor power through mass layoffs. Labor unions could no longer function as the core of the left's concern. Poverty emerged as a new focus.

CEDLA was one of the strong critics of MNR policies. In her introduction to the analysis of informal-sector trends, Silvia Escobar de Pabón laid out her critique broadly, "The social effects of the crisis and the economic measures applied from August 1985 in the framework of the New Economic Program have manifested themselves in: open unemployment, underemployment, reduction in salaries and real incomes, withdrawal of legal protections for the labor force, and a deepening of the phenomenon of tertiary labor [involvement in trading rather than production]."[20] Effects such as these became rallying points for activists concerned about poverty.

Some of the economists who backed the New Economic Policy, together with World Bank analysts, insisted that the social costs came not from the adjustment but from the poor economic policies that preceded it.[21] Bolivians would have to pay these costs sometime, if ever they were to build a sustainable economy. Whether the hardships suffered by the poor resulted from pre- or post-1985 policies, it was clear that it fell to the new government to provide solutions.

The businessmen who led the MNR saw that to ensure continued popular acceptance of their adjustment policies they would have to compensate for the social costs of adjustment. Although the MNR had become more economically conservative, it retained a populist strain. Concern with the social costs of adjustment provided an important motivational spark to launch microfinance programs. Microfinance fit neatly into the overall new economic policy as another measure to mitigate the costs of adjustment. And although government was not involved in the creation of microfinance programs, a number of the architects of the MNR strategy were among key players who launched Prodem, through a startling alliance with activists. Thus, while microfinance was not overtly a part of the New Economic Policy, it filled a policy niche perfectly.

But it was the activists who did the work. Throughout the activist community militancy was put aside in favor of experimentation with concrete actions to combat poverty, including microenterprise development. Pancho Otero, the first executive director of Prodem and BancoSol, remembers the feeling of optimism and energy among activists, their sense that at long last it might be possible to make something happen. The activists may not have overtly acknowledged the implicit support their efforts lent to the New Economic Policy; indeed, many of them were openly critical of the policy. But in creating successful microfinance institutions, they helped give the new policy a fair chance to succeed.

NOTES

1. Jeffrey Sachs and Juan Antonio Morales, *Bolivia: 1952–1986*, International Center for Economic Growth (San Francisco: Institute for Contemporary Studies Press, 1988), 9–10.
2. Calculations based on World Bank, *Economic Memorandum on Bolivia*, Report No. 5680-BO1985 (Washington, D.C.: World Bank, 1985), 106.
3. Sachs and Morales, *Bolivia*, 12.
4. Detailed accounts of these events may be found in Herbert S. Klein, *Bolivia: The Evolution of a Multi-Ethnic Society*, 2nd ed. (New York: Oxford University Press, 1992); and Christopher Mitchell, *The Legacy of Populism in Bolivia: From the MNR to Military Rule* (New York: Praeger Publishers, 1977).
5. World Bank, *Economic Memorandum*, 1.
6. World Bank, *Economic Memorandum*, 3.
7. Sachs and Morales, *Bolivia*, 28.
8. Klein, *Bolivia*, 275.
9. See World Bank, *Assessing Aid: What Works, What Doesn't, and Why*, World Bank Policy Research Report (New York: Oxford University Press, 1998).
10. Klein, *Bolivia*, 276.
11. Silvia Escobar de Pabón, *Crisis, Política Económica y Dinámica de los Sectores Semiempresarial y Familiar: La Paz—Cochabamba—Santa Cruz, 1985–1989* (La Paz: Centro de Estudios Para el Desarrollo Laboral y Agrario (CEDLA), 1990), table 5.
12. Klein, *Bolivia*, 319.

13. Roberto Casanovas Sainz and Silvia Escobar de Pabón, *Los Trabajadores por Cuenta Propia in La Paz: Funcionamiento de las Unidades Económicas, Situación Laboral e Ingresos* (La Paz: Centro de Estudios Para el Desarrollo Laboral y Agrario (CEDLA), 1988), 21-22.

14. Casanovas Sainz and Escobar de Pabón, *Trabajadores*, 20.

15. For example, Meagher writes that informalization is "a process of socio-economic restructuring instigated by the state and various groups within the formal sector in an attempt to maintain and expand their share of income in the context of economic crisis" (Kate Meagher, "Crisis, Informalization, and the Urban Informal Sector in Sub-Saharan Africa," *Development and Change* 26 [1995], 259–84).

16. Hernando de Soto, *El Otro Sendero* (Buenos Aires: Sudamericana, 1987).

17. José Blanes Jiménez, "Cocaine, Informality, and the Urban Economy in La Paz," in *The Informal Economy: Studies in Advanced and Less Developed Countries*, ed. Alejandro Portes, Manuel Castells, and Lauren A. Benton (Baltimore, Md.: Johns Hopkins University Press, 1989).

18. Escobar de Pabón, *Crisis*, tables 6 and 7.

19. Mitchell makes this point a central argument of his political analysis of the MNR (see *Legacy of Populism*).

20. Escobar de Pabón, *Crisis*, 1, author's translation.

21. World Bank, "Bolivia Poverty Report," Report No. 8643-BO (Washington, D.C.: World Bank, 1990), ii.

CHAPTER THREE

MAKING CONTACT:
PRODEM LEARNS TO SERVE
MICROENTERPRISES

IT IS POSSIBLE TO MARK the start of the microfinance industry in Bolivia as one day in February 1987, when Prodem made its first twenty loans to four groups of market women in La Paz. Prodem was not the first microenterprise lending program in Bolivia. FIE is slightly older, while Fades started at nearly the same time. The cooperatives are always quick to remind that they have been lending to microenterprises since the 1960s. Prodem, however, was the first to develop a lending product that connected to microenterprise clients in a big way; to turn that product into an efficient, high-volume operation; and to become financially viable. Prodem and its offspring BancoSol, in demonstrating what successful microfinance institutions look like, influenced nearly all facets of the industry. Monica Velasco, a member of the original Prodem team, observes that everyone in Bolivian microfinance today is indebted to the market and the culture that Prodem created.

This chapter describes how Prodem was launched, and how it learned to serve its clients. It seeks to uncover Prodem's "secrets" at two levels. First, Prodem developed an extraordinarily successful lending methodology. Clients flocked to its doors in unprecedented numbers and repaid their loans exactly on time at prices that allowed the institution to begin covering its costs within two years. As mentioned earlier, Prodem's solidarity group loan is the same product that took BancoSol to the top of Bolivian banking statistics in the mid-1990s. Second, Prodem became a solid institution with a vibrant corporate culture and a dense network of support within Bolivia and internationally. This institutional strength allowed Prodem to deliver its product efficiently, to refine it over time, and to set and meet increasingly ambitious goals. It provided the foundation for the creation of BancoSol.

Prodem's ability to excel grew out of a unique partnership between businessmen and activists. When these two very different groups of people began to overcome their mutual suspicions and find common ground, they drew on the strengths of each side to create a core set of values. Most of the analyses written about Prodem and BancoSol remark on their strong corporate cultures, but none has attempted to convey the essence of those values to the reader. This chapter seeks to bring those values to life, drawing on interviews with the people who created the institution.

EARLY EXPERIMENTS AND MODELS

Credit Unions

The credit unions, or credit cooperatives, were early attempts to provide financial services to Bolivia's lower-income population. The cooperative movement started in Bolivia during the late 1950s and early 1960s, linked to the Catholic Church. Many if not most cooperatives were founded by priests as parish-oriented organizations. Nearly all the cooperatives in Bolivia today have religious names—Jesús Nazareno, San Martin, La Merced. The philosophy emphasized thrift, collective decision-making, and protection of members against usury.

When credit unions began, they focused on the low end of the market. However, in the 1960s rural-urban migration was still in its early stages, and the main low-end market consisted of salaried workers who needed financial services to save—and sometimes borrow—money for buying and furnishing homes, for medical emergencies, and for old age. As it began to emerge, the informal sector lay outside the main focus of credit union activity. This emphasis is reflected in the products of credit unions—savings accounts and loans based on a multiple of savings.

Over time, the credit union movement suffered a number of problems. The cooperative form of governance tended to be vulnerable to unscrupulous leaders and to require more sophisticated management than was available to small, grassroots organizations. A number of cooperatives collapsed, some from fraud, others from incompetence. A more pervasive problem came from policies that favored borrowers over savers. For reasons including their hatred of usury, the availability of low-cost funds from donors, and a tendency for boards to be borrower-dominated, the credit unions offered savers low returns, as well as inconvenient and sometimes even uncertain access to their funds.

Internal problems aside, however, the hyperinflation nearly finished off the credit unions, as the value of assets held in financial form disappeared overnight. Many credit unions survived in the same way individuals did: they turned their financial assets into tangible assets. They purchased real estate, or opened other businesses, like health clubs. By the end of 1985, credit unions had few financial assets left. Although this period was a nadir for the cooperatives, several of the stronger institutions have since rebounded, particularly in Santa Cruz. They are proud to have rebuilt themselves without significant external subsidies. Francisco Perez, consultant for the World Council of Credit Unions, argues that both banks and NGOs received government and/or donor help to capitalize after the hyperinflation, but the cooperatives had to manage on their own. Today, the leading cooperatives are on their way to receiving the Superintendency's seal of approval as institutions free to raise deposits from the public (not just from members). Moreover, as chapter 6 will discuss, the credit unions have at last discovered the informal sector and the techniques of microcredit.

However, in the late 1980s, when microcredit started, the credit union movement was in a sadly weakened state. The initiators of microcredit fairly or unfairly regarded cooperatives as vaguely corrupt organizations that served the middle class. Considering credit unions largely irrelevant for their purposes, they sought a different model.

Rural Revolving Funds

Throughout Bolivia during the military regime of the 1970s, another type of credit institution began to appear, the rural revolving loan fund. With the military in power, many donors sought out NGOs to avoid channeling their support through government, a process repeated throughout Latin America. NGOs proliferated, especially in rural areas, doing a little of everything—rural development, health, water supply, and community organizing. Catholic parishes and local associations started programs. Many of these organizations began lending, especially for agriculture. They set up small revolving loan funds— with a few thousands of dollars (typically $30,000 to $50,000) and hired credit specialists to go out and lend the money.

Pancho Otero, Prodem's founding executive director, began his career in microfinance working in remote villages for a series of these revolving loan funds. He recalls that the good will behind these programs did not stop them from doing nearly everything wrong. They were rigid. Loans had one specific purpose, usually a particular farm input like potato seed, often delivered in kind rather than in cash. If a farmer already had potato seed or wanted to plant something else, he was out of luck. As befitting programs with an entitlement philosophy, benefits were rationed. Each recipient was entitled to a certain amount of credit, no matter how much land he could plant. Clients found creative ways to evade the rules, like loan applications submitted in the names of babies still in mothers' arms. The programs charged low interest rates, believing it immoral to charge high rates to the poor who could not afford them. Donors like the IDB encouraged this interest-rate policy, often setting ceilings on rates, although this eliminated any chance for the program to cover costs. Administration was slow and cumbersome. Head-office employees judged applications from clients they never saw. They based decisions on proper preparation of paperwork and conformity to rules. While the papers shuffled from desk to desk in a far-off town, villagers waited, anxiously watching the planting season advance. Otero, not one to submit meekly to authority, chafed under rules he increasingly believed to be nonsensical and left program after program, dissatisfied.

More formally, one would now say that these programs illustrated the old paradigm of directed development credit. The fundamental flaws of this old paradigm were articulated clearly by the voices of Dale Adams, J. D. von Pischke, and colleagues from Ohio State University beginning in the early 1970s, although the message did not successfully penetrate the mountains of Bolivia or the halls of the IDB for more than a decade. In the broader Bolivian development scene, these revolving funds never amounted to much. They were self-limiting because their low interest rates in a high-inflation environment (even before hyperinflation) eroded the value of their funds, leaving them with little or nothing after only a few years. They came and disappeared, reaching very few people, but perpetuating the belief that the poor were unbankable.

The First Finca Village Banks

An initial experiment in microcredit came from a rural development consultant named John Hatch. It led, indirectly, to the founding of Finca and the village banking methodology now used in ProMujer and Crecer in Bolivia, as well as a host of programs around the world. This experiment, which took place at the height of hyperinflation, was one of the wildest rides in the annals of development finance. Although Hatch's model now operates in Bolivia, its first Bolivian experiment was aborted.

In the wake of a drought in 1983, The US Agency for International Development (USAID) tasked Hatch with designing a fast-acting rural development program using local currency to assist affected families. Hatch, a believer in participatory development, had the idea (after his second bourbon on the plane to Bolivia, he claims) of creating informal, community-based finance funds. These village banks would receive a loan from USAID, which they in turn would lend to each family in amounts sufficient to buy 100 pounds of seed potatoes, repayable after the harvest. As different from rural revolving funds, the community would manage the loan fund and families would be free to use the loans for whatever purposes they chose. Hatch sketched out his ideas and received the go-ahead from USAID, together with a grant, in pesos, of the equivalent of $1 million.

The timing of this grant, just as inflation began to escalate, turned the project from an interesting experiment into a race against time. Hatch recalls that when he got the funds, the ratio of pesos to dollars was about twenty to one; a year later the ratio was closer to 2 million to one. During a five-week bank strike in which the funds were unavailable, the grant lost over half of its value. If the program was to have any use at all, the funds would have to be disbursed fast.

Hatch and his team developed a system of rapid mass disbursement, the closest program on record to the proverbial dropping money from the plane. Five teams would send promoters into a village to organize residents to form a village bank. In the morning a truck loaded with sacks of paper bills would roll into the village. The promoters spent the morning training the group in managing a village bank and then allowed the clients a few hours among themselves to elect officers and make some other decisions. If all went well, they ended the day by hauling out the sacks and giving instant loans off the back of the truck, worth about $50 per family. To maintain the fund's value, loan repayment was indexed to the price of potatoes, plus interest of 2 percent per month. Each borrower affixed his thumbprint as a signature, and Hatch and his team drove off to another village. In three days, a team could disburse a truckful of money. At night, the promoters used the money bags as mattresses, in order to keep them safe.

In this way the program, now beginning to be known as Finca, reached 32,000 borrowers in 420 groups in a 17-week period.[1] During the first year, Hatch recalls, repayments were very high, and repayment day would be the occasion for a village celebration with coca leaves, dancing, and a mountain of banknotes being counted on a table. Unsurprisingly, for reasons including Hatch's own background as rural developer rather than financial manager along with the time pressure for disbursement, this early program lacked proper controls and had barely begun any institutional development. It was criticized by a new team at USAID, who closed it down, leaving Hatch with a simmering grudge toward USAID.

Although this program was too loosely run to be the basis of a successful institution, it did contain the seeds of a solid concept for community groups managing a loan fund within a standardized framework. Hatch went on to refine and develop the concept into an international NGO, making several significant changes in philosophy, most notably a shift to targeting women.

Finca now has programs all over the world, and several major international NGOs have adopted its model, including, in Bolivia, ProMujer and Freedom from Hunger's Crecer program.

Hatch looks back on his cowboy days nostalgically, remarking that his big missed opportunity was not to get Paul Newman and Robert Redford, as Butch Cassidy and the Sundance Kid, the bank robbers who fled to Bolivia, to help raise funds for his Bolivian people's banks.

Acción and the Solidarity Group Model

The first microfinance experiment that really took root in Bolivia was Prodem's. The lending product Prodem introduced to Bolivia, solidarity group loans, was not its own invention but was adapted from a model Acción International had been developing in several other Latin American countries. Nor did Acción invent the methodology; Acción "discovered" it in a small program in El Salvador.

Acción, a US non-profit organization now exclusively devoted to microfinance, began in the early 1960s as a kind of private sector equivalent of the Peace Corps. A wealthy American businessman, Bob Blatchford, became seized with a desire to do something about poverty in the Latin American countries in which he operated. He assembled a group of well-heeled friends and colleagues, and founded Acción with the intent of sending young volunteers to work abroad. By the 1970s, Acción's focus had shifted toward research and community development, and it started its first microenterprise program, UNO, in Brazil. UNO was generally seen as successful. It was featured in an influential USAID analysis, "Ventures in the Informal Sector and How They Worked Out in Brazil"[2] But it served too few people at too high a cost to convince donors to invest substantially in microenterprise development.

At this point in the late 1970s, a small office in the research section of USAID became convinced that small and microenterprises were an increasingly important segment of the economy in developing countries. It was frustrated, however, that USAID could not offer effective models for assisting the development of the sector. Michael Farbman, chief of the office, decided to sponsor a research project, which he named PISCES (Program for Investment in the Small Capital Enterprise Sector), to search the world for effective models. Acción received the contract to explore the scene in Latin America. It fell to Acción employee Jeff Ashe, to, as he put it, "Go out and shake the trees." As it turned out, his work proved to be the means through which both he and Acción found their true calling.

Ashe, a tall, stoop-shouldered man with a slightly disheveled, professorial look, is one of the real innovators of microfinance. His characteristic bemused smile turns to enthusiastic animation whenever he starts to talk about the practical details of how to make a program work better. He recalls that most of what the PISCES team found was "just awful—ill-conceived, expensive, paternalistic, top down. We'd see sewing machines covered in cobwebs." But in a small office in the middle of the main market of San Salvador, they found a program operated by a credit cooperative, Fedecrédito, making loans to small groups of clients, using only their cross-guarantees as security. Ashe called it "one pearl amidst the dross." It seemed to be providing a service that clients valued. Moreover, it was the first program he had seen that had achieved a significant scale. The group guarantee was not the only feature that distinguished this program. It also had a strong sense of efficiency and accountability. It offered field staff 1 percent of all loan collections, and as a result, its field staff recovered nearly all loans, something Ashe rarely saw.

Another program PISCES discovered, this one in Asia, contributed to the development of the model that eventually served as Acción's mainstay. The Money Shop, a commercial bank in Manila, had a small stall in each market, staffed by a manager, a bookkeeper, and an accountant. This team developed a close knowledge of the local scene and relationships with leaders in the market area. They drew on this knowledge in selecting reliable customers. The combination of a lean staff, simple premises, and local knowledge made the Money Shops very profitable.

Ashe combined the principles from these two programs into a proposal that he presented inside Acción. He is too self-effacing to acknowledge that he was innovative, preferring to call his contribution "the sponge model of development—you suck it up and then you squeeze it out." To Ashe's surprise, almost no one bought the proposal. His fellow researchers in PISCES, the Hellinger brothers from the left-leaning NGO, Development Gap, positively hated it because it was not participatory and did not address long-run development of businesses through training and lending for long-term investments. Theirs is still an important critique of microfinance, as we will discuss in other chapters. Ashe's colleagues at Acción simply hesitated to take a gamble on something so different from what they had done before.

According to Ashe, only one Acción colleague, Steve Gross, was willing to try it out, in a project he was developing in the Dominican Republic with the Dominican Development Foundation. Gross and Ashe together created a solidarity group program to serve the ubiquitous *tricicleros* of Santo Domingo, men pedaling three-wheelers equipped with large baskets of goods for sale. The program "took off like a shot," recalls Ashe. Unfortunately, for institutional reasons, this program soon withered, but it served its purpose in demonstrating that the model worked. Acción began taking the model to other

Latin American countries. In each country it encountered resistance, usually on the grounds that the people of that country were too individualistic to form groups and guarantee each others' loans. In case after case, clients proved the doubters wrong. During the years from 1980 to 1986 the solidarity group methodology gradually became Acción's dominant approach. By the time Prodem began, twelve Acción programs were applying it in Peru, Colombia, Ecuador, and Honduras.[3]

The solidarity group model that emerged from Acción's early experiments contained much more than a new form of guarantee. It included the idea of operating close to the ground, using local knowledge to select good clients. The product was a simple loan delivered quickly and easily, appealing broadly to people in the market, free from the weight of training requirements and restrictions on usage. The model also emphasized keeping costs low with a lean staff, plain offices, and efficiency. Finally, it included the idea that staff would have incentives to enforce on-time collections. In short, it was both a loan product and a delivery method.

PRODEM'S ALLIANCE OF BUSINESSMEN AND ACTIVISTS

Prodem was born with an impressive array of backers, including some of the most influential businessmen and politicians in Bolivia, a team of highly motivated activists, Acción International, and, as the main financier, USAID. Prodem cannot claim the kind of rags-to-riches origin that has become part of the myth of Grameen Bank. The message from Prodem's creation is more realistic: Successful institutions do not grow from nothing. They require careful assembly of key ingredients. The quality of the ingredients in the mix, as well as the care taken in assembling them, have a profound effect on the chances that something important will emerge. Prodem's team combined technical know-how (Acción), commitment and local knowledge (the activists on the staff), influence and a business perspective (the Bolivian board members), and an adequate amount of start-up funding (USAID), all critical elements for building a solid institution. Moreover, in Prodem's case, the representatives of each of these elements included a number of extraordinary individuals. Perhaps the most extraordinary group were the business leaders who formed the board of directors.

During the years of military rule in Bolivia the elites of the business sector had been associated with the military regime, in the public's minds and in reality. The close-knit group of mining magnates, industrialists, and bankers had supported the idea that military rule was necessary in Bolivia at the time. However, as the 1970s drew to a close, members of this group began to perceive that it was time for Bolivia to return to democracy. The loss of industrialists' support for military rule was one behind-the-scenes factor bringing Bolivia back to elections.

The decision to found Prodem followed discussions between one of these industrialists, Fernando Romero, and the chairman of Acción International's board of directors, Jack Duncan. Duncan, an American businessman, had traveled for years in Latin America for W. R. Grace and Co., representing extensive mining, transport, and other interests in Bolivia. Romero, an eclectic and vigorous entrepreneur with an intellectual bent, also had interests throughout the Bolivian economy, in agribusiness, finance, and at one time as owner of the local Coca-Cola company. Duncan convinced Romero to assemble a group of his friends and colleagues to hear Acción's proposal for creating a microenterprise credit program.

At a meeting of the business forum, the Federation of Private Entrepreneurs of Bolivia, Duncan and Steve Gross made their pitch, marshaling their experience in other countries and results of a feasibility study conducted in Bolivia by Robert Christen, to present the most convincing case possible. They asked for people willing to join a board of directors. In an important move that is still unusual for international NGOs, they put a price on participation. Board members would have to ante up. The amounts requested—several thousand dollars each—were not high enough to represent significant investment by any of these wealthy individuals but were enough to ensure that members would not join frivolously. A handful of people came through and eventually contributed a total of $80,000 to Prodem's launch.[4]

The small group who joined the Prodem Board was already working together on a larger project—reforming Bolivia. Prodem's Board contained several of the most important reformers in the MNR who launched the New Economic Policy and a few reform-minded members of ADN. It included several past and future ministers, including ministers of finance, and a future president of Bolivia, Gonzalo Sanchéz de Lozada. The group was full of American-educated neo-liberals who sought market solutions to economic problems.

According to Sanchéz de Lozada, involvement in Prodem was part of a larger change in the stance of some members of the private sector. Sanchéz de Lozada's views about social responsibility were shaped by his education at a Quaker boarding school in Iowa, years that also account for his heavy Midwestern accent even when speaking Spanish. As the leading thinker among the group, he injected his Quaker values and his University of Chicago economics into the Bolivian debate: "The private sector had been identified with the military regime. The more creative businessmen had to fight to break that link, and that brought us to the consciousness of the great income distribution divide. There was a responsibility which we had to accept. This is one of the things that brought me into politics." One might say that this sense of responsibility was part of MNR's rediscovery of its populist roots, within the context of its neo-liberal economic outlook. Evidence of this rediscovery has appeared in several government initiatives, beginning with the Emergency Social Fund and continuing during Sanchéz de Lozada's administration with his Popular Participation program and Bonosol privatization/pension reform program (discussed in chapter 8). Microcredit represented an approach to "the great income distribution divide" that neo-liberals could embrace.

Another member of the board, David Blanco, an ADN member who had served as minister of finance under the more right-wing Banzer regime, speaks of a sense of obligation to improve Bolivia's social condition but also notes bluntly that the group saw microcredit as a way to reinforce the concept of the free market. Hearing his words, radical critics of the informal sector might find confirmation of their suspicions that the private sector uses the informal sector as a pacification strategy. A more sympathetic interpretation would be that, as true believers in private enterprise, Blanco and his colleagues wanted to make its benefits available to more Bolivians. Whatever the exact motivations, involvement of big business in a "do-gooder" initiative such as Prodem was a departure from the norm. "Bolivia had no Anglo-Saxon tradition of philanthropy. We've got confession to get us to heaven," quips Sanchéz de Lozada.

The businessmen were skeptical at first. Banker Blanco couldn't believe that a solidarity group guarantee would really work. Everyone blanched at the proposed interest rates. Sanchéz de Lozada recalls, "I had misgivings. It was on the edge of usury. But then the market women told me—I used to pay 10 percent per month to the moneylender." Blanco says that eventually they began to understand that the problem these women faced was access rather than cost.

For Romero, the new organization became a personal vision. During the early days of the Paz Estenssoro administration, Romero helped design the Emergency Social Fund, which provided funding for community projects throughout the country. He then ran the fund from a specially created cabinet-level post. As his office on the twelfth floor of the Central Bank filled with activists—men with ponytails, ethnics—he gradually became sensitive to the viewpoints of those who worked with the poor and better able to relate to the kind of people who would become Prodem's staff. Sanchéz de Lozada claims he's not sure whether Romero actually convinced them that Prodem would work, or whether they gave him their money to get him off their backs, making him prove his claims.

The second half of the alliance that created Prodem—the activists—did not appear until the project actually began. In the meantime, Acción and the board had secured a total of $560,000 from USAID in direct grants and local currency from the PL 480 food-aid program.

The politics of resistance to military rule in Bolivia had created a large and varied group of people with leftist views and a burning desire to change society. As Maria Otero, now president of Acción, recalls, "There was a little Che Guevara in everyone." The centers of socialist thinking in the country included universities, liberation theologians of the Catholic Church, and most prominent of all, the labor unions. Some of these people were grassroots political organizers, while others, like the researchers at CEDLA, were part of the intelligentsia. Others were social workers. After the changes in 1985, the energy drained out of the extreme left. The labor movement, in particular, had lost its driving force. Activists moved toward the mainstream and many went to work for NGOs.

The first activist to join Prodem was Pancho Otero, whom Acción hired as executive director, the only Prodem staff member to be an Acción employee.[5] An early evaluation of Prodem, in good "bureaucratese," called the choice of Otero "fortuitous in particular" and described him as "a Bolivian national with a high level of commitment."[6] David Blanco called him an apostle. Over the years Otero has been called just about everything—Pancho Loco, a revolutionary with a brilliant idea, incorrigible—and many other sobriquets. Otero is unquestionably a charismatic figure. His passion, charm, and insight were among the key ingredients in the success of Prodem and subsequently BancoSol.

Otero's background prepared him well for starting a microfinance institution. He had spent most of the previous decade as a rural credit officer in remote areas of Bolivia, where he developed strong bonds with the rural clients, spending Saturday afternoons doing things like loading mules with huge sacks of potatoes. (Today, he gleefully demonstrates the technique.) He says that during these years he "learned to really like these people. It was a great life." Here he also discovered by direct experience most of the pitfalls of old lending models. But unlike most rural credit workers, Otero's prominent Bolivian family background allowed him to move easily among Prodem's elite directors. After attending high school and university in the United States, it was easy for him to communicate with Americans at USAID. With the squarish build of a laborer, stubbly beard, and a knowing twinkle in his eye, Otero delighted in almost physically confronting elites and bureaucrats with the real field perspective.

Otero chose a small group of people to launch Prodem's operations. He searched for activists like himself rather than for bankers or financial specialists.

He recalls that "the country was full of young, motivated people out doing extension and pastoral work." Monica Velasco, a member of the founding team, points out that at the time there was a large supply of young adults with university education, while good jobs were scarce. Velasco is a beautiful woman with dark, Joan Baez hair and eyes. Even today she echoes the sixties and seventies. She worked together with Otero and the third team member, Mario Usnayo, a young man of Quechua descent who, like Otero, had been out working with credit groups.

Many observers of Prodem's early success, including the staff themselves, believe that the choice of activists rather than bankers helps explain how Prodem connected so quickly and effectively to its clients. Jorge Baldevieso, who came to BancoSol during its early days, refers to the "professional salad" assembled there. Manuel Cuevas, a human-resources specialist hired to help Prodem become BancoSol, listed the kinds of people he found on the Prodem staff: "social workers, teachers, sociologists, graduates from the school of life, ex-nuns and priests, Trotskyites and theologians."

It was not easy for the activist staff and the businessmen on the board to work together. The businessmen continued to be skeptical, while the activists' habit of suspicion toward the businessmen flared from time to time. According to Otero,

Some of the activists looked at the Board of Directors and said nothing good could come out of that group. They still viewed them as the thugs of the country. And it was true that the Prodem philosophy came from the activists, not from the Board. In fact, it was hell trying to get the Board's attention. They were high on being the new government's kitchen cabinet. It was a privilege for me to sit with them and hear them struggle with the future of the country, but if they called me to meet with them over lunch, they wouldn't get around to Prodem until dessert.

Although Prodem was the product of an alliance between these two groups, the groups operated largely separately, each playing by its own rules.

The picture of Prodem is not complete without also understanding the importance of Acción's contribution, both as the initial promoter and animator, and later as the source of technical know-how and oversight. We will describe that contribution below.

PRODEM BEGINS OPERATIONS

The team of Pancho Otero, Monica Velasco, and Mario Usnayo started by learning Acción's solidarity group methodology. Bill Tucker, who was developing Acción's then-successful program in Peru, came to train the Prodem staff.[7] Velasco remembers that the methodology appealed to her because it fit the Aymara culture. It was similar to the Aymara version of a rotating savings and credit society, the *pasanaku*, in which a small group of people make regular contributions that are pooled and rotated among the members of the group. "When we asked people what they needed, they said capital, but they had never thought in terms of credit. We explained borrowing through the concept of the *pasanaku*, which also helped explain the solidarity guarantee."

One of the most unusual things about the start up of Prodem was the decision that the management team would operate the program at first. Otero, Velasco, and Usnayo, who were hired to become senior managers, acted as the loan officers in the early days. The benefits of this decision were many. It ensured that as the program grew, everyone on the staff would have direct field experience—which contributed to staff solidarity as well as to a deeper understanding of clients and operations by senior management. During these initial months the team also had time to adapt the methodology acquired from Acción to the Bolivian setting. They trained the first people hired to be loan officers, using their fresh, firsthand experiences. The willingness to work this way reveals how strongly the team members saw themselves as grassroots activists, seeking direct interaction with clients. It is surprising that this method of launching a program is not used more often. In all likelihood, few new microfinance program managers feel comfortable going one on one with the poor.

Mario Usnayo remembers the initial floundering attempts to find the right clients.

We went to the poorest people in the market. They wouldn't believe us and wouldn't come. We went to the next poorest people. After some promotional activities, we waited, looking out the window, but only a few people straggled in. So we decided to go to an association. We chose the *Asociación de Comerciantes Rodriguez*, a group of fruit and vegetable vendors. The association organized its members into groups. But these forced groups didn't work, so we started again with different people. We succeeded in convincing four groups of five people to come together, and made our first set of loans to twenty people. That was the last promotional work we had to do. From that point on, word of mouth brought people to us.

The product was so immediately successful with clients that Prodem was able to cancel the publicity campaign it had planned. Six months later, Prodem had 700 clients, a waiting list of at least 260, and no delinquency.[8]

Prodem's first loans were for the boliviano equivalent of $50, for a term of two months. The second loan would be $100, and the third $150, with gradually lengthening terms. After that loan officers would base the amount on each borrower's repayment capacity. Clients paid interest of 2.5 percent monthly on declining balance and were required to put up 5 percent of the loan as forced savings.

KEYS TO PRODEM'S SUCCESS IN LENDING

Microenterprise loans based on the principles used in Prodem's solidarity group program are a genuine financial innovation, developed during the 1980s and spread throughout the 1990s. Much of the professional literature on microcredit distills the principles behind this innovation so others can replicate them.[9] Although Prodem did not originate the core innovation, it breathed life into it—applying it extremely effectively and improving it. In the early years the institution was full of talk. Managers and field staff met nearly weekly to re-hash every facet of their operations, and important refinements arose from these exchanges of ideas. Prodem staff remember some of the moments of revelation in which they discovered elements of the methodology that clicked into place. They think of these as essential breakthroughs.

Perhaps the earliest breakthrough was the discovery of enormous demand among women vendors. In the first year, 85 percent of all clients were female fruit and vegetable sellers.[10] The team chose vendors in part because they were among the poorest people in the marketplace. And, as discussed in the previous chapter, the numbers of female market vendors were increasing daily in La Paz, making them the largest single group in the informal sector. Moreover, the benefit to these vendors from access to credit was clear and immediate. Most vendors bought from wholesalers, the *mayoristas*, who drove up every two or three days with big trucks. The vendors, or *minoristas*, bought on credit but had to pay next time the truck came in. The implicit interest rate involved in transactions with the *mayoristas* was well above Prodem's rate. In other words, these clients already had access to a kind of credit, but on highly unfavorable terms reflective of the unequal market power of the wholesalers and retailers. The first effect of Prodem's credit was to help vendors deal with these wholesalers from a more secure position. Prodem's clients, who could buy in bulk and pay cash, received better deals. The fruit and vegetable sellers became the cornerstone of Prodem's work, a solid client base from which Prodem gradually expanded to reach other kinds of clients.

The breakthrough most people recognize is, of course, the solidarity group guarantee. In implementing that feature Prodem was fortunate to begin in La Paz with its predominantly Aymara population, and it was perceptive enough to link the group guarantee with the cultural values of those people. According to Velasco, the Aymara hold honesty in high regard and carry a strong sense of mutual social obligation. They have a tradition of reciprocal assistance: if one person helps another, that person must return the favor in an even more generous way. Thus, the idea that one person would help a group member who couldn't make a loan payment fit with cultural practices. Moreover, clients either participated in or knew about *pasanaku*, in which they formed groups to pool financial resources.

Another profound though not always well-understood innovation in microcredit is the shift in the basis for lending from project to person. The old revolving loan funds lent for specific investments, often selected by the lender, and they devoted significant effort to ensuring that the borrower actually made that investment. This approach is epitomized by loans given in the form of potato seed rather than cash. Prodem used two completely different criteria: character, as evidenced by the client's ability to find a group of people willing to join her, and equally important, current capacity to repay. Prodem saw that it was risky for lender and client alike to base loans on income from a new project. If the project didn't work out, Prodem would lose a client, and the client would lose doubly—a failed project and a debt too large to repay. Rather than expose clients to this kind of risk, Prodem's loans were based on the capacity of clients' existing activities to generate income. As a Prodem officer in 1999 said in his routine client-orientation talk, "You can't come back to Prodem and say, my watermelons didn't grow and therefore I can't pay. Your loan is not based on an assessment of whether watermelons are a good investment. It's based on your ability to repay even without the investment." Prodem devised a simple system for loan officers to analyze clients' cash flow and calculate appropriate loan amounts.

Basing loans on repayment capacity brought a change of view about the process of economic growth among the poor, a more realistic recognition that growth is a long-term process. Rather than emphasizing one particular investment, the Prodem philosophy held that a long-term relationship between lender and borrower would give the borrower the financial flexibility needed to grow gradually, taking advantage of opportunities in a slower but safer way. This philosophy is reflected today in BancoSol's advertising slogan: *Juntos crecemos* (We grow together).

For loans based on character and capacity, the old model of loan processing and approval didn't fit. The old model relied on extensive documentation and centralized decision-making. According to Prodem, only people at the branch level knew enough about the client and the setting to make a good judgment. Therefore, Prodem pushed loan approvals out to the field. It did not dispense with the traditional credit committee, however, recognizing that a check on individual field officers was important for accountability. The credit committee was instead a small group of loan officers, sometimes including the branch manager. This group met weekly to review all new loan applications. Otero recalls these sessions fondly. Discussions could grow heated, as advocates for a particular client spoke with passion while other loan officers challenged their assumptions. "The credit committees were two hours every week of Microcredit 101."

An added benefit of decentralized loan approvals was faster turn-around, something very important to clients. According to the first evaluation of Prodem, the time between completion of applications and disbursement was nearly always less than two weeks.[11] In 1987 two weeks was a dramatic improvement over old models, which often forced clients to wait for months. Twelve years later, most lenders speak in terms of days rather than weeks, and consumer lenders sometimes quote hours.

Although Prodem did not start with the aim of becoming a commercial operation, it did seek to be efficient and financially viable. This commitment showed itself first of all in the interest rate. At 2.5 percent per month, Prodem's loans were far more expensive than those of the traditional revolving loan funds or credit unions. Yet they were far lower than informal rates, and necessary for covering Prodem's costs, which were unfortunately relatively high. These rates exposed Prodem to moral indignation from other NGOs and even sometimes from donors. Prodem was helped by the emerging recognition of the role of transactions costs in lending. Ohio State University and others pointed out that the interest rate was actually only a small fraction of a poor client's total transaction cost in obtaining credit. Time and opportunity costs, as well as out-of-pocket costs for transport, made the process of obtaining credit very expensive. If Prodem could bring down a client's transaction cost, that client would gladly pay the financial charges. In reality, the interest-rate argument was settled not by theories but by throngs of clients whose demand for Prodem loans was not diminished by the interest rate.

Even with higher rates the very small loan sizes (from $50) required unprecedented efficiency. Field staff had to carry many clients in order to cover costs. Prodem started with a natural advantage, as the informal markets of La Paz are extremely dense, with thousands of potential clients. It is hard to conceive of a setting with easier access to so many microenterprise clients. Some loan officers could visit their entire caseload of roughly 300 entrepreneurs in the space of a five-block walk.

Prodem improved on this location advantage by developing a tight weekly schedule and adapting it to the rhythm of the market. The staff began by visiting clients on Mondays through Wednesdays, disbursed loans on Thursdays, and accepted repayments on Fridays. Usnayo remembers, "One day it hit us. Market vendors bought on the days the big trucks came—Wednesdays and Fridays. They sold over the weekend. On Mondays they had money. So we switched the schedule. Monday mornings for repayment, then disbursement on Tuesday mornings. We hit the nail on the head with this because it really fit the market." The biggest benefit of the switch was that it supported the follow-up of late payments. By midday on Monday, each loan officer would know which clients had not paid on time and begin visiting those groups that afternoon.

This observation brings us to the feature for which Prodem became legendary in microfinance circles, its nearly perfect repayment record. During the mid to late 1980s loan programs associated with Acción, as well as a few other microenterprise credit programs around the world, had begun to demonstrate convincingly that poor people could and would pay their loans back on time. A growing number of programs kept arrears at sustainable levels, below 5 percent of portfolio. Prodem, however, maintained an arrears rate below 1 percent for its first several years, and it measured that delinquency from the first day a payment was missed, a far stricter standard than most. Grameen Bank, for example, did not report a loan as delinquent until one year after its full repayment had come due.

There is no single explanation for Prodem's repayment record. A variety of factors contributed, starting with the strong emphasis on honesty and social obligation among the clients, which gave force to the group guarantee. Early evaluators emphasized the importance of the loan-tracking system, whose weekly reports made immediate follow-up possible.[12] Every Monday morning the system produced a report for each loan officer showing the status of all clients expected to make payments that day. When the repayment window closed, the loan officer and the supervisor could easily see who hadn't paid. A system that could deliver information this useful and timely was well ahead of most microcredit programs at that time. Equally important, the originating loan officer was also responsible for collecting the loan. This practice differs from standard banking, in which credit and collections departments are usually separate. When loan officers are responsible for repayment on time from their own clients, they select clients more carefully and have greater incentive to pursue bad payers. An accountability loop is closed.

Zeal for good repayment performance was heightened through the talk inside Prodem. One slogan, known to clients and staff alike, was "zero tolerance," echoing an American anti-drug campaign. This slogan gave the message that late payments of even one day were simply not acceptable. Whenever a client missed a payment, the loan officer and the solidarity group were not to rest until they resolved the situation.

Another important slogan was the question, ¿*Quieren pero no pueden o pueden pero no quieren?* (Do they want to pay but can't, or can they pay but don't want to?). This question was the basis for critical thinking among staff and client groups. In each case of delinquency the staff and fellow group members had to determine which statement described the late payer. As Otero recalls, "We were merciless with *pueden y no quieren* [they can and don't want to], even though this was difficult for some staff. Sometimes a staff member would be crying on Monday night because she had been so hard on a client." All staff, including guards and secretaries, were encouraged to get to know clients and to be aware of what was going on in the community. Staff had the authority to find creative ways to induce borrowers to repay, within reason. They might take an office guard to visit a client, giving the impression of police involvement. Usnayo remembers one credit officer asking clients to swear to repay in a solemn ceremony. A small breakthrough occurred when loan officers realized that many of their *no quieren* late payers had other family member in their groups. Prodem quickly made it a policy to prohibit family members joining the same group. For the clients who wanted to pay but couldn't, Prodem staff would talk through solutions with the group, but in most cases the group guarantee came into effect. There are many examples of late payers temporarily bailed out by their group colleagues, as the solidarity group guarantee required.

The solidarity group methodology involves various mutually supporting elements. The scheduling arrangements support efficiency and quick follow-up of late payments, which are in turn supported by the solidarity guarantee, and so on. Jorge Baldevieso reports that people wanting to copy Prodem's success went looking for the seed that explained everything but could not find it because it was not *one* seed but rather a collection of techniques that together formed a coherent whole.

Perhaps Prodem's most important contribution to the methodology was to imbue it with a set of values. Prodem made the methodology's implicit values explicit and used them as motivating tools. Through Otero's talents as a communicator, the methodology became more than mechanics. It became a cause. The organization was full of people conscious that they were breaking barriers, doing something unprecedented, changing their country. The *mistica* that animated Prodem survives today. Its phrases can still be heard in the mouths of young loan officers from BancoSol, the new Prodem, and even other microfinance institutions.

TRUST AND A NEW SOCIAL CONTRACT

Although the Prodem team members spent their days running an institution and perfecting a lending methodology, if asked what they were doing, they were likely to answer in broad, philosophical terms. For Prodem, it was not enough to apply innovative techniques to a previously unsolved financial-sector problem. Prodem staff members believed their work was about changing the social contract between poor people and mainstream society.

Traditionally in Bolivia, the dominant social contract subjugated the poor to the labor needs of the rich. As the poor gradually won rights, they progressed from subjugation to mere exclusion or neglect. Mainstream institutions ignored the poor, despite their presence on every corner. Stories abound, even today, of bank officials turning people in traditional dress out of banking halls unless they first took a bath or changed their clothes. If they wouldn't let them in the hall, they certainly wouldn't lend to them. They barely accepted their limp, dirty bank notes as deposits. These attitudes were glaringly obvious.

Not quite so obvious was the fact that the implied social contract was little better among institutions of mainstream society concerned with assisting the poor. It was based on ameliorating bad conditions, with the poor as passive recipients of largesse from government, church, or charities. The food aid that had flooded Bolivia during many years of economic hardship epitomized this type of relationship. However, the image of the poor as passive and incapable also underlay economic development programs such as the old revolving loan funds. Their rigid rules suggested that the poor were too ignorant to know what investments to make, too untrustworthy to be given free use of their loan proceeds, and too destitute to pay for transactions on commercial terms.

Prodem's mission was to replace these kinds of relationships with a new social contract in which poor people were active participants in their own development, entering into relations as legitimate partners with formal institutions. Sanchéz de Lozada captured it succinctly. "The essence of microcredit is that poor people know their problems and their businesses and know what to do about them. When you lend money to them you give them both the responsibility and the authority to act for themselves." Fernando Romero says, "The original aim was to facilitate people to meet their own challenges."

For Otero, the key word was trust. "It's not just the cash. It's what the cash means, and it means 'I trust your small project.'" The lender's trust challenges the borrower to take responsibility both for honoring the loan contract and for deciding how to use the proceeds of the loan wisely. Although trust requires individual, personal responsibility, it does not take place in a vacuum. Rather, the program establishes a social context supporting the client. In the process of defining her future, the borrower has the backing of group members and the lender. Prodem staff thought in terms of a long-term growth relationship beneficial to both client and institution. For Otero, lending on trust was the essence of empowerment and the beginning of "a deep structural change in society."

Prodem staff members often contrasted their mission with conventional banking. They took pride in turning conventional bank wisdom upside down. Jorge Baldevieso remembers that Otero posted a list of 30 things a bank does that microcredit doesn't. If conventional banks kept unwashed people out of their offices, Prodem would welcome them. If banks spoke only Spanish, Prodem would also speak Aymara. Most significantly, Prodem would challenge the dependence of the banking industry on collateral by asking only for a group's mutual guarantee. Baldevieso observed, "The laws of banking are written on the basis of mistrust, but the more they are written that way, the more people misbehave. It's a vicious circle." Later, when Prodem transformed into BancoSol, its internalized antipathy toward banks and bankers, which was such an asset in the early days, created deep tensions in the organization.

The promoters of Prodem hoped to demonstrate that the old patronizing ways of working with the poor should be jettisoned, not only in finance programs, but across the spectrum of development issues. Although they saw the implications of their work as wide-ranging and revolutionary, they did not generally apply their concepts in other areas. They hoped others would pick up and incorporate them.

A DIFFERENT KIND OF INSTITUTION

The concepts of trust and responsibility are in some sense present in every solidarity group program. Prodem's distinction lay in the intensity with which it articulated and communicated these ideas. If ever there was a mission-led organization, it was Prodem in its early years.

Fernando Romero observed that Bolivians were accustomed to depending on patrons—he called it being "functionally irresponsible"—and that the syndrome of hierarchy and passivity pervaded business organizations. He wanted Prodem to set a different example. Prodem's institutional development should embody the same principles of trust and responsibility for employees that it conveyed to its clients.

Otero and the human-resource specialists he brought on board, Manuel Cuevas and Eliana Otondo, read extensively in the business management literature. They read Deming on "total quality management" and translated his ideas into "total portfolio quality"—asking staff to commit to achieving a default-free portfolio. More important, they followed Maslow and his observation that once a person had satisfied basic human needs, the most important needs were social and psychological. Cuevas saw that most Bolivians thought of work as unavoidable, not as rewarding in itself. He hoped Prodem would be a leader in changing such attitudes by satisfying employee needs for self-fulfillment.

The Prodem team set out to create an institution unlike the rigid, hierarchical organizations prevailing in Bolivia. Prodem would stand for a single set of values, applied up and down the organization, from clients to directors. The principles of trust and responsibility translated into the concept inside Prodem of *cada uno es su proprio gerente* (everyone is his own manager) or *autogerencia* (self-management). Just as clients know their businesses and can be trusted to make good decisions, so do staff. Field staff made the critical loan-approval decisions, and they decided how to get their work done, within a policy framework. But it was also important that *autogerencia* operated within teams (loosely analogous to the group guarantee idea) under the slogan *O ganan todos o no gana nadie* (Either everyone wins or nobody wins).

Cuevas remembers that a number of companies attempted to sell him the latest time-card systems. They were incredulous when he said that Prodem worked without timecards, and asked him, "How are you going to control your staff?" In fact, this question became increasingly contentious for Prodem as it matured. During the early years management operated through delivery of extraordinary psychic rewards. Otero had an extraordinary ability to motivate staff. He never tired of telling them they were doing the most important work in the country. When they made loans to clients who had never had credit before, they believed they were transforming lives and forging a better society. Otero stressed that everyone mattered to the organization, urging secretaries and office clerks to go into the field to get to know clients so that they would share the organization's mission. Credit officers and branch managers would pinch hit as tellers during the busiest disbursement and repayment times, sending the signal that everyone worked on the same team. The atmosphere was informal, with everyone on a first-name basis.[13] There were no ceilings on upward mobility—even a guard could become a loan officer if he showed aptitude. In response, the staff put their hearts into their jobs, excited to be part of a revolutionary process.

An outside analyst observed, "Both clients and credit officers believe that the program belongs to them and that only through hard work by both clients and employees can the program survive."[14] Otero remembers telling staff to work "as if Prodem belonged to you," and now regrets that staff ownership did not become part of Prodem's legacy. He regards this failure to translate the spirit of ownership into real ownership as an important missed opportunity.

On the other hand, he remains glad that Prodem did not institute a monetary incentive system, as many other microfinance institutions have done. Such systems measure each person's performance on objective indicators like maximizing the number of new clients and minimizing the number of late payers. Although Prodem tracked these indicators, its human-resources team saw incentives based on them as antithetical to the spirit of *autogerencia*.

Nevertheless, an organization cannot thrive on esprit de corps alone, especially when it is growing fast. Velasco remembers that Prodem had to "play catch up" with the systems and controls essential to managing money and thousands of transactions. Prodem would fail if it became confused about how much money clients owed and when. It could not afford for a staff member to steal money without catching the culprit quickly, or to keep staff who couldn't carry their weight in client caseloads. It could not keep costs down without knowing where costs came from. Good management in all these areas depended on good systems and controls. *Autogerencia* required accountability.

Attitudes about incentives and systems reveal a divided soul within Prodem that only came to the fore during the transition to BancoSol. This conflict still haunts BancoSol today. It is a division between those who stress trust, values, and mission as the guiding principles of the organization and those who recognize the necessity of systems and controls. (Some see an analogy here to the division between trust-based lending and paper-documented, collateral-based lending.) A great deal of trauma within the organization has resulted from the ongoing struggle between these two points of view.

Otero found the process of implementing systems tedious at best. However, Prodem was fortunate to have supporters who insisted on high standards in systems and controls and who could help develop systems and controls. Velasco recalls the businessmen on the board of directors pushing managers to think about efficiency. Acción provided technical know-how regarded as excellent in areas ranging from MIS systems, to loan methodology, to management and communication. In fact, in many of these technical areas Acción and Prodem were struggling together to add professionalism in finance to their community development origins. In business school jargon, they were "learning organizations" with learning based on exchange among implementers, supplemented by experts. The interaction was at times intense. During the first year alone Prodem received six technical-assistance visits from Acción and its affiliates in other countries. Prodem staff also made six visits to the other affiliates to see their operations firsthand.

REFLECTIONS ON THE EARLY SUCCESS OF PRODEM

By the end of 1991, after operating for almost five years and immediately before the start of BancoSol, Prodem had become a star among the handful of successful microfinance institutions around the world. With 22,700 loans outstanding and a portfolio of $4.6 million, its outreach was among the highest in Latin America, and it was increasing its client load by 50 percent per year with no end in sight. It operated eleven branches, reaching Bolivia's major cities, with a staff of 116 people.[15] It flaunted its absurdly low default rate of .0002 percent. It was breaking even financially. Although operating costs, at 23 percent of the portfolio, were very high by banking standards, interest income covered them.[16] By this time Prodem had survived a variety of growing pains and had a highly developed sense of institutional self-confidence.

It is important to recognize that in the early years, before BancoSol was conceived and launched, expectations for microfinance institutions were much lower than they are today. At that time the successful application of the solidarity group methodology represented the leading edge, making it possible to contemplate cost recovery for the first time. An Acción/Calmeadow Foundation publication from 1988 describes how the new methodology featured costs "at one-fifth to one-tenth the cost per dollar of the 'traditional' methodology."[17] At this stage Prodem's financial goal was simply to reach a level of operations that would allow it to cover its costs. All the Acción-affiliated institutions aimed to reach unprecedented numbers of clients, in a plan they called *El Gran Salto* (the Big Jump). It was only through striving for large scale that they realized they would have to set their standards of performance at a more commercial level. This realization ultimately led to the creation of BancoSol. The unanticipated level of success of Prodem was in fact instrumental in allowing Acción to recognize that it could raise its sights to more ambitions goals.

No single factor explains Prodem's success. Certainly Prodem began in very favorable conditions: a hungry and growing market, a receptive culture, economic stability, and lack of competition. It applied an effective methodology in the delivery of a product that fit the market very well. Yet those conditions do not explain why Prodem became an excellent institution rather than just a good one. Other institutions beginning with the same attributes would not necessarily fare so well. The chief lessons to be learned from Prodem's experience concern the quality of its leadership, its extraordinary assembly of players: the enlightened businessmen/politicians, the charismatic executive and his activist team, and the technical experts and promoters from Acción. All were highly talented people with a complementary balance of skills, personal qualities, and influence. As Otero noted, "The cocktail was well mixed." In contemplating the origins of microfinance institutions, one must wonder why they are not started more often through systematic assembly of similar elements.

It is also useful to consider what Prodem was not. As it tells every client today, it is neither governmental nor religious. It was not donor-initiated. Although USAID, the United Nations Development Program, and others fully backed its start up and early growth, donors did not originate the project. Nor was it an Acción-run project: Acción promoted the creation of Prodem and watched over it constantly to assure its sound development, but Prodem was from the first a Bolivian organization. Finally, Prodem considers itself a nonpolitical organization and is adamant that politicians should not dominate microfinance organizations. This may seem ironic, when some of the founding directors of Prodem were among Bolivia's most prominent politicians (though they were political technocrats rather than elected legislators). Prodem's answer is that it was not associated with any political party. Its directors came from several parties and served in their capacity as businessmen rather than as party members. Members of the board generally stepped down when serving in the cabinet. However, it is undeniable that Prodem's political connections were very strong. That they did not lead Prodem astray is the result of the vigilance of the activists, Acción, and donors, as well as understanding by the politicians that using Prodem for partisan gain would be self-defeating. Rather than endorsing political involvement in microfinance institutions, Prodem's example shows that it takes a unique set of circumstances to make it work.

The explanation for Prodem's excellence also requires the observation that each group had important reasons of its own to commit itself wholeheartedly to the institution. For the politicians, it was an experiment in transforming their relationship to the Bolivian people. For the activists, it was a chance to break away from the paternalism of the past. For Acción, it was part of forging a progressive organizational identity, with Prodem as its flagship. These motivations brought forth intensive effort and commitment, which certainly contributed to Prodem's success. Undoubtedly the circumstances that allowed these actors with these motivations to come together in Prodem had much to do with the broader transformations taking place in Bolivia. The coincidence of these motivations cannot be duplicated at will by even the most competent program designer.

NOTES

1. Interview with John Hatch.
2. Judith Tendler, AID Evaluation Special Study No. 12 (Washington, D.C.: USAID, 1983).
3. Maria Otero, *The Solidarity Group Concept: Its Characteristics and Significance for Urban Informal Sector Activities*, Acción Monograph Series No. 1 (New York: PACT, 1986), 13.
4. Henry Jackelen, Robert Blayney, and John H. Magill, "Evaluation and Preliminary Project Design for the USAID/Bolivia Micro and Small Enterprise Development Program" (Washington, D.C.: Development Alternatives, Inc., September 1987), I–2–3.
5. Maria and Pancho Otero are brother and sister, hired at Acción independently but, by coincidence, almost simultaneously.
6. Jackelen et al., "Evaluation," II–1.
7. The Peruvian program, Acción Communitaria de Peru, nearly collapsed under high Peruvian inflation but has since revived and become MiBanco, an institution similar to BancoSol.
8. Jackelen et al., "Evaluation," I–16–17.
9. For example, Joanna Ledgerwood, *Microfinance Handbook: An Institutional and Financial Perspective*, Sustainable Banking with the Poor (Washington, D.C.: World Bank, 1999); Maria Otero, *The Solidarity Group Concept*; and Maria Otero and Elisabeth Rhyne, eds. *The New World of Microenterprise Finance: Building Healthy Financial Institutions for the Poor* (West Hartford, Conn.: Kumarian Press, 1994).
10. Jackelen et al., "Evaluation," III–5.
11. Jackelen et al., "Evaluation," 21.
12. Jackelen et al., "Evaluation," 31.
13. Amy Glosser, "The Creation of BancoSol in Bolivia," in Otero and Rhyne, *The New World of Microenterprise Finance*, 230.
14. Glosser, "Creation of BancoSol," 230.
15. Prodem, "Twelve Years Promoting and Developing the Microenterprise Sector" (La Paz, 1998).
16. Shari Berenbach and Diego Guzman, "The Solidarity Group Experience Worldwide," in Otero and Rhyne, *The New World of Microenterprise Finance*.
17. Acción International and the Calmeadow Foundation, *An Operational Guide for Micro-Enterprise Projects* (Toronto: The Calmeadow Foundation, 1988).

CHAPTER FOUR

BUILDERS OF
ECONOMIC DEMOCRACY

PRODEM WAS ONLY THE MOST prominent of several impressive microcredit programs started in Bolivia during the late 1980s and early 1990s. This chapter relates the origins of seven other institutions. A look at all seven constitutes a *tour d'horizon* of most of the principal perspectives in the microfinance field at large.

The people who started these institutions were a special breed of activist. These builders of economic democracy were not marching in the streets or analyzing policy changes in government offices. They were deeply absorbed in building their own institutions and serving the needs of their clients, whatever they understood those needs to be. Each group of founders diagnosed Bolivia's development problems according to its own views and responded to those problems by creating an institution. In the end, these people created significant structural change, bringing a whole class of Bolivians into the circle of the mainstream financial sector. It is interesting to observe that although their social vision may have been broad, their responses were focused and practical: build an institution, provide a service, help specific clients. They were social entrepreneurs.

The seven institutions profiled here held different views of the role of microfinance in economic development and adopted different operating methodologies. However, over time, these institutions have tended to converge, at least operationally. They have gradually moved closer to the dominant microfinance paradigm, particularly in their methodologies and attitudes toward financial viability. The institutions gradually shed the variety of methodological features that distinguished them in favor of three basic lending methods: individual lending, solidarity groups, and community banking. Minimal the idea that credit should be provided with very few other training or tec services—has influenced every institution. Definitions of financial viability have sharpened, and every institution has reached farther in achieving it than its founders envisioned at the outset. The convergence has not been complete, however, and remaining differences reflect the deeply held views of each organization.

It is important to ask why this convergence has occurred, and what it has meant. We will revisit this question at the end of the chapter, after introducing the institutions.

THE SOCIAL SIDE OF MICROFINANCE: PROMUJER AND CRECER

The founders of ProMujer came from the same activist tradition as the Prodem staff. In Bolivia, top businessmen are linked by family ties and so are activists. In fact, the executive director of ProMujer, Carmen Velasco, and Monica Velasco from the original Prodem team are sisters. Tracing the family connections among microfinance institutions is an interesting exercise in itself. Prodem, ProMujer, Idepro, and Caja Los Andes all involve a member of the Velasco family. Prodem, BancoSol, Acción International, and Fassil all have an Otero or Otero relative in a leading position, and there are other interlinkages as well. This is not to say that these organizations are family fiefdoms—far from it. However, it does show how tight-knit Bolivian society remains, and how even socially progressive people are still connected to traditional Bolivian elites.

The extremely dedicated women who started ProMujer were searching for a response to poverty more effective than food aid. While Prodem arose from careful assembly of the right ingredients, ProMujer arose from a journey of trial and error, according to Rich Rosenberg, who counseled ProMujer during its formative years.

Velasco and Lynne Patterson, who founded ProMujer, had been working in El Alto and the slums of La Paz on mother-and-child health. Velasco worked with mothers' clubs. Young women with babies and toddlers met twice a week in these clubs, usually affiliated with churches, to receive donated food. The mothers sat passively on benches week after week, sometimes year after year, waiting for the food in a classic portrait of "abject" poverty. They rarely tried to generate their own income or find jobs. Velasco was deeply discouraged by the dependency she saw food aid perpetuating, but she didn't see a way out. "At least we had the sense to stop the program," she says, "because we realized it wasn't helping."

At first Velasco sought the solution through consciousness-raising in the Paolo Friere tradition. She and Patterson raised funds from USAID and others to create an NGO devoted to training and consciousness-raising among mothers' club members in empowerment, health, and early childhood development. At this stage they regarded income and economic issues as outside their sphere. But an important realization came when they developed a module on family planning. Their clients wanted more children to give the family more workers and more income. When ProMujer staff examined this notion by looking at the costs of having children, they saw how desperately their clients needed income of their own. Yet these women, most of them quite young, had very little confidence in their ability to do anything productive. A few sewed, but not as a business. Most could not read or write.

ProMujer began searching for an income-generation link. At that time, around 1990, Prodem and a few other microcredit programs were operating in El Alto, and ProMujer considered referring its clients to them. However, the mothers' club members didn't qualify for Prodem loans, which required an ongoing business at least one year old. Patterson and Velasco decided to launch something of their own. They considered and rejected the Trickle-Up Program, because it involved grants, which in their view perpetuated the paternalism they wanted to dismiss. They were more attracted to the ideas of Finca founder John Hatch, with his village banking model.[1] His ideas fit ProMujer's operational approach: the mothers' clubs could become community banks. ProMujer decided to adapt the community-bank model to Bolivia, raising funds from monetized USAID food aid (selling donated food on the open market and using the proceeds to finance development programs). Donors were finally recognizing that direct food donations created dependence among clients and undermined incentives for local production.

ProMujer began community banking on nonbusiness terms, reflecting the social welfare backgrounds of Patterson and Velasco. Although they wanted to avoid paternalism, they thought charging interest to poor people was exploitative. Their first loans carried no interest. At this point the program was completely unsustainable, having no income at all. Meanwhile, ProMujer's clients were actively lending to each other from their group savings (known as the internal account) at 4 percent per month. ProMujer realized that clients could pay interest to ProMujer, since they already charged each other. When ProMujer initiated interest charges, Velasco remembers, "we were scared to death that clients would rebel and walk away. We were so worried that our whole management team went group by group to the weekly meetings to explain. But the change had no real effect." Clients were just as willing to participate as before.

This change was one of the first in the journey of ProMujer to become a well-run microlending operation with an education and empowerment agenda. Each step involved shedding another aspect of welfare thinking in favor of a more businesslike approach. At first, ProMujer only wanted to maintain the value of the loan fund. Then, after a visit to Grameen Bank in Bangladesh, Velasco began to think seriously about operating as a business. The managers started using phrases like *product development* and *market niche*, and mastering techniques such as information system development and financial projections. They shortened the training time for clients from six months to ten days and increased its emphasis on business skills. This process was hastened by the examples of Prodem/BancoSol and Procredito/Caja Los Andes operating in the same neighborhoods with a much more explicit business approach. These examples showed what good performance in a microcredit program could be, and at the same time revealed how to achieve that performance.

Rosenberg remembers the long dialogue that ensued when ProMujer's leaders sought USAID microfinance funding. At first, Rosenberg turned them away, saying they might be fine educators but were not taking a sustainable approach to lending. But Velasco and Patterson were determined to learn. "Every time they came to me," says Rosenberg, "I beat up on them. They called me *El Diablo*, but they kept coming back for more. I was very moved by their perseverance." Eventually, convinced by the strides ProMujer was making, he helped secure more funding. Over the course of the years, ProMujer reduced costs dramatically through efficiency gains, which brought it to a break-even position by 1998.

Yet ProMujer had no intention of becoming a carbon copy of Prodem or Caja Los Andes. Its mission remained clearly with the people who were too poor or downtrodden to start businesses without help. It wanted to be the first rung on the ladder, making its slogan, You can start with us. ProMujer also stuck to its gender agenda. Velasco believed that the clients' problems were strongly linked to their acceptance of traditional attitudes about women's roles. Thus today ProMujer continues empowerment training. The link to health remains, as well. Health specialists circulate to the weekly community bank meetings, providing one-on-one consultations as well as educational messages on everything from finding a health clinic to dealing with a child's teacher.

Crecer, a rural village banking program, reflects a similar philosophy with a few twists. Crecer is a project of Freedom from Hunger, a California-based non-profit organization with programs in five West African countries, as well as Uganda, Honduras, and the Philippines. Freedom from Hunger began life in 1946 as Meals for Millions, a food-aid charity. During the late 1980s, Freedom from Hunger made the same kind of journey as ProMujer, from social welfare to microcredit, concluding that it could not treat hunger separately from income. After a period of experimentation and soul searching, the organization decided in 1989 to focus exclusively on community banking, adapting

John Hatch's Finca methodology. But it still clung tightly to its original anti-hunger objective. It developed a methodology it calls "credit with education" (Freedom from Hunger staff say this as nearly one word). Community-banking clients receive lessons during their weekly repayment and disbursement meetings on basic health and nutrition topics: breastfeeding, immunization, diarrhea, family planning, and the like.

Freedom from Hunger launched Crecer in 1990 on a peninsula jutting into Lake Titicaca. It has since spread to Oruro and Cochabamba Departments, searching out rural areas with very poor residents. With a few minor differences, its community banking model is the same as ProMujer's.

The Meaning of Empowerment

Freedom from Hunger has devoted a great deal of energy to justifying the education side of credit with education, including applying for a trademark for the phrase itself. In its hierarchy of objectives, credit is only a means to better health and nutrition, crying needs among Bolivia's poor. For Robert Ridgley, Crecer's acting director for a time, a defining moment of his tenure came during a training session for promoters (loan officers) on diarrhea control. The health educator explained that the local Andean custom in treating diarrhea, to give solid food in hopes of hardening stools, was exactly opposite the recommended oral rehydration therapy. One of the promoters began to weep. She had lost two children to diarrhea by following her mother's advice about solid food. To Ridgley, this incident illustrated the centrality of health education to Crecer's work.

Chris Dunford, president of Freedom from Hunger, defined Crecer's mission as "to alleviate poverty, specifically to provide very poor women with money and information to overcome chronic hunger and malnutrition in their families." According to Dunford, "This mission gives us very little flexibility."[2] If loans are repaid but there is no evidence of healthier children, Crecer will have failed. For this reason, Freedom from Hunger has placed great effort into analyzing the impact of its services on health and nutrition indicators, even taking "anthropometric" measurements of the babies of clients and non-clients, checking height and weight according to age. These impact studies pay far less attention to changes in clients' businesses. It sometimes seems that Crecer wants to be regarded as a health program disguised as a credit program.

Carmen Velasco would not go as far in subordinating the income objective to social objectives. ProMujer aims for broadly based change, both social and economic. Despite differences in emphasis, however, both programs believe their low-end clients need the extra educational messages, group work, and counseling.

The ProMujer and Crecer view of empowerment reminds Pancho Otero of some volunteering he did as a teenager in Washington, D.C. He worked in a church program that brought inner-city children into a center for a short morning session that included Bible lessons and a snack. The church's motivation was to teach these kids some moral and religious values. But, Otero says, "They didn't come for the lessons. They came for the *milk*." In other words, programs like ProMujer and Crecer should admit and embrace what they are really doing for their clients. If they view credit as a means to lure people into hearing messages, they underestimate the value of the credit itself. "Telling people to boil beans and get vaccinated is not empowerment," Otero asserts. "Empowerment is becoming a member of a society that respects you." In his view, a microloan supports the client's own self-esteem-building effort: her business. "It's Calvinist, but true," he says. "Self-esteem comes from work, and credit increases the client's ability to work."

Undoubtedly the differences between these views become exaggerated in the debate. ProMujer and Crecer would readily acknowledge the importance of increased income and the empowering effects of the loan itself, while Prodem staff would acknowledge that the very poor can benefit from health, education, and social-action messages (though not necessarily provided through a credit program). They also acknowledge that some people are too poor for Prodem to serve. In fact, ProMujer cooperates closely with BancoSol, using it as the program's bank and helping its clients move on to BancoSol when they outgrow the ProMujer group.

Social Aims and Financial Viability

Differences in view sharpen, sometimes uncomfortably, however, when the subject turns to financial viability. Both these programs wrestle with the financial-viability beast under self-imposed handicaps: they work with poorer clients needing smaller loans, and they believe in providing ancillary services. They are caught between acknowledging the importance for sustainability of breaking even, and concern that full financial viability would require them to sacrifice their most precious goals.

ProMujer has placed considerable effort on becoming financially viable. It produces financial reports following the regimen of the Superintendency of Banks for FFPs. It claims to have reached a break-even point during 1998, showing a 5 percent return on assets (after adjusting for the cost of subsidized capital). Rosenberg affirms that ProMujer's claims of financial viability are likely to be accurate, because it has been committed seriously to transparency in reporting. Nevertheless, ProMujer continues to rely on subsidized funding. Most of its loan capital comes from grants or loans that are mildly to deeply concessional. It excludes the cost of health workers in evaluating the profitability of credit operations. ProMujer says that it will aim to become as viable as it can while remaining true to its mission. It does not expect to reach commercial-level profitability but hopes to come close.

In its 1995 request to USAID for funding for Crecer, Freedom from Hunger made an even stronger statement. Crecer would prove that a village banking program could become fully financially viable. It saw Crecer as a test case not only for Freedom from Hunger, but for all village banking NGOs. With Crecer in Bolivia where microfinance seems to work like a charm, Freedom from Hunger thought it would have the best possible chance of demonstrating viability. And because Freedom from Hunger rather than a local partner operated the program, it would have greater control over the test.

For Freedom from Hunger, however, becoming financially viable is not the same as becoming "subsidy free." In a speech he made in Bolivia, Dunford pointed out:

Because our name is Freedom from Hunger, not Freedom from Subsidy, we have to stop a moment to think about where all this is leading *us* and the *microfinance movement*. . . . The reality is that subsidy is available. Traditional businesses have thrived on it for centuries. There is a market for subsidy to traditional social services. It is called philanthropy or charity. Freedom from Hunger has more or less thrived on this market for 52 years, far longer than the average life span of a for-profit business.[3]

More bluntly, as Ridgley says, "As long as subsidies are being offered, why shouldn't we accept them?" Crecer, he asserts, will never pursue financial viability at the expense of improving rural women's health.

Freedom from Hunger's statements are highly unusual—many organizations take subsidies, though only a few announce this in their speeches. The embrace of subsidy represents a defensive strategy by an organization that resents the popularity among funders of more commercial operations, such as Prodem, Caja Los Andes, and BancoSol, fearing that those funders may stop supporting organizations like Crecer. Today, Crecer has reached a slightly lower level of financial viability than ProMujer but still projects that it will break even in the next two years.

Of the two similar organizations, most observers agree that ProMujer has a stronger base for the future.[4] ProMujer has enjoyed support from expatriates close to Bolivia and, importantly, the commitment of a talented chief executive, Velasco. Crecer, on the other hand, has not found a local champion. It is the only significant microfinance program still operating as an international project rather than as a Bolivian organization. Institutional development has been slowed by changes in personnel and by Crecer's preoccupation with achieving growth and financial viability targets quickly to please donors, which has diverted attention from painstaking institutional development tasks.

THE ENTERPRISE DEVELOPERS: FIE AND IDEPRO

The origins of FIE and Idepro represent a significant critique of the Prodem approach from a different direction. At the time when Jeff Ashe and Steve Gross were developing Acción's solidarity group methodology, the prevalent form of microenterprise credit in Latin America combined training and credit. Frequently, as in the influential Carvajal Foundation program in Colombia, credit was only available after training had been completed. Most such programs emphasized enterprise growth, provided long-term loans for investment in productive assets, and favored manufacturing businesses. The motivating aim of such programs was the transformation of informal sector businesses into larger, more productive enterprises. These programs had little use for tiny commercial enterprises, seeing them as making no significant contribution to economic development. As Acción's solidarity group methodology began to prove successful, a schism emerged between the "minimalists," like Acción, who advocated mainly short-term credit to traders, and the "credit plus" group, who saw credit as only one ingredient in an enterprise transformation process it tried to support.

FIE emerged on the credit-plus side in the mid-1980s, when this debate was at its peak. The five women founders came from the same activist roots as those of ProMujer and Prodem. They had been working in the same kinds of social programs with health and refugees. The story of their disillusionment with the effects of food aid is by now a familiar theme. Pilar Ramirez, the key figure behind FIE, speaks of the negative effects of food aid in even stronger terms than Carmen Velasco, saying that food aid demeans, infantilizes, and disrespects its beneficiaries. Her choice of terminology reveals her professional training as a psychotherapist. Ramirez explains further that the position of power of the donor over the recipient defeats any possibility of empowerment. She first heard of Grameen Bank in 1984, while attending a master's program at Harvard. The idea of credit appealed to her because it offered the possibility of a more equal, respectful relationship between the provider and the client.

Ramirez, a petite woman with a feisty spirit, wanted to launch her program as a fully Bolivian effort. Although she and her colleagues consulted many international microenterprise-development experts, they did not take an international partner. At one point they considered a potential partner organization, but when its leader insisted that Ramirez and her group of colleagues, whom he characterized as housewives, give control of the organization to experienced private businesspeople, Ramirez walked away. Ramirez is exceedingly proud of FIE's independence, even though this independence has made it more difficult for FIE to raise funds from major donors.

FIE's first break came from Oxfam America, which encouraged the group to submit a proposal to work among rural peasant communities. Ramirez, who had always been very politically active, knew the women's arm of a peasant union in the altiplano community of Ayo Ayo, whose dynamic leader, Lucila Morales, was concerned about the loss of youth to the cities. Morales's idea was that if young people could earn enough money from off-farm employment to buy such basic items as bicycles and radios, they would be more likely to stick around. Morales and Ramirez developed the idea for a community enterprise, a knitting and sewing company, and Oxfam gave them their first grant in 1985. FIE started providing technical assistance in production and management.

This kind of community-based income generation project was a typical model from the 1970s and 1980s. It has gradually fallen out of favor in the development community: most such enterprises lacked real market orientation; ownership and management problems often became intractable, and the intensity and cost of technical support required was very high relative to the number of people assisted. The first FIE project, for example, provided just 39 jobs.

Nevertheless, this sewing business established FIE's fundamental character as a hands-on enterprise-development organization. With funds from the Inter-American Foundation, FIE moved on to a project to assist unemployed miners in establishing other businesses. The mining company was "relocalizing" laid-off miners, a euphemism for sending them back to their original homes. When they returned, few knew how to run a business. FIE helped clients get started in machinery repair, a trade many miners knew, as well as in more standard trades such as carpentry, fishing, poultry, and livestock. Ramirez remembers there was always a waiting list of people wanting help to set up pig farms. Nevertheless, the miner project was not successful enough to be the basis for FIE's future.

These early initiatives taught FIE some important lessons, but they ultimately proved to be detours. FIE had taken them on in part because they were the only funding possibilities it could find. In 1988, Ramirez was finally able to start an urban informal-sector loan project, something she had wanted to do from the start, with a small project loan from the InterAmerican Development Bank. FIE adopted the credit-plus approach. It sought mainly manufacturing businesses and provided intensive technical and business training prior to extending loans at subsidized rates. Ramirez acknowledges that these features of the program came from a leftist ideological stance. FIE's founders believed they were "defending the productive base of the country." Their choice of individual loans also reflected personal beliefs that it was paternalistic to force people to form groups.

Over the years, however, FIE moved away from credit-plus to a minimalist profile. It recognized that its intensive training delayed microenterprises from getting on with their plans and that business training made little difference to client productivity. The training requirement was shortened from one month to four days. Eventually, FIE split training and credit into two departments operating separately, with separate client intake. It gradually altered its interest-rate policy. FIE's founders began to see themselves not only as social activists but as business entrepreneurs. They also recognized that FIE's exclusive focus on manufacturing effectively excluded women from the program, and, accordingly, they opened their doors to market vendors.

Today, FIE's main distinguishing features are its continuing emphasis on manufacturing enterprises (50 percent of clients as opposed to 20 percent at BancoSol),[5] and its nonfinancial services department. Its original ideological stance persists, but that stance has been subordinated to the dominant microfinance approach through the combination of lessons from FIE's own experience and the influence of successful competitors like Prodem, BancoSol, and Caja Los Andes.

Idepro, founded in 1991, represents an attempt to return to earlier objectives by people who had experienced minimalist microcredit but were not satisfied to leave the enterprise-development agenda unfinished. Idepro's origins lie with CEDLA, the activist research organization that discovered the importance of the informal sector in the mid-1980s. Together with several other organizations, CEDLA founded Idepro in 1991. The executive director of CEDLA, Roberto Casanovas, was one of the original CEDLA researchers who documented the patterns of growth in the informal sector.

CEDLA's view of the informal sector gave precedence to the larger end of the microenterprise spectrum, and especially to the manufacturing enterprises within it. In Casanovas's view only this portion of the sector has potential to generate real development in terms of productivity and employment. Accordingly, he and his colleagues set up Idepro to make larger, longer-term loans to such businesses. In establishing its lending program Idepro benefited from the experience of one of the founding managers of Prodem, Monica Velasco. Her move from Prodem to CEDLA and then Idepro was perhaps the first of what has become a tradition of outward transfers of staff expertise from Prodem/ BancoSol into other Bolivian microfinance programs.

Velasco brought her knowledge of how to work with the informal sector and manage an NGO lending operation. However, she also brought a strong critique of Prodem's focus. She left Prodem in part because of its lack of interest in providing training and technical support to its clients, and because "I couldn't imagine myself in a bank." At Idepro she created a nonfinancial-services department, where she now concentrates her effort. She admits that Idepro has yet to develop methods that work well. "We are learning a lot, but we are still farther behind on this kind of service than we were ten years ago on credit at Prodem." Nevertheless, she is convinced that nonfinancial services are the way to go. "My surprise has been to discover that the enterprises with the greatest potential to grow are not the ones who seek credit most. The ones who can really grow want technical assistance and technology."

The minimalists won the old debate about credit-only vs. credit-plus. Even the most dedicated enterprise-developers learned that integrating training requirements into credit programs not only prevented them from reaching large scale and covering costs, but was also unpopular with clients. But that nagging economic development question won't leave the leaders of FIE and Idepro alone. They continue to search for breakthroughs in enterprise development methods, while taking advantage of the lessons they have learned from the minimalists.

PROCREDITO AND INDIVIDUAL LOANS

Procredito came relatively late to the Bolivian microfinance scene, launching operations in January 1992, only a month before Prodem launched BancoSol. It made up for its late arrival through aggressive professional drive. The founders of Procredito set out to prove two things. First, they wanted to prove that a microfinance program could move quickly from NGO to licensed financial institution. They succeeded, establishing Procredito's offspring, Caja Los Andes, as the first licensed FFP in 1995, a process we will discuss in chapter 5. Second, they wanted to show that individual microlending was superior to group lending. The debate about this question continues, but Procredito represents very strong evidence in favor of the individual case.

The German consulting firm Interdizciplinare Projekt Consult (IPC), which started Procredito, is an ardent proponent of individual microlending. Its founder, Claus-Peter Zeitinger, is a man for whom there are no gray areas. Zeitinger is not content for his individual approach to be seen as one of several effective methodologies. He wants it to be recognized as the best. Although many people in microfinance have found themselves in an adversarial relationship with Zeitinger at one time or another, all acknowledge him to be one of the pioneers of the field. He has built IPC into the largest team of highly trained technical experts in microfinance anywhere. IPC has been the driving force behind several pioneering microfinance institutions: the Cajas Municipales of Peru, Financiera Calpia of El Salvador, Centenary Bank of Uganda, and numerous programs in Eastern Europe and Russia.

During the early 1990s Zeitinger positioned IPC as a rival to Acción in Latin America, particularly in competition for resources from the Inter-American Development Bank's new microfinance initiative. He viewed the involvement of NGOs in microfinance, the use of group lending, and the talk of empowerment as "essentially romantic" and based on emotion.[6] He was disturbed that the growing popularity of these approaches distracted policy makers from what he considered the real work of microfinance—creating microfinance capacity in the formal financial sector, either in specialized institutions like the Cajas Municipales or in the "downscaling" of commercial banks. For IPC, microfinance was a serious, financial, and, above all, professional business. NGOs and other amateurs should at best be temporary players.

When IPC began exploring possible involvement in Bolivia, it did so with the explicit aim of converting an NGO into a financial institution. It first considered establishing a relationship with FIE because of FIE's individual lending approach, but FIE's independent-minded founders did not want to submit to the degree of control that IPC demanded, nor did IPC buy into the enterprise-development side of FIE. Instead, IPC assembled a group of Bolivians, including Jorge Crespo, a senior Bolivian diplomat, together with funding from German Technical Cooperation (GTZ), the Swiss Development Corporation, the IDB, and the Andean Development Fund, to create a new organization, Procredito. IPC installed a full management team of its own staff in the new organization, taking a much more management-intensive role than Acción had taken with Prodem. In January 1992, Procredito began lending.

Procredito's operations built an excellent case in support of individual microlending. In IPC's view it was self-evident that individual loans are better for clients than group loans. Who would choose voluntarily to go through the trouble of forming a group and keep it going? Who would accept risk for other people's debts if it could be avoided? Who would choose to link his or her own schedule for receiving loans to the schedules of four or five other people? Clearly, according to IPC, no one would take a group loan if offered an individual loan instead. And, in fact, there is abundant evidence that whenever asked, the majority of microfinance clients around the world say they would prefer an individual loan.[7]

The more difficult question was whether individual lending worked from the lender's perspective. Group lenders made two main claims about the ne-

Table 4.1 Individual vs. Group Lending

	Group Lender Claims	Individual Lender Claims
Effects on Clients	Group guarantee secures loan without asset pledges: accessible to poorer people	By accepting any kind of collateral, it is possible to make individual loans to people equally poor
	Group acts as source of support and advice; a fall-back during bad times	Clients spared the trouble of group formation and maintenance costs for clients
		Clients not burdened with other people's debts
		Loans can be tailored to individual in terms of timing, amount, and duration
Effects on Lending Institution	Group guarantee is best repayment incentive	Combination of informal collateral and personal guarantee can be just as effective
	Easier client screening, as groups perform much of that task	With loan officers screening clients, lender learns more about borrower
	Lower cost to reach same number of borrowers	Lower cost to reach same number of borrowers
		Easier to grow with top clients; not constrained by other group members; therefore easier to reach profitability

cessity of using groups: first, that the group guarantee is the only effective way to secure loans made by very poor people lacking assets, and second, that group loans allow a lending program to be more financially viable while reaching those people. Procredito disputed both these claims, and set out to prove them wrong. Table 4.1 provides a summary of claims about the merits of group and individual lending.[8]

At Procredito, and subsequently Caja Los Andes, most loans are secured by both a personal guarantee and a *prenda*, a general lien on assets. These criteria sound at first just like the criteria conventional lenders use, which normally exclude poor and informal-sector clients. However, Procredito applied them very differently. Where conventional lenders require personal guarantors to be people of substance, who have assets to back up loans, Procredito accepted other poor people as guarantors. Where conventional lenders treat collateral as a store of value that they can obtain to cover the amount of the loan, Procredito saw collateral mainly as a motivating tool. Clients would prefer to repay loans rather than lose their possessions. Thus, conventional lenders are highly concerned with the market value and legal documentation of collateral, while Procredito looks mainly at the value of the collateral to the client. Under the *prenda* it lists items clients would not want to lose, such as household appliances or machinery used to earn income.[9] With this approach Procredito claimed that even very poor people could provide acceptable guarantees. It embodied this thought in its marketing slogan, You are our best guarantee.

Moreover, Procredito's management emphasized careful analysis of repayment capacity as more important in loan decisions than the guarantee itself.[10] It trained its loan officers extensively in the analysis of household and enterprise cash flows. Zeitinger advanced the argument that this approach "permits the financial institution to learn a great deal about its clients and to translate these learning effects into increases in productivity and cost savings,"[11] primarily by lending right up to repayment capacity rather than following a more conservative series of fixed steps, as solidarity lenders tended to do. He believed group lenders would not be able to grow with their best clients.

In actual practice Procredito/Los Andes lends to clients from similar levels as those of its main group lending rival, BancoSol, but is positioned slightly upmarket from BancoSol. Los Andes starts clients out with larger loans and maintains a higher overall average loan size.[12] Ohio State University comparisons of these institutions in 1995 showed that more of BancoSol's borrowers were below poverty thresholds.[13] It is possible that these differences reflect the willingness of Caja Los Andes to move up with clients to larger loans and to serve small businesses rather than an inability to reach the poor. However, the general sense that Los Andes occupies a higher end of the market squares with comments from clients and lenders. BancoSol's former CEO, Hermann Krützfeldt, commented that in interviews with clients about preferences for individual loans many clients believe they lack sufficient assets to qualify for a loan from an individual lender. He sees a large and continuing market for group loans. Nevertheless, the rise of direct competition among lenders has given individual lenders a distinct advantage.

The other aspect of Procredito's claim about individual loans concerned financial viability. Procredito claimed that it could lend just as efficiently and as safely as any group lender. Its argument rested on three points: it could keep delinquency low, so it would not have to pay high loan-loss costs; its loan officers could serve just as many clients as loan officers in group programs; and its willingness to increase loan sizes as clients grew would allow it to spread costs across a larger loan portfolio. Procredito and Los Andes have done an excellent job of demonstrating all these claims. The delinquency rate, at 0.33 percent of the portfolio over 30 days in 1996, represents stellar performance. The actual productivity of the loan officers was very similar to that of Prodem/BancoSol, at an average of 350 clients per loan officer, with some loan officers in central La Paz reaching as many as 700 clients. Its loan officers receive monetary incentives based on achieving low delinquency, a large number of loans, and a large portfolio volume. Costs fall within the same range as costs at

Prodem/BancoSol, allowing Procredito/Los Andes to charge interest rates at or slightly below the levels of its main competitor, while reaching profitability within a short time.

Participants in the microfinance industry emphasize the contrasts between Prodem/BancoSol and Procredito/Caja Los Andes in corporate culture as well as in lending methodology. While Prodem had built its corporate culture around the inspiring ideas of trust and responsibility, Procredito's culture revolved around cold professionalism and incentives, a decidedly unromantic approach.

Nevertheless, by magnifying the differences in style and emphasizing the group vs. individual question, observers overlook the fundamental similarity of Procredito and Prodem. These two organizations had more in common than most of the other microfinance organizations in Bolivia, and the similarities grew as each became a formal financial institution. In methodology, both lenders were minimalists. They did not believe in requiring clients to undergo business or technical training or in restricting loan uses. They based loan decisions on repayment capacity and used access to gradually larger loans as repayment incentives. Their methods for managing delinquency were virtually the same, relying on immediate follow-up by loan officers, facilitated by sophisticated information systems. These elements for securing high repayments may in fact be more fundamental causes of low arrears than guarantee type. At the institutional levels, both lenders were committed to efficiency and financial viability. Because it started five years later, years in which thinking about microfinance and commercial viability had progressed substantially, Procredito began with a clearer vision of its ultimate corporate form, and as a result, it took less time than Prodem to reach profitability and the transformation stage.

RURAL LENDERS: FADES AND SARTAWI

The picture of the origins of Bolivian microfinance institutions would be incomplete without a note on two rural organizations, Fades and Sartawi. Although we will discuss the experience of these organizations in greater depth in chapter 7, we will now point out how their origins and evolution reflect the same themes behind some of the other NGOs.

A consortium of Bolivian activist institutions, including FIE, CEDLA and four others, created Fades in 1986. Their understanding of rural realities placed associations and cooperatives at the center of rural development. Thus, Fades's original answer to the problem of reaching into rural areas was to be a second-tier lender to grassroots organizations—bean producers, users of a common irrigation system, or displaced miners—as well as to local NGOs. Fades would help such organizations finance whatever they found most important, including production, marketing, and community projects. In the early days Fades financed bridges, irrigation schemes, roads, and a great deal of community-owned machinery. It followed an eclectic array of lending methodologies. Nearly everything was an experiment. It also followed lending policies left over from the days of the rural revolving funds, with low interest rates and little attention to collections. At this stage Fades was an innovative organization that was learning a great deal about the culture and organization of rural life in Bolivia, but it was performing badly as a lender, with high defaults and low sustainability. In the early 1990s Fades began to offer direct microcredit using standard solidarity and individual methodologies, and this has now become its largest line of business. In 1994 it hired a new executive director, Edgar Zurita, an entrepreneurial man of Quechua descent who had been the main force behind Sartawi. Under Zurita's leadership delinquency was driven down and the most problematic lines of business were discarded. Thus, over time, Fades has focused its operations, taken up standard microcredit products, and improved its financial viability. Although it remains a unique organization on the Bolivian scene, it looks a lot more like Prodem today than it did ten years ago.

Much the same thing can be said about Sartawi, whose Aymara name means "to lift oneself up." When it first started in 1985, in Batallas near Lake Titicaca, as a program of Lutheran World Relief, it looked like many other NGOs. Sartawi did a little of everything: agricultural extension, women's empowerment, training, agroforestry, and the like. Its credit programs, begun in 1988, followed the old revolving loan model. They were mainly directed to specific agricultural inputs, such as fertilizer, with subsidized interest rates. These loans did not perform well. In late 1990 Sartawi launched the solidarity group loan program that today remains its main service. According to Rosenberg, Sartawi was on its way to becoming a stronger institution by the mid-1990s when a fight broke out among factions within the board and management, resulting in the departure of Sartawi's executive director, Edgar Zurita, who went to Fades. It is clear that Zurita represented a great deal of the organization's leadership talent, because since that time Sartawi has struggled while Fades has flourished.

UNDERSTANDING THE CONVERGING PATHS

Over the years these seven microfinance institutions, although started with very different objectives and philosophies, have come to resemble one another more closely. This convergence reflects the influence of what has now become the dominant paradigm in Bolivian microfinance. This paradigm did not originate in Bolivia; rather, international microfinance promoters, primarily Acción and IPC, introduced it. Their affiliates, Prodem/BancoSol and Procredito/ Los Andes, began squarely within the dominant paradigm. Their intent was always to become sustainable financial-service providers.

The other institutions profiled here began with a wide variety of approaches: FIE with technical assistance to a single community-based enterprise; Fades with lending for community infrastructure projects; ProMujer with empowerment training. Over time, each of these institutions dropped most of the operational practices that differentiated it from the dominant paradigm while retaining underlying differences in philosophy.

In the area of credit methodology several important changes took place. First, the lenders moved to support individual enterprises rather than community-based enterprise. Even the community-banking programs, ProMujer and Crecer, which create community groups, use those groups to support the individual businesses of the members. Lending for group enterprises remains only in a few of the loans of Fades and another NGO, ANED. Most adherents of the dominant microfinance paradigm harbor a deep distrust of collective enterprises. Second, the lenders provide credit with few or no nonfinancial services. The nonfinancial services that remain have been drastically streamlined (ProMujer and Crecer) or separated from credit (Idepro and FIE). Third, most of the lenders have adopted wholesale the solidarity group or individual loan techniques of microfinance. By 1998 the vast majority of Bolivian microcredit went out as solidarity group loans (67 percent) or individual loans (26 percent), with only 9 percent as association or other kinds of loans.[14]

What caused this convergence of methodology? Rosenberg attributes it almost entirely to the example Prodem/BancoSol and later Procredito/Los Andes provided. Carmen Velasco and Pilar Ramirez attribute the changes in their institutions to their own trial-and-error experience. Both are probably correct. ProMujer and FIE did learn by experimenting, though the shape of their experimentation was undoubtedly influenced by what they saw happening "down the street." Finally, an overwhelming conclusion is that the dominant microfinance paradigm simply proved to be a more efficient way to get credit into the hands of low-income people.

Some indication of *how* efficient is reflected in the growth trends of the seven microfinance institutions profiled here (see Table 4.2). One obvious point from these figures is that the organizations that began with the dominant microfinance paradigm grew the fastest and farthest. By 1997, Prodem, BancoSol, and Caja Los Andes were the three leading microfinance institutions in terms of loan portfolio and number of clients. The institutions that started with other approaches really began to accelerate their growth only when

Table 4.2   Scale of Microfinance Institutions
(Portfolio amounts in millions of U.S. dollars)

	1992 Portfolio	1994 Portfolio	1997 Portfolio	1997 Borrowers
BancoSol	8.7	33.2	63.1	76,000
Prodem	n/a	2.6	18.2	38,000
Procredito/Los Andes	0.1	2.9	20.4	28,000
FIE	2.1	4.1	12.1	22,000
Fades	n/a	3.1	6.5	23,000
Idepro	0.4	1.5	5.0	10,000
Sartawi	0.6	1.1	2.6	6,000
ProMujer	n/a	0.1	2.3	14,000
Crecer	n/a	0.2	1.3	9,000

Source: Finrural and Cipame, *Microfinanzas: Boletin Financiero.* La Paz, 1998.

they shed their older methodologies.

As methodologies were becoming increasingly similar, so were attitudes about financial viability. On this dimension change swept across the microfinance scene more quickly than most institutions found comfortable. In the mid-1990s most of the institutions struggled to achieve financial viability even as the definition of viability was becoming more and more rigorous. The previous chapter noted that the original thinking about financial performance among the founders of Prodem was simply to prevent the donated loan fund from losing value through excess default, administrative costs, or inflation. In the late 1980s few of the other institutions had even thought that far. The subsidized interest rate policy at a number of the institutions reflected the lack of concern with financial viability.

Prodem was clearly a driving force for change in attitudes about financial viability. It quickly reached the first hurdle—covering out of pocket expenses—and stayed on a path to even higher performance levels. Prodem's path opened a new world to the promoters of microfinance, because it showed that it would eventually be possible to move microfinance away from the shelter of donors into commercial territory. At that point, around 1990, one could almost see the light bulbs turning on inside the heads of microfinance promoters who realized that the field had just entered a new realm. A somewhat more commercial definition of financial viability emerged, one that placed a value on loan funds in recognition of the fact that banking is based on covering the spread between the cost of raising money and the cost of lending it. Earlier definitions had ignored the cost of money. Finally, with the conversion of Prodem into BancoSol, a more stringent standard appeared, that of genuine profitability embodied in returns to equity sufficient to attract private investors. Only then would microfinance be a genuinely commercial activity. We will discuss the issue of returns to investors in chapter 5, but the important point here is that each time Prodem and then BancoSol and Procredito met another financial viability hurdle, they raised the bar for others. As Freedom from Hunger's Chris Dunford described it:

Years ago, we thought it would be a major breakthrough just to recover all the recurrent costs of field operations. Then, we set our sights on recovering all recurrent operating costs of the total Crecer institution. Then, as our loan portfolio grew with loans from the commercial bank BISA and other lenders charging commercial and near-commercial rates, we determined that financial sustainability means covering all recurrent financial and operating costs of Crecer, including the hidden costs of inflation and set asides for loan loss reserves.[15]

The institutions invested in becoming more financially viable through three main strategies: aligning interest rates with real costs, making staff more productive, and improving financial management.

The results of this evolution in Bolivia have been dramatic. During the years from 1993 to 1997 the incidence of subsidy in microfinance programs plummeted. Using the subsidy-dependence index developed by Jacob Yaron, a Funda-Pro study analyzed the financial viability of the leading microfinance institutions (see Table 4.3).[16] The subsidy-dependence index measures the amount of subsidy (overt and hidden) embedded in a program. A score of zero represents a fully commercial operation. All costs are covered, including inflation and an adequate return to shareholders. Negative scores represent high profitability, while positive scores indicate that the institution still relies on subsidies of some type. It is important to recognize that many private commercial banks have years in which their scores are positive, usually in the nearly independent range. These would be years of low profits, such as many businesses experience at one time or another.[17]

At the start of this period there were no subsidy-free microfinance institutions, but by the end of the period there were six. Such figures may not be surprising, as the profitability of leading Bolivian microfinance institutions is widely known. What may be more surprising is the movement at the other end of the spectrum. By the end of this period none of the significant microfinance institutions remained in the highly dependent category, and most

Table 4.3   Subsidy Dependence of Microfinance Institutions

	1993	1994	1995	1996	1997
Independent (0% or less)	0	1	0	3	6
Nearly Independent (1-20%)	5	4	5	2	2
Dependent (21-100%)	2	4	5	6	6
Highly Dependent (+100%)	4	4	3	3	0
TOTAL	11	13	13	14	14

Source: Tania Rodriguez Auad, "Autosostenibilidad Financiera en Instituciones de Microfinanzas en Bolivia," Serie Credito No. 3 (La Paz: Funda-Pro, 1998), 39.

of those that had moved into the dependent category were on trajectories that would place them in higher categories within a few years. This is the kind of pattern that policy makers in many countries postulate but that until now has rarely been realized across a whole nation.

In Bolivia by the late 1990s it was simply no longer acceptable to run credit programs in the old, highly dependent manner. Although managers of microfinance institutions still complain about lenders who spoil client discipline by lending at below-cost interest rates and being lax about collections, most people had a hard time actually naming any such lenders. The institutions they named have generally either changed policies or shrunk to insignificance.

All the institutions profiled in this chapter embrace the pursuit of financial viability. For some, the embrace may not be wholehearted but rather a realistic recognition that it is not tenable to hold out against a rigorous definition when so many institutions achieve it. A few institutions, notably ProMujer and Crecer, insist that they cannot reach the fully commercial definition of viability if they are to remain true to their mission of reaching the very poor. The industry environment in Bolivia is sure to continue pushing them hard to come as close as they can.

The convergence among Bolivian microfinance institutions reveals the power of innovations for extending credit to microenterprises that are represented in the methodologies of Prodem/BancoSol and Procredito/Caja Los Andes. These innovations permitted the achievement of scale and sustainability by all the institutions that adopted them. It also reveals the power of the push for financial viability. When they pursued viability seriously, all institutions achieved far more than they initially aspired to.

Our discussion in this section has focused on improvements in cost coverage, defining financial viability as achieving a positive bottom line. However, this is only one side of the picture. Real financial sustainability also requires a shift in the sources of funding from donors to commercial sources, including depositors, shareholders, and capital markets. As the Bolivian organizations reached higher levels of cost recovery, they realized that they could not become independent of donors incrementally, through gradual improvements. They would have to make fundamental transformations in their organizations. These transformations are the subject of chapter 5.

The convergence among microfinance institutions has not, however, changed the moral purpose or theories of development that launched each institution. FIE and Idepro may have changed the way they deliver credit, but they still hold the same views about informal-sector manufacturing businesses as contributors to economic growth. While progress in the financial area has been dramatic, it has not been matched by learning in the areas of these other objectives. The pragmatic decision to separate credit from training offers little help in showing how enterprises contribute to economic development. Nor does the adoption of efficient techniques and rigorous performance standards diminish the commitment of ProMujer and Crecer to changing the behavior of the very poor. The tool of microfinance, however, sits somewhat uncomfortably atop the objectives and motivations of these institutions, creating ongoing tension within them. It fits most solidly with institutions whose objective was always fundamentally financial.

The stories of the origins of Bolivia's microfinance institutions hold important lessons about the conditions for institutional development. They show that good institutions don't grow in a vacuum. The environment of Bolivia in the late 1980s and early 1990s provided a rich mix of ideas, skills, motivations, and attitudes. One can imagine the talk that went on at bars and coffee houses in La Paz—for nearly all these institutions began in La Paz—starting with disgust at food aid dependency, disillusionment with socialist militancy, and the beginning of openness to the ideas of private enterprise. This kind of shared experience created the exceptional individuals behind nearly all the successful microfinance institutions: Monica and Carmen Velasco, Lynne Patterson, Pilar Ramirez, Roberto Casanovas, Edgar Zurita, Pancho Otero, and others. The success of each of the institutions associated with these individuals arose in large measure from their talents and from the continuity of leadership they provided. Only two institutions, Procredito and Crecer, have not had the same kind of dominant leader, relying instead on international partners. It is interesting to note the importance of the external technical partners. In general, the institutions with international partners (Prodem, Procredito, Crecer, and to a lesser degree ProMujer, which has a US-based board of directors) progressed faster than those that decided to go it alone (FIE, Fades, Idepro, and Sartawi).

Only one organization, Prodem, possessed both an experienced international partner and a dynamic local leader. Its combination of these two factors may go a long way toward explaining why it was so successful.

NOTES

1. For more on village banking, see Candace Nelson, Barbara McKnelly, Kathleen Stack, and Lawrence Yanovitch, "Village Banking: The State of the Practice" (Washington, D.C.: SEEP, 1995).
2. Christopher Dunford, "Microfinance: A Means to What End? Sustained Pursuit of Different Objectives for Microfinance" (Unpublished speech, Davis, Calif.: Freedom from Hunger, 1998), 4.
3. Dunford, "Microfinance," 6.
4. For example, James Hochschwender, "Preliminary Analysis of Microfinance Institutions in Bolivia" (Washington, D.C.: Chemonics, 1997).
5. Claudio González-Vega et al., "Bolivia's Microfinance Market Niches: Clientele Profiles" (Columbus, Ohio: Rural Finance Program, Ohio State University, 1996), table 5.
6. Reinhard H. Schmidt and Claus-Peter Zeitinger, "Creating Viable Financial Services for Poor Target Groups in LDCs: The Experience of NGOs," Sustainable Banking with the Poor Occasional Paper No. 8 (Washington, D.C.: World Bank, 1996), 3.
7. See, for example, González-Vega et al., "Bolivia's Microfinance Market Niches"; and Craig F. Churchill, *Client-Focused Lending: The Art of Individual Lending* (Toronto: Calmeadow, 1999).
8. For a detailed treatment of the arguments in favor of individual lending, see González-Vega et al., "Bolivia's Microfinance Market Niches" or Churchill, *Client-Focused Lending.*
9. González-Vega et al., "Bolivia's Microfinance Market Niches," 78–79.
10. Mery Solares de Valenzuela, "Caja de Ahorro y Préstamo Los Andes," in Claudio González-Vega, Fernando Prado Guachalla, and Tomás Miller Sanabria, eds., *El reto de las microfinanzas en América Latina: La visión actual* (Caracas: Corporación Andina de Fomento, 1997), 112.
11. Schmidt and Zeitinger, "Viable Financial Services," 10.
12. González-Vega et al., "Bolivia's Microfinance Market Niches," 64, 68.
13. Sergio Navajas et al., "Poverty and Microfinance in Bolivia," Economics and Sociology Occasional Paper No. 2347 (Columbus, Ohio: Ohio State University, 1996), 6.
14. Funda-Pro, "Annual Report" (La Paz, 1998), 33. Document does not state whether these figures represent number of loans or amount of portfolio.
15. Dunford, "Microfinance," 6.
16. Tania Rodriquez Auad, "Autosostenibilidad Financiera en Instituciones de

Microfinanzas en Bolivia," Serie Crédito No. 3 (La Paz: Funda-Pro, 1998).

17. The subsidy-dependence index is scaled according to the percentage change in interest rate required for an institution to be subsidy-free. For example, an institution charging 20 percent whose subsidy-dependence index was 10 percent would have to raise its interest rate to 22 percent (that is, 20 percent x 1.1) to be subsidy-free.

CHAPTER FIVE

THE BOLIVIA MODEL OF MICROFINANCE TRANSFORMATION: IDEALS AND REALITY

AS THE MICROCREDIT NGOS in Bolivia took off, each one began to bump against its limits as a donor-funded non-profit organization. The programs tried to grow quickly to satisfy the huge demand they had discovered. Their appetite for new loan capital was tremendous, well beyond amounts bilateral and multilateral donors were prepared to give. Prodem, which had started with a grant of $560,000 from USAID, was by 1990 managing a portfolio of $2.4 million and looking to double that in the next year, with continued rapid growth for years thereafter.[1] Where could it get the money?

Moreover, the NGOs couldn't tolerate the uncertainties and delays that accompanied donor money, which often arrived months or even years after its originally promised date. Microcredit emphasized continued, rapid access to credit as a basic element of service quality and an important repayment motivator. The institutions needed ready access to funds. Beyond these practical issues, the NGOs embraced independence from donors as a matter of principle. The sustainability and autonomy they sought required a broader, more commercial funding base.

Microfinance professionals at that time were also recognizing something they should have known from the beginning: the importance of savings. Bolivian microcredit leaders traveled to Bank Rakyat Indonesia, a pioneer in savings for the poor. Many of them came back convinced that low-income people wanted better opportunities to save and that savings services could touch even more people than credit. Moreover, savings could provide a reliable source of funds for the institution.

As they began exploring new funding sources, the NGOs quickly pinpointed the basic, intractable constraint: their own organizational identity. The structure of NGOs differs from that of any formal financial institution, because NGOs, however well-endowed they may be, have no owners with capital at risk. Lacking owners, their accountability structures are not up to being entrusted with what bankers call "other people's money." An NGO's assets cannot easily be seized in case of default, and thus they provide little security to lenders. For these reasons Bolivia, like most countries, does not permit NGOs to accept deposits or participate in money markets. The same weakness in ownership, together with still rather amateur financial management among NGOs, made banks hesitant to supply more than a fraction of the NGOs' required funding.

The solution, obvious in retrospect but radical at the time, was to transform the NGOs into licensed financial institutions. Starting with Prodem, the Bolivian microcredit NGOs developed an approach to transforming their operations into financial institutions that has become known in microfinance circles as the Bolivia Model. This model is one of the main features that distinguishes Bolivia from some of the other countries where microfinance is internationally known, especially Bangladesh (where microfinance institutions have remained outside the financial sector) and Indonesia (where the dominant model is a state-owned bank). The Bolivia Model has influenced similar transformations in numerous countries, from Kenya to Cambodia.

Briefly put, the model involved using some or all of the NGO's capital to purchase shares in a newly created financial institution, making the NGO the lead owner of the new institution. Other new owners would join in. The new financial institution would be licensed by the banking authorities to accept deposits from the public and would be able to raise funds in money and capital markets. The NGO's staff, operations, and loan portfolio would move to the new institution, leaving the NGO as owner/investor. However, as an asset-rich organization, the NGO would have resources to launch a new round of developmental activities, deepening its original mission.

Although the Bolivia Model is hailed as an example for microfinance institutions around the world, it is often only partially understood.[2] The model seems deceptively simple, but in reality it raises any number of vexing questions. What is an effective ownership structure? Are NGOs appropriate owners of financial institutions? Should donors allow their funds to capitalize a for-profit institution? Should the new institution qualify under existing financial institution legislation, or should the government create special regulations just for microfinance institutions? How should the NGO's main asset, its loan portfolio, be transferred? Are banking authorities equipped to supervise this new type of institution? How can the organization reconcile its original development mission with its new form as an investor-owned, for-profit institution? What new mission should the founding NGO take on? Should it actively assist the financial institution, or should the two separate? These questions generated countless hours of debate in each instance of transformation in Bolivia. In the turmoil old friends have parted company and new alliances have formed. Behind the personal interplay, important principles are at stake.

THE FIRST TRANSFORMATION: PRODEM TO BANCOSOL

The idea of turning Prodem into a bank first emerged in 1988, a time when Prodem staff were facing serious funding crunches.[3] They spent anxious weeks casting about for a donor who could provide funds quickly (Canada came to the rescue at least once), and months of conserving funds by slowing client intake and squeezing down loan sizes, risking both lower earnings and client dissatisfaction.

Prodem had some access to commercial loans from banks, but these were too limited to maintain its desired rate of expansion. In 1991, the year before BancoSol started and also the year of Prodem's greatest access to bank loans, it had a total of $710,000 in commercial loans from Banco Boliviano Americano (BBA), the bank of Prodem chair Roberto Capriles and board member David Blanco. These loans covered less than one-third of Prodem's total funding requirement. That year Prodem issued about $2 million in loans each month, expanding its portfolio from $2.4 million to $4.6 million.[4] Moreover, the loans were still closely linked to donors. Acción International's Bridge Fund, a guarantee mechanism set up with funding from USAID, Ford Foundation, and others, guaranteed repayment of the loans to BBA. These loans offered virtually no leverage; to back its guarantees the Bridge Fund maintained a deposit (supplied by donors) approximately the same size as the loans themselves. Without the guarantees, Prodem's "collateral" for a loan from a bank was its own loan portfolio, which consisted of unsecured loans that bankers and banking authorities considered too risky to use as security. Moreover, no bank wanted to face the unpleasant possibility of chasing down an NGO whose aim was to lend to the poor and whose owners were not liable for the organization's assets. Unless Prodem were to enter the financial markets as a full-fledged member, it could not hope to gain access to the amounts of finance it would need.

Planning for a bank began in earnest in late 1989, just after Bolivian presidential elections, a time when the politically active members of the Prodem board could focus systematically on a new project. Fernando Romero, the board's chairman, led the process with the help of Calmeadow Foundation and Acción. Lest anyone think that it is a simple process to transform an NGO into a commercial bank, a few facts about the process may be illuminating. Prodem established a separate planning entity, Cobanco, with a budget of more than

$600,000 and a staff of two full-time professionals plus consultants. Cobanco allowed Prodem senior management to concentrate on running a fast-growing organization, while protecting the bank project from languishing if management could not pay it full attention. Both cost and effort were perhaps higher than they would need to be today, because at that time there was no model. The partners were feeling their way step by step.

To Be or Not to Be Commercial

At first the concept of the new bank focused more on gaining access to money markets than on operating as a fully commercial institution. Early sketches portrayed an institution that would continue to rely on subsidies. Surprisingly, the Acción International Board, made up mainly of US businessmen, was particularly reticent. Fernando Romero recalls that "Acción's board members came to the table with very altruistic motivations, in the tradition of philanthropy. Their thoughts were that credit was good, but that you couldn't go so far as to make a business out of poverty." Ironically, one of the most skeptical Acción board members at first was Michael Chu, now BancoSol's chairman of the board.

In Romero's view one person led the advocacy for a commercial approach and, in fact, for the original concept of the bank: Martin Connell, the founder of the Calmeadow Foundation. Connell was a successful Canadian businessman who started Calmeadow to pursue his vision that microfinance could be a commercial operation. Calmeadow helped fund Cobanco and provided an experienced banker, Doug Salloum, as one of the Cobanco staff. Connell convinced Romero, and then he, Connell, and Salloum set about convincing the members of the Prodem board. Many of the board members were Bolivian bankers, but they could not fit microlending and banking into the same conceptual framework. Just as definitions of financial viability changed over time, so did definitions of what it meant to be genuinely commercial. Acceptance of the principle came first, followed by the difficult process of swallowing, bit by bit, the concept's full meaning.

The central issues on which the commercial question rested were interest rate and return on equity. At first the Bolivian board members proposed an interest rate lower than the rate Prodem was already charging. They feared negative public reaction if a bank lent money to poor people at 20 percentage points above the rates mainstream banks charged wealthy people. They worried that a commercial bank would be more visible and vulnerable to negative public opinion than Prodem had been as an NGO. They felt their own reputations as socially responsible businessmen could be at risk.

Directly linked to the question of interest rate was that of returns to shareholders. An early draft of the feasibility study had been prepared by Lauren Burnhill of the InterAmerican Investment Corporation (IIC), the private-sector arm of the Inter-American Development Bank, the first external investor recruited into the project. USAID's Rich Rosenberg noted that the study estimated the rate of return at 14 percent, which just happened to be IIC's minimum acceptable rate but was lower than any private equity investor would demand. Later, in discussions with board members Capriles and Romero, Rosenberg asked, "What is your objective in creating this bank? Do you want to create a mechanism to serve 70,000 people, or do you want to provoke competition?" Romero and Capriles answered, "Provoke competition." They agreed that a fully commercial operation would have to earn the kind of return on equity that would make private investors pay attention.

The board members, soon to become BancoSol investors, agreed to include an interest rate of 4 percent monthly on boliviano loans and 2.5 percent on dollar loans, equivalent to the rate Prodem had been charging. Feasibility studies put the expected return on equity closer to 20 percent. These pricing policies represented acceptance of the commercial vision.

Later a subtle difference would appear between Rosenberg's perspective and that of Romero and Capriles. For Rosenberg, the challenge was to create a thriving microfinance industry, independent of donors, by attracting private capital into multiple, competing institutions. "The proof of the pudding," he said, "is competition." BancoSol board members, however, focused on creating a level of profitability that would attract private, profit-motivated investors to BancoSol, so that it would become a genuinely private bank. Both their visions have since come true, though perhaps not exactly as foreseen.

Money and Owners

Through months of meetings and rewriting plans, Cobanco put together a capital base and an ownership structure. To launch a bank, the Superintendency required minimum capital of $3.2 million. The suppliers of that capital would become the owners of the new bank. At that time, for the people involved in the NGO, $3.2 million seemed like a lot of money.

The largest source of funds would be Prodem's loan portfolio, derived mainly from grants, which was Prodem's only substantial asset. Donors had granted these funds for the purpose of lending to the poor, however, not to capitalize a private, for-profit commercial bank. Prodem had to seek permission from donors to allow their funds to be used to purchase shares in BancoSol. Some officials inside donor agencies were not immediately convinced that donors should provide what amounted to a major start-up subsidy for the new bank.

USAID was the main hurdle, as it had been the main source of loan funds.

Everyone in USAID had a different opinion about the propriety of such a use. On the one hand, the creation of a bank devoted to microenterprises represented the fulfillment of USAID's objective in funding Prodem and gave USAID a perfect exit strategy. It was a better outcome than the project designers had ever hoped for in terms of numbers of people served and leverage for USAID's initial investment. On the other hand, the thought of using US taxpayers' money as shares of a private, for-profit corporation made government lawyers queasy. Even though the money had been given to Prodem as a grant (so USAID would not own any shares itself), the grant agreement restricted Prodem from using the funds for anything other than their original purpose. The grant agreement could be amended, but some within USAID questioned whether capitalizing a private bank could ever be considered a legitimate purpose. The rules were not entirely clear. Rosenberg, who was deeply allergic to the kind of bureaucratic thinking that began swirling around within USAID, championed BancoSol inside the organization. He ultimately secured approval. After USAID approved, the other main funder, the Bolivian Social Emergency Fund, followed suit.

Prodem would supply $1.4 million of the initial capital, becoming the largest owner of BancoSol, with a 41 percent share. The remaining owners differed substantially from the ownership groups of most new banks. The next largest shareholder was the InterAmerican Investment Corporation (IIC), which, as anchor investor, helped convince both other investors and the banking authorities. The Bolivian businessmen who had been on the Prodem board came forward with significant support. Each of five "founders" put in a small personal investment (about $10,000), not substantially more than they had originally raised to launch Prodem, but several businesses associated with these board members contributed more, for a total of $1 million. Next came three non-profit organizations specializing in microfinance, the essential technical partners, Acción and Calmeadow, and a third, less-involved group, the Swiss small-enterprise-development organization Fundes. Together these three contributed about $900,000. Finally, the Rockefeller Foundation contributed $200,000, and SIDI, a French foundation, $150,000. Cobanco had courted a host of others, and when BancoSol opened, these were listed as "in negotiation," but most of these investments failed to materialize. The biggest disappointment was the reticence of the World Bank's private investment arm, the International Finance Corporation (IFC), whose staff members agonized for months over the investment, unable to come to terms with BancoSol's unconventional business (a missed opportunity some in IFC came to regret).

The ownership structure of BancoSol has been hailed as a model for other microfinance institutions. Therefore it is worth noting a few points about what the structure did and did not include. It did not include true private investors who were interested in BancoSol primarily as a business venture. The Bolivian organizations that invested were all involved with Prodem as a social endeavor, through the personal interest of their leaders. Although these businesses did expect BancoSol to become profitable, it is doubtful that many of them really counted on using that money again. They were staking their reputations more than their purses. The remaining investors were "do-gooder" organizations of one kind or another. At that time BancoSol could not attract investors strictly interested in profit. The moderate expected returns on equity did not match the enormous perceived risk—enormous because unknown. In any case the founders did not seek such investors. They were leery at this stage of allowing partners who would not be as dedicated to BancoSol's social mission as they were to its bottom line.

It is also important that Prodem did not control BancoSol. Often in considering transformations, microcredit NGOs put forward plans in which the NGO becomes the sole or majority owner. These plans arise out of a fear of loss of control and loss of mission. BancoSol was fortunate to face scrutiny from the Bolivian Superintendency of Banks, which was rapidly becoming a model among developing nations. The Superintendency was particularly concerned about the ownership structure. It challenged Cobanco to defend the reputations, viability, and commitment of the owners and the balance of control among them. In particular, it wanted assurances about the heavy participation of NGOs, normally not considered appropriate owners of financial institutions. It asked whether the NGOs could act as responsible owners, making decisions on a businesslike basis and taking action in the event of a problem (especially raising emergency funding). These questions challenged Prodem, Calmeadow, and Acción to deepen their own understanding of ownership. The result was a stronger shareholding structure with participants that brought much more to the table than BancoSol could have counted on from Prodem alone. Yes, there was clearly a loss of control, as we will see. But most of the people involved in the start-up would agree on the benefits wider ownership has brought.

Finally, participation as owner posed a special challenge to Acción, as the original international partner of Prodem. The prevailing development philosophy among politically correct international NGOs was to build local institutions, turning over governance and management to newly empowered local people. Opportunity International, for example, also a promoter of new microfinance institutions, originally set a five-year limit on its involvement with any one affiliate. At that stage success was defined as graduation of institutions to self-governance. Anything less smacked of paternalism or, even worse, imperialism.

BancoSol, however, definitively changed that picture for Acción. After all, this transformation was happening at a time when reformers saw foreign ownership as one means of modernizing the Bolivian financial sector. Did the same concept apply for microfinance? Acción staff believed strongly that BancoSol needed a technical partner on its governing board. The Bolivian investors, although they knew banking, did not understand microfinance. They might make policy decisions that would move BancoSol away from microfinance, even without intending to do so. Neither did the IIC and the other institutional investors know the business, and Acción observed that the institutional investors would likely be relatively passive. Prodem itself could have been the guardian of the technical end of the business, but as we will see, Prodem's interests grew apart from those of Acción and BancoSol.

Naturally it was also in Acción's self-interest to stay involved. Prodem had been Acción's top-performing affiliate for several years, and BancoSol would be Acción's crowning achievement. It needed BancoSol for its own reputation and ability to continue attracting support for its programs throughout Latin America. Yet Acción, a non-profit whose own funding was often more precarious than that of the organizations it assisted, had no money to invest in BancoSol. Its $250,000 was a significant stretch, and it was not enough to qualify Acción for a seat on the board of directors. Acción's president, Bill Burrus, worked tirelessly to raise additional money, finally obtaining a grant from the McArthur Foundation. With Acción's investment in BancoSol, a piece of idealized development thinking yielded to business realities.

The Challenge from the Superintendency

After attracting investors and creating a sound ownership structure, the next major challenge was preparing BancoSol to comply operationally with the requirements of the Superintendency of Banks. At first, the staff of the Superintendency and the superintendent himself regarded microcredit as something strange, risky, and not really suitable for a commercial bank. Their skepticism was greeted by an equal skepticism about banking authorities on the part of most of Prodem's staff. They began dancing around each other warily, like boxers at the start of a match.

Prodem's operations did not always comply with fundamental banking requirements. In some cases this noncompliance was an integral part of the nature of microlending, and in others it was the result of Prodem's informal style. The task was to sort out which features would have to change to bring BancoSol into compliance with banking laws, while protecting its ability to carry on its main line of business.

For example, Jacques Trigo, former superintendent of banks, remembers his shock on learning that Prodem's administrative costs were close to 20 percent of assets, compared to the 5 percent range for a conventional bank. Prodem's costs resulted directly from the high cost of making very small loans. They were a basic feature of microcredit, although at that time there were no industry statistics available to convince banking authorities that such high costs were normal.[5] In fact, high administrative costs were also an important stumbling block for IFC. Although no regulation required administrative costs to be in a certain range, bank examiners normally viewed high costs as a signal of a badly run bank. Examiners would have to undergo a major shift in their way of thinking to feel comfortable with such costs, and bank examiners are not commonly trained for flexible thinking.

A practice less integrally related to microcredit was Prodem's fluidity in staff functions. Tellers doubled as receptionists and would often get up to escort visitors. If a teller took a day off or ran an errand, another staff member might step in. Prodem used these practices to help reduce costs, and they were part of its team-style operations. As Otero recalls, however, they violated sacred principles of internal controls, enshrined in regulations. Regulations required tellers to stay in their cubicles whenever they were on duty. Issues like this were sometimes resolved by compromise. Prodem would develop a more rigorous procedure, which the bank would signal as acceptable. Perhaps tellers could leave their posts if they locked their cash drawers.

One core issue remained unresolved at the time of BancoSol's opening: the treatment of Prodem's portfolio of unsecured loans. According to participants from the BancoSol side, the Superintendency never really understood microlending, and the lack of understanding came to a head over the safety of the loan portfolio. Banking regulations required that most loans be "well-guaranteed," which meant backed by legally registered collateral or guarantees of sufficient value to protect the bank against loss. Banks could make loans without this kind of backing only to a very limited extent. If the value of unsecured loans exceeded 10 percent of the bank's equity, a bank would have to set aside provisions of 100 percent of every boliviano over the limit. In the eyes of the Superintendency, every Prodem loan was unsecured. Enforcement of this regulation would prohibit BancoSol from doing more than a tiny fraction of its planned business.

BancoSol's designers worked urgently with Superintendency staff to show them that a portfolio of solidarity group loans could be safe. They explained how the solidarity guarantee gave strong assurance of repayment. They urged bank examiners to look at the systems Prodem had for tracking problem loans and at Prodem's extraordinarily low loss record. It had lost less than $2,000 in its five year history. Still, the authorities hesitated to make changes in such a fundamental precept. The superintendent and his key staff were convinced that the BancoSol experiment was important enough and that its backers were competent enough to go forward. Rather than change the regulation, they agreed to wink at BancoSol's noncompliance. Nevertheless, the threat hung over BancoSol's head long after it had already commenced operations.

One day in 1993, a year after the launch, Otero received a letter from the Superintendency instructing him to close the bank because of inadequate provisions against unsecured loans. Someone from the Superintendency's legal department had issued the letter, for the first time invoking this provision against BancoSol. Close to midnight, Otero and his then-deputy, Hermann Krützfeldt, caught up with the superintendent and convinced him to put the letter back on the shelf. A year later the Superintendency issued an amended regulation exempting loans of less than $2,000 from the limitation. BancoSol could make as many smaller loans as it wanted. Still, the issue was not fully put to bed, and only in 1998 did the Superintendency finally produce a regulation stating that a loan backed by a solidarity group guarantee could qualify as "well-guaranteed." With that regulation the banking authorities finally began to come to terms with the essence of microcredit.

These and other technical issues, like BancoSol's currency mismatch (too many of its liabilities in dollars, compared to loans in bolivianos), remained unresolved, but the superintendent decided that he was convinced on all the crucial points. On the day in early 1992 when the Superintendency finally delivered the license to Prodem, the jubilant Cobanco staff celebrated with a high-spirited evening of carousing and self-congratulations. A more dignified formal inauguration took place shortly thereafter in BancoSol's new headquarters, a beautifully restored historic La Paz mansion.

The celebrations yielded to the hard and sometimes divisive work of transforming Prodem's operations into a bank. On its opening day BancoSol began operating the main urban branches and regional offices that had formerly belonged to Prodem. It took over staff, buildings, and clients from the headquarters and from branches that were operating profitably. The newer branches and branches in smaller locations remained with Prodem.

The Culture Clash

Various observers have emphasized the shift in corporate culture as Prodem became BancoSol.[6] For some of Prodem's staff, ingrained hatred for banks proved too strong to overcome. Monica Velasco simply could not see herself working in a bank. She left to help found Idepro. Others stayed behind in Prodem. Among some of the staff brave enough to transfer to BancoSol, the continued requirements to become more formal chafed against their understanding of what Prodem had been all about. The anti-banking ethos Prodem had cultivated now made it more difficult to become BancoSol. According to Otero, the staff would make arguments like the following, "How long does a bank take to make a loan? Forty days. How long do we take? Four days. So why should we become a bank?"

Looking back, Otero insists that there was no significant change in corporate culture. "Yes, the back office changed radically. And the Superintendency required us to obtain signed loan contracts and promissory notes. Okay, we hadn't done that before. But the mission was the same. It was traumatic for people because they couldn't see that these changes were a matter of form, not essence."

Tensions grew as BancoSol began to bring in experienced bankers for specialized functions, such as asset and liability management and internal control. Over time, a rift grew between the old staff from the NGO, who lived by the Prodem values, and the new staff who readily adapted to the banking environment.

BancoSol brought in human-resource specialists to help create a unified corporate culture that would embrace the new identity as a bank. One of those specialists, Eliana Otondo, recalled their use of the image of a tiered wedding cake. Prodem had built the bottom level, with the three core values of *autogerencia*, communication, and teamwork. The second tier, added under BancoSol, included service quality and profitability.

Despite their best efforts, however, divisions among BancoSol staff linger today. The staff who were associated with Prodem or the early BancoSol days still lament the increasing influence of bankers. One senior employee asserts bitterly that he can no longer aspire to be a regional manager, as one by one these positions are reserved for bankers. In his view, a series of such decisions gradually diluted the understanding of microcredit among the staff.

Some BancoSol observers have generalized from its experience and concluded that the cultural divide is inherent in a transformation from NGO to financial institution. However, another hypothesis is that the divide resulted from the very vitality of Prodem's original corporate culture, particularly its vehement anti-bank sentiments. Otondo notes: "The conflict was inevitable because the earlier culture was so strong. New people couldn't understand how strong it actually was." To illustrate that the divide was not inevitable, she points out that "after BancoSol split off, Prodem also began to introduce some of the controls BancoSol had put in place. Within Prodem, staff accepted the changes because they didn't view them as threats to their vision." Rather, Prodem staff saw them as relatively neutral operational improvements. Another illustration, as we shall see, comes from Procredito, which did not experience the same kind of culture shift when it became Caja Los Andes. Its corporate vision had always included the creation of a formal financial institution.

Over the years the banking side of BancoSol's corporate personality has increased in dominance, especially with the departure of Otero. Although Otero was enthusiastic about the creation of BancoSol and embraced the concept of operating at a commercial level, he was not a banker by training or desire. He poured his heart into the clients and the staff and became enthused about new initiatives, but he was not the kind of manager to watch over the fine details of the bank's financial condition.

Shortly after BancoSol started, its founding champion, Fernando Romero, stepped down as chairman of the board to assume a cabinet post in the new Sanchéz de Lozada government. A powerful businessman and banker, Julio Leon, replaced him. According to Rosenberg, Leon worried when he saw how much work was involved in bringing BancoSol's operations up to banking quality and how great the risks would be, not least to his own reputation, if BancoSol failed. He asked Gonzalo Paz Pacheco, one of the top bankers from his own bank, BISA, to join the BancoSol board of directors and keep a close watch on BancoSol. Together these two men concluded that BancoSol needed the day-to-day support of an experienced banker as financial manager, and they hired a capable young banker, Hermann Krützfeldt, to do this. Several months later Otero resigned, leaving Krützfeldt to take his place. The scenario enacted in BancoSol was the classic stuff of business school case studies: the transition of a small, entrepreneur-built company into a more established corporation. Otero, a charismatic, entrepreneurial leader, gave way to the competent but unglamorous professionalism of Krützfeldt.

A New Incarnation for Prodem

The creation of a new financial institution may be the major focus of the Bolivia Model of transformation, but the complete model also addresses the fate of the original NGO, especially the relationship between the NGO and its offspring. Prodem's sponsors quickly perceived that the NGO now had an opportunity to focus on a new mission. However, it took some time to decide what that mission would be and how Prodem NGO would interact with BancoSol. After considering a variety of ideas, some zany, Prodem decided its next mission would be to test microfinance in rural areas. No one had yet offered services sustainably outside the major cities and towns. This rural experiment, which has give Prodem a second life, is discussed in chapter 7.

At first Prodem and BancoSol planned to remain closely linked. In Otero's view, Prodem and BancoSol together could achieve more than either could alone. In fact, Otero views the Bolivia Model as a unique way to use the success of the commercial side of microfinance to keep pushing toward the realization of the full vision of microfinance—access to finance for even poorer people, especially those in his beloved rural areas. The plan grew from the observation that not all Prodem's branches were "ready" for BancoSol at the time of its launch. A number of branches were still new and lacked the volume to operate profitably. Prodem would bring each of these branches up to a profitable level, then sell the branch and its portfolio to BancoSol in return for more shares. Through this process Prodem would contribute to BancoSol's success, while, as owner of BancoSol, it would have a valuable endowment and a source of dividend income to finance its push into the frontier. A virtuous spiral would begin, with each iteration closer to universal access.

More mundanely, this process was a practical strategy to keep BancoSol from taking on too much at once. It also allowed the bank to earn profits sooner, because only mature branches would appear on BancoSol's books, and in that way it provided an ongoing start-up subsidy for BancoSol. In fact, although in public, and even in private, BancoSol embraced commercial principles, there was still perhaps a lurking fear that the bank experiment would not work. Prodem could be a cushion. In addition, Rosenberg, in his blunt style, suggests that the directors kept Prodem as a machine for milking funds from donors, something BancoSol could not do.

However, within the first two years of BancoSol's life, Prodem's evolution took a turn away from the model as Otero saw it. The turning point was the choice of Eduardo Bazoberry to head Prodem in its second life. Bazoberry, a cousin of Otero's, is in his own way as much an activist, entrepreneur, and visionary as Otero, though with a harder, more aggressive style. One question to Bazoberry and he is off for half an hour, pacing the room and jabbing points home with his cigarette, revealing ambitions by no means modest. His analytic mind and personal energy ensured that Prodem would be a place where new ideas surfaced, were thoroughly tested, and, if they stood the test, would become reality. Bazoberry quickly became personally identified with Prodem and wanted to create a distinct Prodem vision. An old family rivalry between the cousins was reborn in rivalry between Prodem and BancoSol. Bazoberry and Otero agreed that there would be no hidden subsidies. BancoSol would pay full price for any services it received from Prodem. Eventually, Bazoberry determined that Prodem would have no operational connections to BancoSol at all. It would be lead shareholder, nothing more. After the sale of the first few branches, in accord with the original plan, Prodem declined to continue producing branches for BancoSol. In short order Prodem became a microcredit institution on its own, with a substantial portfolio and increasing success in serving rural clients. Although they shared the solidarity group methodology with the same vision and values, and although many of the sponsoring directors were the same people, Prodem and BancoSol were fast becoming competitors.

In Rosenberg's view this outcome was even better than the original plan. He notes that Prodem and BancoSol were fortunate that Otero and Bazoberry had such a strong rivalry. He and other observers see the original model as a dangerous one, in which organizations can use the close links between an NGO and a for-profit subsidiary to hide problems. In fact, Corposol/Finansol, an Acción affiliate in Colombia, collapsed for this very reason.[7] In the Corposol case, the NGO and its transformed formal financial institution were linked operationally and through NGO control of the financial institution's board of directors. The NGO directed the financial institution into a number of highly risky lines of business, while the financial institution parked its problem loans on the balance sheet of the NGO in order to appear more profitable to other shareholders and banking authorities. When the ruse was discovered, it was already too late.

In Bolivia the arm's-length relationship between Prodem and BancoSol prevented this kind of maneuvering, and the personal distance between the principals in turn ensured that the relationship would stay arm's length. As for Otero's desire to see a virtuous cycle pushing deeper into unserved territory, it is being fulfilled, albeit in a slightly changed form. Prodem has indeed used its endowment as a basis for developing rural lending. Now, as Prodem has become a *fondo financiero privado* (FFP), the cycle begins again: Prodem FFP operates commercially, while its lead owner, the well-endowed Prodem Foundation, pursues a new development role. While Otero foresaw a continuous spiral, the process in fact has involved the spin off of independent circles.

CAJA LOS ANDES AND THE CREATION OF THE FFPS

The story of the creation of Caja Los Andes from the NGO Procredito illustrates the Bolivia Model in action for a second time, with enough variation to throw light onto several basic issues. It also provides an opportunity to examine how the banking authorities responded to the emerging microfinance industry by creating the regulatory category of *fondos financieros privados*. The birth of Caja Los Andes was less traumatic than that of BancoSol. Caja Los Andes had two major advantages over its older sibling: it was a second child, and it was part of a planned family.

Throughout the early days of IPC's work to create Procredito, IPC staff were also advising the Superintendency on the creation of a new category of institution for microfinance. IPC's explicit intent was to pave the way for Procredito's transformation. This work started in 1991, at the same time the Superintendency was evaluating Cobanco's application to create BancoSol. Therefore, the Superintendency was already learning about microcredit, albeit from a slightly different perspective.

The first concept IPC and the Superintendency developed was the *casa bancaria*, modeled loosely after the *cajas municipales* of Peru, owned by municipal governments, at that time IPC's premier project. Soon, however, a different model emerged from political circles, entitled *bancos departementales*. These would be private financial institutions of limited capitalization. Like the rural banks in Ghana and the Philippines, they would be allowed to work only in one department of the country. The *bancos departementales* appealed particularly to politicians wanting to serve their constituencies. However, the model did not fit the emerging microfinance institutions, which aspired to national coverage. Moreover, these localized banks would lack exposure to competition and would have limited ability to diversify risk. In other countries these same limitations have often been associated with weak institutions. IPC advisors chafed over the emergence of the *bancos departementales*. Nevertheless, Procredito, still based mainly in La Paz, began planning to convert into such a bank. Fortunately, the new Sanchéz de Lozada government quickly scuttled the concept and started redrawing a regulatory framework for microfinance institutions. Pilar Ramírez of FIE remembers that the new superintendent dismissed the *bancos departementales* with the comment, "I'm not going to allow five friends to pitch in $100,000 each and have their own bank."

IPC identified one line in Bolivia's existing credit law that created a type of institution called *fondos financieros privados* (FFPs). No regulations had ever been written to specify what an FFP might be, and indeed, no one seemed to know the intent behind this legal provision. Thus, it was a convenient empty shell for IPC and the Superintendency to fill without having to ask Parliament to amend the credit law. The Superintendency could define the category by issuing regulations.

The Superintendency and IPC developed a framework for the new category, based on three principles. First, the minimum capital would be $1 million, one-third the size of the minimum capital required for a bank. This nice, round figure dovetailed with a calculation about the minimum feasible size for a microfinance institution. If an institution leveraged its capital by a factor of ten, as would be allowed, the minimum capital would provide a base for up to $10 million in assets, or up to a maximum of roughly $9 million in loans (allowing for liquidity reserves). The analysts judged that institutions much below this size would not compete successfully in the Bolivian financial marketplace.

The second, and very important, principle was to require these institutions to meet the same regulatory norms as banks. They would have to maintain standards of "safety and soundness" just as stringent as larger institutions (though ratios were sometimes adjusted to the nature of the business), in ownership structure, portfolio quality, capital adequacy, liquidity, internal control, limitations against insider lending, and other areas. Their objectives of reaching the poor would not exempt them. In fact, if they raised deposits from their low-income clients, they would have to be especially trustworthy.

The third principle was to limit the range of activities of the institutions, excluding them from some of the kinds of services that require more risk or greater sophistication. This list now includes foreign trade, credit cards, checking accounts, factoring, trusts, guarantee of debts, and investments in other institutions. On the other hand, the category did not specify the type of service that had to be provided. Thus, while the framers of the FFP regulations had microfinance institutions, especially Procredito, in mind, they wrote the regulations in a fairly open way, so that a number of different kinds of institutions with different services could use the category. FFPs now include lenders specializing in microenterprise, small enterprise, agribusiness, and consumer credit. Importantly, as supervised financial institutions, FFPs would be allowed to raise deposits from the public.

The government issued the regulations as Supreme Decree 25,000, in April 1995, and three months later the Superintendency awarded Caja Los Andes the first FFP license. The transfer of ownership and equity resembled the Prodem/BancoSol transfer, with a few adjustments. The ownership structure looked very much the same, with Procredito owning nearly half of the equity, international organizations owning an equal part (the Multilateral Investment Fund of the InterAmerican Development Bank, and the Swiss Development Corporation), and private investors, including Bolivian founding individuals, holding the remainder. On the day of the portfolio transfer Procredito exchanged all its good loans for deposits in Caja Los Andes and ceased to exist as an operating organization. The Superintendency insisted on a thorough audit of the loan portfolio before approving this exchange in order to ensure that the new institution's assets would be worth what it paid for them.

Procredito and Caja Los Andes implemented the vision IPC set out from the first, and therefore few issues of corporate-culture change arose to plague it. The transition from NGO to FFP did involve accommodation to technical requirements of the Superintendency, but the staff took these in stride. Caja Los Andes demonstrates the obvious lesson that it is much easier to create a financial institution if you plan to do so from the very beginning. Changes in organizational vision are among the most difficult changes to implement.

Unlike Prodem after BancoSol, Procredito did not look for a new raison d'être. Procredito has fulfilled its chosen objective, to become a holding company for Caja Los Andes. Today, Procredito has a board of directors, an office (one room inside the Los Andes headquarters), and a part-time accountant. It is a well-endowed organization, with equity and deposits in a profitable FFP. Its board of directors is distinct from that of Los Andes. Only one person, Pilar Velasco, sits on both boards. Six years after founding the institution, IPC withdrew as managers, turning management over to the local team it had created but remaining closely involved as a consulting partner, and more recently as equity investor and board member.

THE EVOLUTION OF THE BOLIVIA MODEL

Since the first two experiences of NGO transformation, the Superintendency has awarded five additional FFP licenses. Two of the new FFPs, Acceso and Fassil, are purely commercial ventures, without NGO antecedents, and both started with consumer credit. (They will be discussed further in chapter 6.) All of the remaining FFP licenses involve transformed NGOs. Although each case twists the model developed for BancoSol and Caja Los Andes in slightly different directions, the differences are not substantial.

At FIE, for example, the only significant twist involves the transfer of the loan portfolio. When Procredito had exchanged its loan portfolio for deposits in Los Andes, the Superintendency first required an exhaustive audit of that portfolio to ensure that the transfer represented an equal exchange of value. FIE wanted to avoid this time-consuming and expensive process, so it developed a different mechanism for transfer. At the moment FIE FFP opened its doors, all the financial staff moved from the NGO to the FFP, but the ownership of the portfolio remained with the NGO. Every day the NGO pays a fee to the FFP for the management of its assets. Meanwhile, whenever a client repays a loan borrowed from the NGO, the FFP issues the new loan. In other words, FIE transfers customers rather than loans. Because all the loans are short term, the transfer of customers runs its course quickly, leaving the NGO with cash. After paying off its loans from concessional/public sources, the NGO places its cash on deposit with the FFP. This process was facilitated by the fact that the $1 million capital requirement was relatively easy for FIE to raise without tying up the majority of the loan portfolio. This process has subsequently been repeated for newer FFPs, Prodem and EcoFuturo.

FIE's ownership structure is similar to that of BancoSol and Los Andes: a mix of the NGO (60 percent); a few wealthy Bolivians (30 percent); and an international organization, Swiss Development Corporation (10 percent). The most significant differences are the absence of an international technical partner, reflecting FIE's go-it-alone history, and the fact that the NGO retains majority control. FIE's Bolivian backers include members of the Johnson family, the retired owner of *Cerveceria Paçeña*, Bolivia's main brewery, and others from the family of a local cigarette company. Ramírez jokes about being owned by the vice industries but has a great deal of respect for the individuals involved. Besides, the Superintendency had told her she needed to bring some wealthy Bolivian shareholders into the picture, and she was grateful to have found them. Ramírez considers FIE's transformation faithful to the original concept, much as envisioned by Otero. FIE NGO continues, funded in part by the dividends and interest income from its deposits in the FFP, and concentrates on providing the nonfinancial services Ramírez has always believed to be an integral part of microenterprise development.

At Prodem the transformation into an FFP followed the FIE model, again with the NGO as a majority owner. Prodem raised a similar amount of capital from private Bolivian investors as BancoSol did before: approximately $1.5 million, of which about $75,000 comes from individuals. Raising the initial capital was not an issue for Prodem, whose net worth at transfer was $18 million. Prodem Foundation, which partially owns Prodem FFP, will devote itself to a new mission, starting with developing specific rural industries in which microproducers can share. Although management expresses its continued commitment to the commercial principle, the size and profitability of Prodem FFP and Prodem Foundation's existing endowment will make the foundation wealthy enough to fund a substantial development program without fundraising. And, of course, the Foundation form will allow it to seek donor money.

A final twist on the Bolivia Model concerns the joining of four very different NGOs in a single FFP, EcoFuturo. This group includes two urban NGOs, Idepro and CIDRE, and two rural ones, Fades and ANED. The four work in different settings, using a wide range of methodologies. What they have in common is a general perspective that sees microfinance in a broader economic-development context. Most of the organizations provide nonfinancial services in addition to their lending, and they have some operations they don't believe can be fully financially viable, such as remote rural lending. After a long process of negotiation with the Superintendency they have agreed on a mode of operation. On the day when EcoFuturo begins operations in a given department (La Paz first), the participating NGOs will cease credit operations in that department, turning over their customers to EcoFuturo. Over the first several years EcoFuturo will gradually expand to additional departments. The remaining NGOs will each go in a different direction: Idepro to concentrate on nonfinancial services; CIDRE to become the research organization it was originally; Fades and ANED to work in remote departments EcoFuturo is not yet prepared to enter. The ownership structure is familiar: a group of five Bolivian private investors; the four NGOs; and two international organizations, the Andean Development Corporation (ADC) and Swiss Development Corporation (SDC). EcoFuturo and Prodem are adding an important new wrinkle, an employee stock-ownership plan.

The joining of four quite disparate NGOs to form one FFP is more complex than any of the transformations that have gone before. It shows that both NGOs and the Superintendency have grown increasingly comfortable with the issues involved in bringing microfinance institutions into the financial system.

REFLECTIONS: HAS THE BOLIVIA MODEL FULFILLED ITS ORIGINAL AIMS?

The Bolivia Model is still young. Only BancoSol and Caja Los Andes have sufficient history to yield strong conclusions. Nevertheless, we can already discern the outlines of how—or whether—the model fulfills its original aims with the help of figures like those in Table 5.1.

Certainly the institutions are operating essentially on commercial terms. Their current financial performance is far ahead of the performance represented by the microfinance NGOs in most countries. Both institutions report returns to equity as good as or better than mainstream financial institutions in Bolivia. They maintain a financial structure in line with standards of safety and soundness for financial institutions, with the kinds of protection against risk that safety and soundness require (adequate equity and liquidity ratios, interest rate risk mitigation, and so on). Until the general crisis of 1999, they contained delinquency safely. Thanks to the Superintendency's demands, they meet stringent financial-reporting requirements, which makes their operations relatively transparent. Their management and governance have become more professional. Their dependence on subsidies has ended. All these practices make them safer, more efficient stewards of the resources they manage, with strong prospects for the future.

The figures in Table 5.1 also reveal the heart of the challenge that BancoSol and Caja Los Andes faced during their early years, to manage rapid growth while operating in an increasingly professional and competitive environment. Both institutions have become much more efficient and have passed some of that gain to clients in the form of lower interest rates (seen by declining interest yields). Los Andes reduced costs impressively from 27 percent of portfolio in 1995, the year it became an FFP, to 13 percent in 1999. Behind such numbers

Table 5.1 Evolution of Transformed Institutions: BancoSol and Caja Los Andes

	1992	1993	1994	1995	1996	1997	1998	1999
BancoSol								
Loans outstanding (thousands)	27	49	61	63	72	76	82	73
Total portfolio (US$ millions)	8.8	24.8	33.2	36.7	47.4	63.1	74.1	82.3
Average loan balance (US$)	326	506	544	583	658	830	904	1127
Admin. costs/portfolio	22	21	21	22	20	18	17	16
Interest income/portfolio	n/a	n/a	50	33	47	33	33	29
Return on equity	-9	4	13	9	14	24	29	9
Delinquent loans/portfolio	3.2	2.9	5.1	3.1	2.6	21	4.5	7
Procredito (1992-94)/Caja Los Andes (1995-99)								
Loans outstanding (thousands)	1	2	5	16	24	30	35	37
Total portfolio (US$ millions)	0	1	2.1	6	11.9	20.4	28.6	35.9
Average loan balance (US$)	543	518	391	375	496	680	817	970
Admin. costs/portfolio	n/a	n/a	n/a	27	20	14	13	13
Interest income/portfolio	n/a	n/a	n/a	40	35	32	31	27
Return on equity	n/a	13	11	7	18	36	27	14
Delinquent loans/portfolio	12.1	10.4	10.4	5	n/a	n/a	5.7	6.5

Sources: Caja Los Andes and BancoSol annual reports; mimeographed data from Asofin and Micro Rate; Fiedler, Peter. "Bolivia. Assessing the Performance of Banco Solidario." *Sustainable Banking with the Poor.* Washington, D.C.: World Bank, 1998; González-Vega, Claudio, Mark Schreiner, Sergio Navajas, Jorge Rodriguez Meza, and Richard L. Meyer. "A Primer on Bolivian Experiences in Microfinance: An Ohio State Perspective." Columbus, Ohio: Rural Finance Program, Ohio State University, no date; Asofin, Caja Los Andes, BancoSol, Micro Rate, Fiedler, González-Vega et al. n/a = not available

Notes: Ratios given as percentages. Figures at year end, except Procrédito 1992–94, which are monthly averages.

is a story of intensive, sustained management effort within each institution. Managers reduced costs through combinations of growing loan sizes with their clients, lengthening loan terms, and increasing loan-officer caseloads. BancoSol lowered costs even while introducing savings products (which usually drives up costs). Although both lenders have increased average loan sizes, analysts who have examined the data in detail have not found evidence of a loss of commitment to the poor but rather a natural process of client improvement and a maturing portfolio.[8] It is evident that transformation into formal financial institutions has given both institutions a secure footing for growth and placed them under pressure to improve performance.

Nevertheless, in two key areas, funding and ownership, the agenda remains unfinished.

Is It Still Donor Money?

The institutions have satisfied their most urgent goal: they have gained access to the funds they needed for growth. On opening day BancoSol's portfolio was $4 million; within three years it had grown to $33 million. In its first three years as an FFP, Caja Los Andes grew from $6 to $20 million. This kind of growth would have been difficult for the institutions as NGOs, because it has required a shift in funding sources. However, in the main that shift has involved replacing donor grants with public-sector lines of credit rather than a complete shift to commercial sources. Only BancoSol raises most of its funds from private sources.

It is significant that the early reliance on direct donor grants has all but vanished, because with the disappearance of grants, the major subsidies also disappeared, an important step forward. None of the financial institutions has received substantial grants from donors since becoming licensed, though a few have raised limited support for specialized technical assistance. Donor grants still play a role in the background, as sources of some of the equity investments made by other institutions, including Acción, Calmeadow, ProFund, and the IDB's Multilateral Investment Fund. USAID and the Consultative Group to Assist the Poorest (CGAP) have given grants to Acción to buy equity in BancoSol in order to ensure that Acción's technical and managerial voice continues to be heard in the BancoSol board room. The total amount of grant-based funding, however, is small relative to the amounts that these institutions absorbed during their start-up phase.

Ironically, although subsidies are down, the absolute volume of public-sector support has increased. Transformation has brought in as investors a number of organizations previously uninvolved in microfinance, such as the InterAmerican Investment Corporation, the Andean Development

Corporation, and the Commonwealth Development Corporation. These public-sector development banks operate on mainly commercial principles, albeit under multilateral backing. They share characteristics of both public and private institutions. As dual-personality institutions they have a natural affinity with microfinance institutions and have been influential in introducing the microfinance field to private-sector standards of operation. Yet, fundamentally, they must be considered a part of the donor world.

Similarly, Bolivian-based second-tier organizations like Funda-Pro (established with USAID money) and NAFIBO (a facility of the government of Bolivia) provide a significant amount of loan capital at market rates but are still motivated by public-sector concerns. These wholesale lenders, also called apex facilities, lend to other financial institutions, using donor and/or government funds. They have money earmarked for microfinance, so they cannot apply a genuinely private set of risk and return calculations. Nevertheless, funding by multilaterals and apexes is not heavily subsidized.

Multilaterals, second-tier lenders, and funds from the original NGOs constitute the main sources of funds of the new financial institutions. Reports from Caja Los Andes, for example, show two-thirds of all funds (liabilities plus equity) coming from multilaterals, wholesalers, and the original NGO, while only 7 percent is clearly identified as fully private. The remaining 27 percent is a mixed group of deposits from the public, including both private depositors and donor-linked organizations in an unknown ratio (but almost none from clients). Much of the private funding of Caja Los Andes is raised through the Bolivian capital market.

BancoSol has moved significantly farther toward private funding sources but is still closely linked to public-sector institutions. Its 1997 Annual Report shows that deposits furnished 69 percent of all liabilities. About half of those deposits come from BancoSol clients, while the rest come from better-off depositors and institutions, both public and private. Another 20 percent of funds comes from other financial institutions, including public institutions. Another 8 percent of funds comes from bonds BancoSol has issued. These bonds are hard to classify as public or private. They carry a 50 percent guarantee from USAID, but they have been sold to quintessentially private-sector buyers—through a Wall Street investment bank. While it is difficult to pin down the percentage of purely private-sector funding on BancoSol's balance sheet, a best guess would place that percentage over 50 percent. Although BancoSol has developed an important capacity to bid for funds from private financial markets (including depositors), it still retains support from the public sector to enhance its marketability.

It is important to ask whether the other institutions aim to make the same kind of transformation of funding sources BancoSol has made (and if so, how), or whether they expect that multilaterals and wholesalers will continue to be the main financiers of the microfinance industry. Former Bank Superintendent Jacques Trigo expresses disappointment that the new FFPs have not developed a broader, more stable funding base. He contrasts the FFPs with the cooperatives, which have grown largely on the basis of customer deposits. This stable source of money, he believes, puts coops in a stronger position to survive over the long haul.

Has a Suitable Ownership Structure Emerged?

Gabriel Schor, one of IPC's leaders, sees IPC's history as a search for an ideal ownership structure for microfinance. One might say the same about the Bolivia Model of microfinance transformation. In each instance of transformation the types of investors involved are quite similar; however, there are some crucial differences in approach, with BancoSol and Caja Los Andes representing two different perspectives. Neither institution would claim that it has fully solved the ownership challenge.

The original structure of Caja Los Andes represents IPC's thinking about ownership as of 1995. In earlier experiments (in Peru, Nicaragua, and Guatemala) IPC attempted to develop microfinance services in government-owned organizations, concluding sadly that the incentive structures of these organizations were inherently antithetical to efficiency. IPC also rejected the NGO form, perceiving inefficiency among NGOs to be intimately related to lack of clear ownership.

IPC set out to find an ownership structure that would combine efficiency with mission. Unless the owner of the organization could marry both goals, the microfinance institution would veer off course, either remaining unsustainable or abandoning the target population. IPC wanted to find the "ideal capitalist," who had both mission and a concern for the bottom line. When Caja Los Andes was developing, IPC's thought was to duplicate the characteristics of the ideal capitalist by combining different kinds of owners. The original NGO would maintain commitment to mission. Multilateral investment organizations (ADC and the IDB's Multilateral Investment Fund) would maintain the commercial perspective. Caja Los Andes started with the NGO and multilateral interests balanced at 40 percent each, with the remainder distributed among the private individuals who had been Procredito board members. Ownership was held among only a few organizations and people, and the purely profit-oriented private sector was largely absent. Schor notes that the choice of this structure reflected a European mistrust of purely private investors, as well as the observation that few Bolivian investors were prepared to take the long-term perspective toward business development that microfinance required.

Over time, however, Caja Los Andes learned that the multilateral institutions were not adequate guardians of efficiency. According to Schor, "We over-idealized the role the multilateral organizations could play. They are playing with Mickey Mouse money, and lack a clear and natural incentive to push toward efficiency." The multilateral organizations changed representatives at board meetings often, which hampered informed participation in crucial decisions. Most aggravating were unclear lines of authority among various players within a multilateral organization, making it difficult for representatives to hold consistent positions. Moreover, the crisis of Finansol in Colombia demonstrated that the multilateral investors could not respond quickly with more capital in an emergency, an important qualification for owners of financial institutions. In fact, none of the nontraditional types of owners involved in these institutions had that capability, a significant shortcoming of the evolving ownership model.

For IPC, another problem with the ownership structure was that it left IPC out. No longer part of management and not an owner, IPC was relegated to the role of outside kibitzer. IPC's response has been to create its own ideal capitalist in the form of a private investment fund, IMI. The principals of IPC, together with other individuals they have attracted, have invested their own funds in IMI, which in turn invests in microfinance institutions. IMI has taken an 11 percent stake in Caja Los Andes, and with that, IPC regained a seat on the board.

IPC and Acción have moved in the same direction to solve the dilemma of passive multilaterals and potential loss of influence through direct investment and participation in governance of the transformed organizations. Direct investment by entities such as IMI, ProFund, and Acción help ensure that the owners of the organization have working knowledge of microfinance. Each of these investors embodies the marriage of mission and profitability. The technical partners can often wield disproportionate influence on the board, because of their knowledge and willingness to put in time and effort. The presence of such investors is welcomed by the multilateral organizations, which recognize their own limitations. By funding these technical partners, the multilateral organizations can help ensure that their own direct investments in microfinance institutions are managed safely.

In its current form Caja Los Andes offers an ownership model substantially similar to the other FFPs, and widely applicable to other countries: a close-knit group consisting of the original NGO, multilateral investors, local individuals, and an international technical partner. Conspicuously absent, however, is the profit-motivated private sector. It is in this regard that BancoSol's ownership struggles differ from those of Caja Los Andes.

Although the types of owners BancoSol first assembled were similar to those in Caja Los Andes, BancoSol's somewhat unruly group of participants always aimed to attract private investors with primarily commercial interests. Ownership would evolve as new capital was raised (bringing new investors in) and through built-in steps like IIC's five-year exit horizon. The organizers hoped BancoSol would become a genuine private-sector institution. This hope was a leap into the unknown, risking loss of control. Attempts to maintain control over BancoSol while pursuing private investors have created turmoil at the top of the bank since 1997, when major ownership changes began.

In that year BancoSol faced two major ownership changes. IIC, the lead multilateral investor, had made it clear that it would sell its shares after five years. This sale coincided with the need for Prodem, still the largest shareholder in BancoSol, to sell its shares as a requirement to obtain its own license as an FFP. Bolivian banking regulations prohibit one financial institution from owning shares in another. The directors of Prodem, including some of the original founders of Prodem and BancoSol like Romero and Sanchéz de Lozada, suddenly faced the prospect of BancoSol slipping into unknown hands.

To forestall this possibility, the idea emerged of a merger between BancoSol and Prodem. Proponents of the merger argued that Prodem's rural network would complement BancoSol's urban one, creating a single institution with a dominant market position throughout Bolivia. Because of their origins as one organization, BancoSol and Prodem shared similar products, systems, and values. Calmeadow called in a Canadian bank, Toronto Dominion Bank, to study the proposed merger. Its experts concluded that a merger would add value. However, Michael Chu, a veteran of the mergers and acquisitions wars on Wall Street and the lead negotiator for Acción, concluded that the kind of opportunities for cost savings one would want to see in a merger weren't there. The main advantage of the proposed merger would be to gain a stronger market position.

Ultimately the merger foundered over the question of control. Prodem and its board (including Fernando Romero and most of the original Bolivian founders) put forward one proposal based on the existing Prodem management, while Acción, Calmeadow, ProFund, and the largest private shareholder in BancoSol, Julio Leon, put forward another based on BancoSol's existing managers. As David Blanco, one of the Prodem group put it, the merger talks turned into "a fight of power and prestige" between people who had worked together for years. Finally, neither team could yield its precious gem to the other. For many of the principals, the failure of the merger talks was a deep personal loss, leaving behind animosities where there had been friendships. However, for observers like Rosenberg, who see competition as a beneficial process, the failure was a good thing for microfinance in Bolivia. A combined Prodem and BancoSol would have commanded an inordinate share of the market.

Thus, in 1998, BancoSol shares from IIC, Prodem, and Julio Leon were sold to the highest bidder. Although there was some interest by Bolivian private investors, the winner was another multilateral investor, the Commonwealth Development Corporation, which purchased 20 percent of the bank. According to Fernando Romero, this sale to a multilateral bank was a major missed opportunity for Bolivians. He laments the fact that Bolivian investors did not see BancoSol as a strong enough business opportunity, especially given BancoSol's impressive financial performance during the mid-1980s. Perhaps CDC, as a public institution wanting to join the microfinance movement, was willing to swallow risks that choked Bolivian investors. Romero laments the same thing Schor observed, that Bolivian businessmen are impatient, lacking a long-term perspective—perhaps a legacy of the past, when long-term bets on Bolivia were not good bets.

Former Superintendent Trigo is one of those disappointed by the lack of response by Bolivian investors. He notes that his office accepted unconventional owners for microfinance institutions—NGOs and multilaterals—as an entry strategy, expecting to draw in private investors and depositors' money, but this has not happened in a major way.

Finally, after a long wait, a private Bolivian investor, Ramiro Freitas, purchased 7 percent of BancoSol shares. Freitas is not a member of the old power elite who founded BancoSol. A newer entrepreneur, he made at least some of his money in retail merchandising, where the layaway department gave him a glimpse of the financial habits of low-income people. Freitas is the first genuine profit-motivated private investor in BancoSol, though some point out that he is also seeking prestige and social recognition. As a private investor he represents a first step toward achieving the goal set when BancoSol began, and one would expect to hear some rejoicing from BancoSol's board room.

Instead, Freitas and CDC have split BancoSol's board into two blocs, the microfinance bloc (Acción, ProFund, and others) and the commercial bloc (CDC and Freitas). CDC and Freitas push hard for faster profits and the addition of more conventional commercial lending products, while the other bloc seeks to maintain BancoSol's unique microfinance identity. In sum, BancoSol has lost its original NGO owner (though Prodem still owns some shares, which are for sale and no longer carry a board seat). It has gained a local champion, but he is a champion who does not know microfinance. Acción and ProFund, foreign entities, struggle to maintain control in order to preserve the mission.

Fernando Romero is disappointed that BancoSol has not yet become both a truly private and a truly Bolivian organization. He notes somewhat bitterly that BancoSol's evolution parallels the decision of most Bolivian banks to take international partners. Most observers credit this entry of international banks as a major factor in making the Bolivian financial sector safer and more dynamic. In fact, BancoSol's attempt to build a standard corporate governance culture and structure parallels the attempts of the international banks in their own institutions. According to Romero, genuine corporate-style governance is still new on the Bolivian scene. Although Bolivian businessmen acknowledge the modernizing influence of foreign banks, foreign control is still a sore spot.

For microfinance institutions, the lesson from comparing the ownership models of BancoSol and Caja Los Andes may be that the safer course is to build an ideal capitalist rather than to invite real capitalists in. But the safer course leaves unfulfilled the final promise of microfinance to become a normal private business. The search for the best ownership structure is far from over.

Deepening the Mission

The last, but certainly not least, objective of the Bolivia Model, as Pancho Otero articulated, is to launch a new deepening of the mission. Have the transformations in fact allowed microfinance to penetrate farther? First, it might be important to note that no transformed institution has yet changed its basic clientele or services as a result of adopting commercial standards. Certainly there is pressure to make larger loans, but this pressure comes from sources beyond just the transformations, especially competition, as we will discuss in chapter 6.

Part of deepening the mission involved extending savings services to microfinance clients. The transformations of Bolivian institutions allow the FFPs to offer savings services, provided they can convince the Superintendency they have systems and skills for doing so. However, as noted above, only BancoSol has attracted any significant savings from its informal clients, funding about one-third of its total portfolio with these deposits. By the end of 1998, Caja Los Andes had raised only $700,000 in deposits from microfinance customers, about 3 percent of its total funds. Los Andes and the other FFPs intend to take some more systematic initiatives into the savings area. This savings push is one subject of chapter 7.

As for the virtuous spiral that Otero envisioned, in which the original NGO seeks to reach deeper while the financial institution pays dividends that help finance the NGO's outreach, the evolution of Prodem and BancoSol illustrates this model well. Prodem in its second phase pushed successfully into rural areas, and in its third phase, as Prodem Foundation, it is again poised to take on another mission. The only element of Otero's vision that has not come to pass is that of continual feeding of the financial institution by the NGO, and this is probably for the best.

Procredito, on the other hand, has not yet taken advantage of its status and assets to develop a new mission. It is likely that it will carefully design any steps it does take so as not to compete with the business of Caja Los Andes. For example, Procredito has made a small investment in IMI, which in turn invests in microfinance institutions in other countries. The other new FFPs, EcoFuturo and FIE, do intend to apply Otero's model, but it is too early to tell how well they will succeed.

NOTES

1. Cheryl Frankiewicz, *Building Institutional Capacity: The Story of PRODEM, 1987–1999* (Toronto: Calmeadow, 2001), 6.
2. For an excellent discussion on transformation, see Anita Campion and Victoria White, *Institutional Metamorphosis: Transformation of Microfinance NGOs into Regulated Financial Institutions*, MicroFinance Network Occasional Paper No. 4 (Washington, D.C.: MicroFinance Network, 1999).
3. The process of creating BancoSol has been well documented in Deborah Drake and Maria Otero, *Alchemists for the Poor: NGOs as Financial Institutions.* Monograph Series No. 6 (Cambridge, Mass.: Acción International, 1992); Amy Glosser, "The Creation of BancoSol in Bolivia," in *The New World of Microenterprise Finance: Building Healthy Financial Institutions for the Poor,* ed. Maria Otero and Elisabeth Rhyne (West Hartford, Conn.: Kumarian Press, 1994); and Frankiewicz, *Building Institutional Capacity.* Some of the facts presented in this section, particularly the numbers, are drawn from these sources.
4. Drake and Otero, *Alchemists,* 90.
5. Now such statistics are available through initiatives such as the *MicroBanking Bulletin,* MicroRate, and other analytic studies. Leading microfinance institutions are slowly reducing these costs.
6. See, for example, Glosser, "Creation of BancoSol" and Campion and White, *Institutional Metamorphosis.*
7. This episode is the subject of Jean Steege's paper, "The Rise and Fall of Corposol: Lessons Learned from the Challenges of Managing Growth" (Bethesda, Md.: Development Alternatives Inc., 1998).
8. For example, Peter Fidler, "Bolivia: Assessing the Performance of Banco Solidario," Sustainable Banking with the Poor (Washington, D.C.: World Bank, 1998); Claudio González-Vega et al., "Bolivia's Microfinance Market Niches: Clientele

Profiles" (Columbus, Ohio: Rural Finance Program, Ohio State University, 1996); and Robert Peck Christen, "Commercialization and Mission Drift: The Transformation of Microfinance in Latin America," (unpublished draft, Washington, D.C.: Consultative Group to Assist the Poorest, 2000).

CHAPTER SIX

COMPETITION, COMMERCIALIZATION, AND THE CRISIS IN MICROFINANCE

THE FOUNDERS OF THE BOLIVIAN microfinance institutions never bargained on being in the midst of a competitive maelstrom. However, during the late 1990s, a number of private commercial players entered the microcredit market as the microlenders themselves grew to unprecedented scale. The ensuing competition, coinciding with a general economic crisis, brought fundamental changes to the microfinance scene. These changes challenge some of the cherished assumptions about the way microcredit works and thrust the industry decisively into a new era.

PRECONDITIONS: A MODERNIZING BOLIVIAN FINANCIAL SYSTEM

We have already noted that Bolivia's financial sector reforms set favorable conditions for the creation of advanced microfinance institutions, starting with inflation control. These same reforms also created the conditions for commercial entry into the low end of the banking market.

Until the 1990s, as in many developing countries, Bolivian banking was family banking. Each bank was controlled by a single individual, business group, or family. Some of these finance magnates were also among the founders of microfinance, including Fernando Romero, David Blanco, and Julio Leon. Typically, these men had both industrial and banking interests, and quite often the banks provided funding for their industries. Together, the banks formed a financial oligopoly. Their leaders met each other in richly appointed offices, within a well-understood informal business culture. Predictably, the banks were inefficient, with high administrative costs and few innovations in banking services. However, starting in the late 1980s, financial-sector reforms turned the world of these bankers upside down.

The reforms aimed to restore the confidence of the population in the banking system, confidence shattered during hyperinflation. At the end of hyperinflation the entire Bolivian banking sector had only $60 million in loans outstanding, according to Mario Riquena of the Ministry of Finance. The successive MNR governments gradually rebuilt trust through four major steps. In step one, they liquidated the state banks, which lost money, were corrupt, and lent to elites. The reformers viewed these banks as too hopeless even to privatize. In step two, they began to modernize the legal framework for the banking system. They strengthened the Superintendency of Banks, giving the superintendent significant independence from political control. The new legislation also prohibited insider lending, endemic in traditional Bolivian banking. In step three, during the early 1990s, the government began applying these new legal and administrative tools to weed out weak banks. Fifteen of the 35 banks that had existed in 1985 were closed or restructured, in most cases because of severe undercapitalization. In step four, during the late 1990s, the government began allowing foreign banks to enter the market, sometimes alone, but generally in partnership with local banks. Foreign banks have come from the United States (Citibank), Spain (Banco Santander), and the region (banks from Peru and Chile). Bolivia needed these banks first of all to supply the equity capital local banks lacked, but the government also counted on foreign banks to bring greater efficiency. With access to plentiful and relatively inexpensive capital, banks with foreign partners could invest in modernization and innovation, guided by their partners' knowledge of the latest technologies.

The reforms brought depositors back into the financial system. From $60 million, the total amount of loans outstanding reached $4 billion at the end of 1999.[1] Yet the public remains skittish, as shown by a run on Banco Santa Cruz as late as 1998. An unfounded rumor sparked a massive withdrawal of funds from this otherwise sound bank until the superintendent and other top government officials hurriedly assured the public that the bank was safe. Interest rates and spreads have also fallen throughout the reform period, suggesting improvements in efficiency and more competitive pricing.

Of direct relevance to microfinance, the entry of foreign banks created intensive competition throughout the banking sector. David Blanco reports that Citibank and the other foreign-owned banks began luring prime corporate customers, using their access to cheaper funds, to offer lower interest rates. In response to saturation in the corporate market, local banks started looking downmarket, searching for competitive niches. Yet at this level, too, foreign banks are a formidable force. The foreigners bring technology and techniques for retail banking, particularly consumer lending. These competitive pressures finally brought some Bolivian banks to the doorstep of microcredit, a home-grown innovation they thought they could readily master.

Critics of financial-sector reform programs often charge that without directives banks will ignore the low end, leaving the poor with fewer services than before. Reform advocates contend that market forces will press financial institutions downward. Bolivia's experience proves both views partly right. Competitive pressure in Bolivia is indeed driving banks downmarket. However, Bolivia's experience also shows that before entering, banks need to see and understand how profits may be made in these markets. Liberalization is only a necessary condition. The sufficient conditions are liberalization plus adaptable models. In Bolivia's case, two models dominate the scene: consumer credit and microcredit. The clash between these two models created a major upheaval in the microfinance sector at the end of the 1990s. We will begin by looking at the modest entry of private lenders into microenterprise credit before turning to the more dramatic entry of consumer lending.

COMMERCIAL ENTRY INTO MICROFINANCE

We will look briefly at three institutions that observed the microfinance lenders and decided they could compete profitably in the same marketplace: Fassil FFP, Banco Económico, and Cooperativa Jesús Nazareno. These institutions are all based in Santa Cruz, where the business community is more freewheeling and microfinance institutions are not as strong as in La Paz.

Alfredo Otero, the founder and chief executive of Fassil (actually, Fa$$il), began thinking about starting his own financial institution during the early 1990s, when Bolivia was weeding out its weaker banks. Otero (another distant cousin of Prodem's Pancho Otero) had been working for many years in traditional banking. He observed that bank failures were not caused by small loans; in fact, banks with small loans were the least likely to fail. He also saw that banks provided poor quality services to their retail customers and thought he could do better. He assembled a group of eight investors, all local private businessmen, who together met the minimum $1 million initial capital requirement to become an FFP, and opened Fassil in 1996. These businessmen, although not as prominent and probably not as wealthy as the backers of Prodem/BancoSol, put in significantly more of their own money to launch Fassil.

Otero's motivation was neither altruistic nor totally profit-driven. Rather, he portrays himself as a professional banker, motivated by the personal challenge of serving a large market effectively. If in this process Fassil contributes to Bolivian development, Otero says he would be pleased, but it is the professional challenge that brings him to work in the morning. Fassil's strategy was to start with consumer lending in order to obtain profits quickly while building its microcredit portfolio to a profitable level. Gradually, it planned to increase the share of business devoted to microcredit, where it saw its long-term future. In fact, the crisis of consumer lending, described below, led Fassil to shift sooner than anticipated.

Otero makes no apology for his method of acquiring know-how. To learn consumer credit, he and colleagues went to Chile to study experienced consumer lenders and then contracted a team of Chilean design consultants. To learn microcredit, he raided BancoSol. Fassil's microcredit manager, Claudia Ordoñez, started as a Prodem employee and was a BancoSol branch manager when Fassil recruited her. Several of Fassil's credit officers also started at BancoSol.

Ordoñez and her team applied the BancoSol solidarity group methodology at Fassil with few alterations. They adjusted some procedures, such as reducing the credit committee to two people and disbursing loans every day of the week. However, the core values developed at Prodem are very much in evidence today among the staff of Fassil, including the emphasis on the fieldworker's responsibility for results, the solidarity group concept, and the importance of prompt repayment and immediate follow-up. Fassil emphasizes trust and promotes group values to clients through its slogan, Everything is easier when we work together. Fassil also operates a small but successful pawn loan service, offering cash on the spot to people pledging gold jewelry.

When Fassil entered microenterprise credit, competition was increasing quickly through the growth of established microlenders. Yet Fassil lacked the start-up subsidies and access to preferred sources of loan capital that the donor-backed microfinance institutions had. Nor do its investors have the deep pockets of an international banking partner. As one observer put it, "The institution is young and does not have external subsidies to lessen the consequences of a bad decision, as is the case of many nonprofit organizations."[2] The same factors make Fassil vulnerable to external crises as well. The number of microenterprise clients Fassil reaches is still relatively small (8,300 in May 1998).[3] It will be interesting to see how well this example of local entrepreneurship survives competitive pressures.

A perhaps stronger entrant into the microcredit scene is Banco Económico, a commercial bank launched in 1991 to focus on the small- and medium-enterprise sector in Santa Cruz. The 18 private shareholders of Banco Económico are a far different group from the traditional Bolivian banking and industrial elite. With names such as Kuljis, Vicevic, Svarcic, Kakuda, and Fuchtner, in addition to more standard Spanish surnames, the shareholders of

Banco Económico represent a new force in Bolivia, springing from Santa Cruz's policy in mid-century of attracting colonies of immigrants to farm its rich hinterlands. Banco Económico has been successful, with returns on equity higher than any other Bolivian bank throughout most of its lifetime. Between 1993 and 1997, rates of return on equity have ranged between 18 and 35 percent. Measured on this critical indicator of profitability, Banco Económico has outperformed BancoSol, which scored better during those years on return on assets, but not on equity.

Banco Económico is not explicitly a microlender, but it includes microenterprises as a part of its overall target market, making few distinctions between microenterprises and others. It began locating branches near large informal markets, recognizing that many informal operators move large sums of money. It took standard commercial-banking methods and infused them with a strong orientation toward efficiency and service quality. Banco Económico's chief executive, Justo Yépez Kakuda, prides himself on his ability to relate to the local entrepreneurs. Though he wears the suspenders, slicked-back hair, and aftershave of an elite banker, Yépez Kakuda spends several hours a day sitting at a desk on the main banking floor, where clients are encouraged to approach him directly with any issue they may have. He talks of work on weekends with clients and attending feasts and celebrations at their homes. Banco Económico's offices are a beehive of client and staff activity. It was the first bank to break ranks on banker's hours by opening during lunchtime.

Although Banco Económico did not copy directly from microfinance institutions, Yépez Kakuda was an early member of the Prodem board of directors and reports that the time he spent in the markets with Pancho Otero influenced him significantly. Banco Económico's eclectic approach to product design, its emphasis on service quality, and its intimate knowledge of local markets suggest that it will continue to be a strong competitor and source of innovation affecting microfinance.

A third source of commercial entry into the microfinance market is represented by Cooperativa Jesús Nazareno. Jesús Nazareno is the largest of several Santa Cruz-based cooperatives to launch specific microenterprise credit products. Although the cooperatives were started by priests with altruistic motivations, and although they have had connections to donor agencies at various times, it is appropriate to consider them commercial entrants both because their funding derives from private sources (member savings) and because they have started microcredit purely as a market venture. Moreover, the larger, sounder cooperatives with equity over $1 million are in the process of obtaining licenses to be regulated by the Superintendency of Banks, enabling them to accept deposits from the general public.

The cooperatives claim that they have served microenterprises throughout their history. Nevertheless, until recently they have not used microcredit methodologies. Their lending formula has been based on membership in the cooperative, with loan size determined as a multiple of the client's savings deposits. A wide rift exists, in fact, between the cooperatives and the microfinance institutions. The cooperatives resent the subsidies the microfinance institutions have received over the years while cooperatives struggled to mobilize savings on their own. They express outrage at the high interest rates of microlenders. The microfinance institutions, on the other hand, charge the cooperatives with having abandoned the poor in favor of middle-class members, failing to recognize the specific financial needs of the smallest enterprises, and suffering from weak governance and management.

Pancho Otero's view is summed up in his remark that if the cooperatives open up to microenterprises, they make them go in by the back door. And in fact, while Jesús Nazareno's lavish chrome and polished stone headquarters outshines the headquarters of Fassil, Banco Económico, or BancoSol, the entrance to its microcredit department is down the street in a nondescript building under a small, crooked sign.

This physical separation of microcredit from mainstream cooperative operations may reflect a real difficulty the cooperatives have in becoming effective microenterprise lenders. The credit cooperatives have tended to introduce solidarity group lending by hiring staff from a microlender, most often BancoSol or Prodem. Cooperativa San Martin is famous for having hired away the staff of an entire BancoSol branch, although these people did not stay at the cooperative long. The moral of that story, according to one-time BancoSol manager Jorge Baldevieso, is that the existing staff of the cooperative did not understand the microfinance people, and vice versa—the familiar culture clash in another setting. However, other experiments stuck, and by early 1999 at least five of the cooperatives in Santa Cruz offered solidarity group loans as a regular part of their business.

These three experiences—Fassil, Banco Económico, and Cooperativa Jesús Nazareno—illustrate the limited way the private sector is "dipping its toe" into microcredit. Only one institution, Fassil, is staking its future on microcredit. The others experiment with microcredit at the margins of a wider array of markets and services. Yet the new entrants also add their own banking experiences into the mix, which has the potential to bring innovations in quality, efficiency, and product range. They do not always understand the informal market, and when burned, they tend to retreat to the market's upper end. However, their leaders express determination to learn from their mistakes.

THE RISE OF CONSUMER CREDIT

The consumer credit story is much flashier. Consumer credit was an import into Bolivia from the developed world of salaried workers and consumer durables. It arrived in Bolivia through Chile, where it had burgeoned during the past decade. The Chilean consumer credit industry counts about three million clients in a country whose estimated work force is six million.[4] Consumer lenders offer loans of about the same size as microenterprise loans, very quickly and flexibly, primarily on the basis of a worker's salary. While in theory the market for consumer lending is quite distinct from the microcredit market—salaried employees vs. informal enterprises—in practice there has been a great deal of overlap between the two.

A brief portrait of Acceso FFP, the first and largest consumer lender in Bolivia, will serve to tell the story of consumer credit. Acceso represented the entry of foreign capital and know-how. The owner, a large Chilean holding company, Empresas Conosur, operates home-improvement centers (similar to Home Depot), networks of automobile dealerships, and a variety of other businesses that appeal to the growing Latin American middle class. A multinational company with ten years' experience in consumer lending, Conosur is expanding its subsidiaries into Peru, Paraguay, and Bolivia.

From the glitzy style of its billboards to the inner workings of its lending methodology, Acceso was as different as could be from the microcredit institutions. To lead the operation in Bolivia, Acceso chose Andre Le Faye, a young Bolivian whose crisp, white business shirt and clean-cut self-confidence bring to mind a newly minted American MBA. In fact, he attended Texas A&M. The Acceso methodology is a product of the information age, made possible by the availability of credible information about prospective clients and by technology for managing masses of information efficiently. The concepts of trust and responsibility, so central to the Prodem microcredit methodology, do not feature importantly, either for clients or for staff. Such concepts are not particularly relevant when the fundamental basis for lending is the ability to tap a borrower's steady salary as the source of loan repayment.

When Acceso first entered Bolivia, it sought customers among the employees of prime companies. Large, stable employers provided trustworthy information about a loan applicant's employment and salary and were willing to arrange loan repayment through payroll deduction. For customers with less-than-prime employers, Acceso relied on its own sophisticated credit-scoring model. Credit scoring rates each applicant based on his responses to objective questions linked through a model based on extensive past data to the probability that a client will repay. Questions range from simple personal information to employment history, type and location of residence, and credit experience. The model categorically excludes some groups of people, such as single men below the age of 25 or people with a monthly salary below $150, while giving a rating and determining allowable loan sizes to others. Credit-scoring models distill vast experience into a powerful though mechanical predictive process; formerly that experience would have found expression in a set of policies applied through the judgment of a veteran credit officer.

The internal management of loans also differs drastically from microcredit, which is based on the loan officer's responsibility for the whole client relationship (see Table 6.1). Alfredo Otero of Fassil, which introduced a similar consumer-lending methodology, describes it as a credit factory. Acceso, for example, broke loan approval and collection into at least eight separate steps, each performed by a different person. In assembly-line fashion, each person performs his task very efficiently, and various people cross-check the work of others for quality control. The process begins with credit officers, who are really salespeople on a small base salary, making most of their money on commissions. These officers bring customers through the point of completing a loan application. After that, separate staff enter data, verify data accuracy, evaluate the credit (using credit scoring), verify client identity, notarize documents, disburse, and collect. These steps are done so efficiently that Acceso claimed to disburse first loans within forty-eight hours and second loans within twenty-four. In contrast to microcredit, credit officers have no role in the important steps of verification, evaluation, or collection.

Using such a methodology and a work force of over 1,000 people, Acceso reached a total of 90,000 loans outstanding during its first three years, a scale that BancoSol had not achieved in the twelve years since its origin as Prodem. Nor was Acceso alone. Nearly all the Bolivian banks also started consumer-credit operations using virtually identical techniques. Estimates were that in mid-1998 the Bank of Santa Cruz's Solucion program had another 40,000 clients, as did Union Bank's CrediAgil program.[5] David Blanco estimated that at its peak the system had about $150 million in consumer loans outstanding, nearly the same aggregate size as microcredit.

If consumer lending kept strictly to prime salaried employees, the microlenders would have overlapped with it to some degree because many families include both salaried and independent people; sometimes the same individual has both a salary and a business. The overlap was exacerbated by the fact that Bolivia has so few prime employers. To achieve the volumes they hoped for, consumer lenders moved to lower-grade employers and to independents (their name for microenterprises). La Faye estimated that about 30 percent of Acceso's clients were independents. This would mean more than 25,000

Table 6.1   Comparison of Bolivian Microcredit and Consumer Lending

Parameter	Microenterprise Credit	Consumer Lending
Loan terms	Average near $1000; short term; fast turn-around	Average near $1000; short term; fast turn-around
Basis for loan approval	Enterprise and household cash flow; credit history, group guarantees	Salary; credit "score"
Basis for repayment	Motivation for continued access to credit	Ability to garnish wages
Tolerance for delinquency	"Zero-tolerance" policy. Expected delinquency: less than 3–5%	Not worried until after 30 days late. Expected delinquency: 15–20%
Method of follow-up	Immediate, personal visit	A letter in the mail
Staff organization	Loan officer responsibility for client from start to finish	Assembly-line loan processing
Basic philosophy	Trust and responsibility	Information management

clients, putting Acceso on par with the microlending FFPs in number of microenterprise loans. Thus, consumer lenders competed directly with microlenders.

Direct competition is always a challenge, but because the competition represented a very different lending philosophy, the challenge threatened microlenders in two related dimensions: tolerance of delinquency, and over-lending. Prodem staff describe the line between consumer lending and microcredit as a *brecha*, a schism.

Ironically, the profit-oriented consumer lenders were far more lax on delinquency than the "do-gooder"-inspired microlenders. The consumer lenders assumed that a large share of clients would pay late, and they built these expectations into their pricing. According to staff, Fassil's planning models assumed continual delinquency levels around 17 percent, resulting in write-offs of about 7 percent. Other sources report that write-offs in the consumer loan industry are routinely expected to be five times the size of standard commercial bank write-offs. Coming from more developed countries, consumer lenders use automated collection measures for handling most late payments, printing and mailing form letters to delinquent clients, a dramatic contrast to the immediate loan officer visits microlenders make to delinquent clients. Consumer lenders only initiate visits for the small share of delinquencies that continue for weeks. La Faye, for example, did not consider a loan at risk until its delinquency exceeded 30 days. He pointed out that in the rest of Latin America, banking authorities only consider loans at risk beyond 30 days, while in Bolivia (thanks, in part, to the microlenders) the authorities measure risk beginning with one day. Consumer lenders charge fines for late payment that actually increase their revenues when clients are a little late, making a few days or a week of delinquency welcome, not just tolerated.

Given the obsession with on-time repayment prevailing in Bolivian microcredit, microlenders view such practices with alarm. Without the salary to fall back on, microlenders have always felt exposed to changes in attitudes toward repayment that can sweep like contagion through an institution's clientele.

The consumer lenders added to their vulnerability to default through aggressive marketing. They began moving into the independent (microenterprise) sector in a big way, but without changing their basic methodology. Instead of adopting techniques designed for informals, they piggybacked on the screening done by the microlenders. The technique was simple: lure the good clients away from microlenders by offering them larger loans (and faster, and at lower rates, but mostly larger). The consumer lenders thought they would be safe if they targeted clients in good standing among the microlenders. After all, the loss rates of the microlenders had always been exceedingly low. Carmen Velasco of ProMujer says the competitors were offering loans like hot bread. "Come and get it!" BancoSol staff complain that these *desleal* (disloyal) competitors had no concern for the well-being of the client. Microlender staff seethe when new entrants systematically target their best clients as a low-risk strategy to invade the microcredit market. They also note that the big banks can offer cheaper interest rates because they can spread their fixed costs among their large corporate clients. Similarly, these banks can afford to operate microcredit or consumer loans at a loss for a time, because these portfolios are only a small percentage of their overall assets. Microfinance staff worry that big banks can therefore engage in dumping practices to drive others out of the market.

As it turned out, the consumer lenders should have given more heed to the market knowledge of the microlenders. After what in hindsight turned out to be reckless entry, default shot up among consumer lenders and microlenders alike during 1999 and 2000, creating the crisis of *sobreendeudamiento* (over-indebtedness).

OVER-INDEBTEDNESS AND THE DEBTORS' REVOLT

Clients took advantage of the offer of quick and easy credit from so many institutions to borrow from multiple lenders, maintaining two or more loans outstanding at a time. In an increasing number of cases, clients borrowed more than they could handle. Some let repayments slip, or in worst cases, they began "bicycling" loans—using the proceeds of one loan to pay off another. Such behavior seriously damaged the carefully constructed culture of repayment in microcredit.

When delinquency first began to rise at BancoSol, the bank found a close correlation between late clients and clients with loans at other institutions. According to Juan Domingo Fabbri of BancoSol's marketing department, clients do not see multiple loans as risky. His focus-group research revealed, "The logic of clients is that they will earn more by investing more. Multiple loans have even become a status symbol." Moreover, clients who can maintain a relationship with two or more institutions may actually feel that they have reduced their risk by widening their choices. Clearly, at the upper end, there are some borrowers, like the La Paz textile manufacturer described in chapter 1, whose need and ability to borrow exceeds the amounts microlenders have traditionally been willing to provide. Such borrowers have apparently long had a practice of taking out multiple loans. However, for most other borrowers, too much credit is a quick route to financial disaster.

Carmen Velasco says that some of ProMujer's very poor clients have been broken. She recounts visiting delinquent borrowers in Cochabamba at their homes in the evening. At one very poor house the husband came out asking, "Who are you?" The group identified itself as ProMujer staff. The husband began a tirade. "Oh, the people from FIE were just here ten minutes ago. Yes, this stupid woman of mine has taken two loans." They could see the woman sitting on a bench inside weeping. "But don't worry," he said. "Tomorrow she's getting a loan from BancoSol." For Velasco, the worst of this episode was the man's belief that the third loan would solve their troubles.

The recognition that over-indebtedness was becoming a problem dawned slowly on the microfinance lenders, because they had not prohibited multiple loans when there was less competition. Fassil staff, in fact, report that as many as 90 percent of its borrowers have another loan. Fassil had always seen itself as a second lender to proven good clients and still permits its clients to have more than one outstanding loan. Several microfinance institutions, including ProMujer, now declare clients with a loan at another institution to be ineligible. Nevertheless, Velasco describes driving through a poor section of Cochabamba where delinquency had surged, looking for delinquent clients. They found many of them standing in the queues of other microlenders. They began to tour the offices of their competitors, finding a delinquent ProMujer borrower in nearly every line.

Over-indebtedness due to fierce competition increased just as Bolivia's economy started to slide, propelling a significant problem to crisis proportions. In 1999 Bolivia suffered its first serious economic setback after fifteen years of progress, the result of troubles throughout South America, starting with financial crisis and currency devaluation in Brazil. The ensuing recession hit the informal sector particularly hard. After years of relative quiet, Bolivia began to experience heightened social unrest, with mass protests about things like water and electricity prices. Microfinance, too, felt the anger of the powerless. Interactions with clients started to sour, as loan officers spent more and more time wheedling collections from customers faced with too much debt and shrunken demand. These conditions set off a backlash against microcredit.

A handful of "professional" union organizers began gathering members into debtors associations to protest against the consumer and microfinance lenders. These associations grew quickly, because organizers promised members debt forgiveness. The leaders claimed to speak for several thousand borrowers. The associations staged protests, mainly at the offices of Acceso, CrediAgil, and other consumer lenders, but even at Caja Los Andes and BancoSol. They chanted, calling the lenders *rateros* (rats) and throwing refuse at the windows. A few association members engaged in hunger strikes, a tactic with a long history in Bolivia (it contributed to ending military rule in the 1980s). Through such tactics the associations attempted to take the moral high ground by painting the lenders as exploiters of the poor. In petitions to various authorities they accused the lenders of using humiliating tactics against debtors—hiring mariachi bands to perform outside a debtor's house all night, painting the word *debtor* on the house, or broadcasting the names of debtors over the radio. They blamed the lenders for provoking every kind of social ill from suicide to prostitution. They demanded full debt forgiveness.

The affected institutions, working through their newly created association, Asofin, sought aid from the courts to stop the demonstrations. Even though Asofin hired high-priced and well-connected lawyers, the tearful testimony of a few market vendors carried the day. In fact, Asofin had scant legal basis for stopping the associations from mounting street protests. Eventually, the debtor associations forced their way into a dialogue with the Superintendency of Banks and Asofin, in which the microfinance lenders agreed to consider debt relief to association members on a case-by-case basis. Only a handful of cases were ever resolved, however. Shortly thereafter, the microlenders rejoiced when the associations threw their own leaders in jail. Apparently one association was a true pyramid scheme, where leaders illegally collected debt-service payments due to the microlenders and used them to make new loans. Leaders of the other more legitimate association mishandled membership dues, a less spectacular crime, but enough to bring them down.

After a few months hiatus, however, the associations surfaced again, with new leaders and petitions to the president of Bolivia. This time they moderated their aims slightly: while acknowledging their obligations to repay debts, they asked for extended grace periods, longer loan terms, and annual interest rates of 2 percent. The second time around the associations may be more robust. The microfinance industry will have to live with the debtors associations, or at least the attitudes they represent, for the foreseeable future.

THE FALL OF CONSUMER CREDIT

The members of the microfinance community were not the only ones concerned about the consequences of growing delinquency among the consumer lenders. The superintendent issued regulations in early 1999 to place consumer credit on a sounder footing.[6] The most important provision limited the client's total debt service to 25 percent of his salary. Thus a client who already had a substantial car, home, or business loan from a microlender would likely not qualify for a consumer loan. The response to this move varied. Fassil sharply curtailed consumer lending, switching almost completely into microcredit. Acceso, it was widely rumored, went on much as before, simply paying the penalty the regulation carried.

The regulations came too late, however. By mid-1999 the consumer-lending movement came crashing down. When the level of bad debt grew large enough to erode the equity of the two largest consumer lenders, Acceso FFP and the CrediAgil division of Union Bank, the superintendent intervened directly in those institutions. At the end of 1998, Acceso had 88,000 clients, a portfolio of $93 million, and delinquency of 19 percent (already excessive). One year later, it had only 32,000 clients, a portfolio of $32 million, and delinquency of 32 percent.[7]

Acceso no longer lends. It has become a collection agency. And though its offices remain open, their posters of the hand snapping send an ironic message. What seemed too easy to be true turned out to be an illusion, gone in a snap. Nearly all the other consumer-lending operations, including the Presto division of Banco Económico, have disappeared. The Santa Cruz premises of BBA Consumo, David Blanco's pride, are an abandoned, dusty shell.

Acceso's owner, a devout Chilean named Jose Luis del Rio, put up a trust fund of $40 million of his own money to liquidate the debts, thus saving his reputation as a decent person, if not as a successful businessman. Andre LeFaye, the polished young executive director at Acceso, leapt unscathed from the ruins; he has become the representative of Microsoft for Bolivia and was pictured in a recent magazine feature as a developer of upscale housing in an elite section of La Paz.

In retrospect, it is easy to see that the consumer lenders came into Bolivia without understanding it. The models that worked in middle-class Chile were not suited to less formal Bolivia. The lenders were also seduced by the success of the microlenders and arrogant enough to think that their superior technologies could out-compete the charity-inspired institutions. They failed to recognize that their "credit factory" techniques lacked the essential elements that made lending to microentrepreneurs work. Finally, they were unlucky to have run up huge portfolios just before an economic crisis.

Observers like Fernando Romero believe that consumer lending will return, smarter and more cautious. For example, he sees closer ties to retailers of consumer durables, with shared risk, variations on department-store credit, and lease purchase. BancoSol is trying out a new consumer-loan product, limited to the employees of a select few prime companies.

MICROFINANCE IN CRISIS

After consumer credit vanished, as quickly as it had come, it left behind a weakened microcredit industry. Liliana Bottega of Caja Los Andes stated, "Acceso and CrediAgil have closed, but the damage has been done to the system. Who knows if it can recover?" The weakness in microfinance reveals itself through four indicators: the end of growth in numbers of clients, rising portfolios as microlenders go upmarket, the highest delinquency in the history of Bolivian microfinance, and a dramatic fall in profits. To the extent that the difficulties of this crisis result from economic downturn, these kinds of problems prevail throughout the Bolivian banking sector. Nevertheless, this is the first time the microlenders have experienced such stress.

During 1999 none of the microlenders recorded the sizeable client-growth rates of the past. BancoSol and Prodem each lost more than 10 percent of its clients, shrinking from a combined total of 129,000 to 113,000. Yet at the same time, BancoSol's portfolio grew by 11 percent, reflecting its business decision to move into conventional small-business lending. Only Caja Los Andes among the regulated microlenders continued adding clients, though at a reduced rate (13 percent). To achieve this growth, Los Andes had to work much harder than usual, because a larger share of old clients left, and a larger share of new applicants failed to qualify. The NGOs ProMujer and Crecer, whose markets were less affected by consumer lenders, also added clients.

Every microfinance lender experienced unprecedented delinquency during 1999 and continuing into 2000. At the end of 1997 the regulated microlenders had only 2.4 percent of their portfolio overdue by one day. This rate rose steadily, reaching 8.4 percent by mid-1999. The rate dropped slightly by the end of 1999, but only because of loan rescheduling, as discussed below.

The effects of slower growth and higher delinquency showed up immediately on the bottom lines of all the microlenders. BancoSol's return on equity dropped from 29 percent in 1998 to 9 percent in 1999. Fassil's profits dropped from 12 percent to 1 percent. Caja Los Andes, the least affected by the crisis, managed to keep its return on equity at a respectable 14 percent, making it the third most profitable financial institution (including banks) in Bolivia in 1999.

Each of the microfinance lenders has had to respond to increased delinquency through a combination of internal strategies and cooperation with government and other institutions. A first line of defense was greater use of the Superintendency's Central de Riesgo, or credit bureau. By the late 1990s, Bolivia already had a reasonably good system, designed for the formal banks. Because Bolivia had a national system of identification cards covering most of the population, this credit bureau could include members of the informal sector. A person could not easily avoid a bad credit rating by using an assumed name. Through the credit bureau, staff at banks, FFPs, and now the microfinance NGOs can log onto their computers, connect via modem, and immediately obtain a report on the outstanding indebtedness of any prospective applicant. Importantly, the system records outstanding loans, not just instances of delinquency, information necessary for determining whether a client is becoming over-indebted. Unfortunately, the system was never sufficiently complete or up to date to provide a water-tight reference. Although a good system by Latin American standards, it was not good enough to prevent lending to many clients with multiple loans. In fact, some lenders may have used the system to identify desirable clients of other institutions.

Microlenders also attempted to combat delinquency through the greater use of conventional ways of securing loans, spurred by tougher regulations from the superintendent. A first change has been greater emphasis on repayment capacity relative to past group performance. BancoSol's Mario Usnayo notes that when emphasis shifts to repayment capacity over group formation and repayment history, loan sizes diverge among group members, and it becomes harder to keep groups together. A second change was greater emphasis on tangible collateral. A new law will establish a registry of movable goods that would allow clients to mortgage their equipment, an instrument that would improve on the current general purpose *prendaria* lien. Fassil's Ordoñez comments that increased demands for documentation show that the Superintendency still doesn't understand microfinance. The authorities want to see formal documents such as sales receipts for informal enterprises, which, almost by definition, have none.

Delinquency affected internal operations as well. Caja Los Andes and FIE, which relied on monetary performance incentives based on a loan officer's portfolio size and quality to motivate staff, found their systems generating perverse results when delinquency worsened. Staff worked harder, spending inordinate amounts of time on collections, but still failed to meet the targets needed to earn incentives. The system quickly stopped motivating staff and started generating bitter complaints. The organizations had to reformulate staff performance targets, allowing officers with previously unacceptable levels of delinquent loans to qualify and focusing incentives narrowly on collections.

As a last resort, microlenders began to use rescheduling, in which a delinquent client is given more time to pay and smaller monthly payments. Until 1999 the microfinance lenders rarely rescheduled or refinanced loans, considering such practices highly risky. But in the midst of the economic crisis, with many clients of the *quieren mas no pueden* (want to, but can't pay) variety, they saw few alternatives. The Superintendency, searching for ways to get the banking system through a bad time, granted a one-time amnesty on rescheduling for several months. Its standard norms require that rescheduled loans be classified in a risk category that carried a 20 percent provisioning requirement: the lender must set aside 20 percent of the outstanding value of the loan as a bad debt reserve. Under the amnesty, however, a rescheduled loan could be returned to the top risk category, as if it had never been late. BancoSol reported rescheduling $6 million and Caja Los Andes $1 million during 1999. Further rescheduling was introduced as part of the government's economic revitalization program in early 2000. Although rescheduling is in some cases a realistic approach to clients with real debt-service problems, its widespread use sends signals that can have a long-term negative effect on repayment discipline. And regulations allowing rescheduled loans to be treated as on time give an overly rosy picture of the solvency of financial institutions.

While none of the microlenders is experiencing delinquency at the levels that brought down the consumer lenders, their delinquency problems were more severe than the aggregate 8.4 percent published figure for the end of 1999 suggests. Alfredo Otero of Fassil estimates that the microfinance institutions can survive another year of the pain they experienced in 1999, but if the crisis fails to recede by the end of 2000, some institutions, including perhaps his own, will fail. He is looking to obtain soft loans from donor sources for the first time, in order to reduce Fassil's cost of funds, and he is looking for additional capital or perhaps a merger partner.

With these conditions rumors of mergers have been sweeping through the microfinance community. One potential merger moved into advanced negotiations: between FIE and Prodem. FIE, a largely urban, individual lender, and Prodem, a largely rural, group lender, are direct competitors only in a few locations. For FIE, a merger would help cope with increasing demands for professional financial management skills within an organization that retains a strong NGO flavor. For Prodem, the merger would be a step in Eduardo Bazoberry's long-run plan to survive the competitive environment. In Bazoberry's view, stand-alone microcredit institutions cannot be viable in the long run because they cannot sufficiently diversify their risk. He believes that only a bank can offer a wide enough range of products, especially fee-based products, which carry reduced risk. Diversification of offerings is particularly important in rural areas where volumes are small, requiring a successful financial institution to target the entire market range. Knowing that the Superintendency is reluctant to grant additional banking licenses in Bolivia, Bazoberry wants to position Prodem to be the obvious next new licensee. Despite the theoretical attractions of a merger, this one did not go through, nor have other rumored marriages proceeded. The practical barriers to joining two institutions have repeatedly proved greater than the theoretical advantages.

GAINS AND LOSSES FROM COMPETITION: GOODBYE TO "YELLOW PAJAMAS"

The fireworks caused by the rise and fall of consumer lending combined with recession partially obscures a broader and longer-term process at work: the arrival of competition. Competition is a new experience for the microfinance institutions in Bolivia, and indeed, those in most other countries. Microfinance institutions have always competed for donor and commercial funds, but on the client side they have tended to operate as near monopolies, assuming that their main constraint was not the size of the market but their own service-delivery capacity.

The aggressive tactics of the consumer lenders exposed Bolivian microfinance institutions to an extreme level and particular type of competition. However, even without their entry, the growth of the microlenders themselves and the entry of more conservative commercial players like Fassil and Banco Económico would have led toward market saturation. By 1997 the estimated total number of active microfinance loans had reached nearly 300,000, with the number of consumer loans also approaching that level. The total microfinance loan portfolio was about $170 million. If the very rough estimate made by second-tier lender Funda-Pro was correct, and there were about 600,000 microentrepreneurs in Bolivia, market penetration by microfinance alone was near 50 percent. This is a very high level, considering that not all clients want a loan (or qualify for one) at any given time.

The events of 1999/2000 were particularly unfortunate because they make it easy for observers to conclude that commercial entry and competition are necessarily damaging to microfinance. A closer look at the anatomy of competition in Bolivia, however, suggests a more complex conclusion, with both positive and negative features.

The fundamental fact of increased competition in microfinance is that it alters the balance of power between lender and borrower. A Fassil loan officer stated the problem succinctly, "Before, the institution selected the clients. Now the client selects the institution." In this reversal of roles, fundamental tenets of microfinance come unstuck. Microfinance expert Robert Christen calls this the end of the "yellow pajamas" myth. At first, he says, microlenders believed a client would do nearly anything to gain and keep access to loans, even stand outside in yellow pajamas. But when a client has a choice of institutions, the tables are turned. Clients move to the lenders that offer the best service and the best deal. This new freedom of movement plays havoc with the established methods of microcredit. Although microcredit methodologies fit their clients better than older models, they have also sacrificed some client convenience in order to minimize lender risk. Group guarantees, immediate follow-up of delinquency, and small initial loan amounts all pose inconveniences to clients and are effective only if the client needs a long-term relationship with a particular lender. Today, clients may care more about their credit rating at the credit bureau but less about a long-term relationship to a particular institution. BancoSol's motto, *juntos crecemos* (we grow together) is losing its zing.

The presence of alternative lending methodologies in conditions of competition has particularly strong consequences for group lenders. Solidarity group loans, pioneered by Prodem and BancoSol, require clients to put their own assets at risk for their colleagues. If groups go wrong, as they often do, clients can lose a great deal of time, not to mention stress and financial loss, in repairing the situation. Village banking methods, like those of ProMujer and Crecer, are even less flexible. They tie the timing of a woman's access to credit into a schedule with 30 or more other women and require weekly attendance at meetings.

Jorge Crespo of Caja Los Andes asserts that individual lending gives Los Andes and FIE a tremendous market advantage over BancoSol and Prodem, a view long advocated by IPC and shared by Claudio González-Vega and other financial economists at Ohio State University. Their views are validated by the stronger performance of Caja Los Andes relative to BancoSol and Prodem during the crisis.

A closely related disadvantage concerns loan size. Solidarity group loans begin with a formula for the first few loans, moving gradually to greater reliance on repayment capacity as the determinant of loan size. Caja Los Andes uses repayment capacity from the start. This means that Caja Los Andes is often willing to offer new clients a significantly bigger initial loan than is BancoSol, and to increase loan size more quickly.

BancoSol moved slowly to respond to these competitive challenges. Former managing director Hermann Krützfeldt reports that when the competition first increased, some people on the staff wanted to jettison solidarity group lending. However, market research showed a significant portion of clients who cannot or do not want to provide the tangible guarantees that individual lenders usually require. Market researcher Domingo Fabbri says that these clients use the credit history of their group essentially as an equity capital base on which to leverage larger loans. Krützfeldt rules out any possibility that BancoSol will abandon solidarity group lending. It is BancoSol's bread and butter.

Nevertheless, BancoSol felt the need to do something, and it began studying a variety of new products. By mid-1999 it introduced a host of products, generally aimed at a higher market than the target market for solidarity group loans. It moved into competition with conventional lenders like Banco Económico by raising its ceiling on individual loans from $30,000 to $100,000 and adopting loan-appraisal methods from mainstream banks. It introduced housing loans, a line of credit, and consumer loans. Throughout this period, solidarity group loans remained the largest share of the portfolio, but that share was shrinking.

Senior managers at BancoSol regarded these moves as protective, a strategy to give BancoSol greater risk diversification, rather than a change in mission. Maria Elena Querejazu, then one of the senior management team, argues that adding more conventional business protects BancoSol against cyclical risks inherent in microfinance. She and Krützfeldt note that in a recession the group mechanism may even augment risk. Krützfeldt explains that during normal times, when one person has problems the other members can help him out. However, in bad times, when all members are weak, the need to help one member can be too much for the others. One drags the others down. They back up their observations by pointing out that the majority of BancoSol's delinquency since the crisis has been concentrated in its solidarity portfolio. In financial economists' terms, they contend that group lending is a great way to deal with idiosyncratic risk but not systematic risk.

Others note that the distribution of delinquency merely reflects the youth of the individual loan portfolio, as new loans always look sound. These critics question the wisdom of moving too quickly into business markets BancoSol does not understand well and is not structured to serve. One long-term employee lamented, "The end of the world was when BancoSol gave a $50,000 loan to a member of the Roda family," the Rodas being a well-known wealthy family. Outside observers offer opinions to the effect that "BancoSol is losing its compass." "It's losing its essence." Or even, "BancoSol is living off its past and eating its future."

Some of the innovations BancoSol is exploring fit the trend toward formality. These include the adaptation for microenterprises of credit-scoring models, together with hand-held computers loan officers can take to the field. With hand-held computers, a loan officer would enter data about a client, link via satellite to the main headquarters system, and obtain a credit score for the client right away. In a majority of cases the score would allow the loan officer to approve or deny credit on the spot. Loan turn-around would become even faster, and in some sense the loan officer would be "empowered" to make decisions in the field. However, such a system might also reduce the loan officers' discretion, making them increasingly into data-management clerks, as they are at consumer lenders, and losing the culture of *autogerencia*.

ProMujer, faced with a challenge to the rigidity of its group methodology, is also searching for an effective response. It seeks to enhance flexibility by increasing the use of client internal accounts in which clients can borrow from the pool of funds managed by the village bank itself. Such borrowing can happen at any time and with little paperwork. However, ProMujer's main bulwark against competition is its attempt to segment the market. By aiming at clients who are too poor or inexperienced to qualify for loans at the main microlending institutions, ProMujer hopes to claim that market niche for its own. The difficulties with this strategy are that ProMujer does not have a proven method for selecting such clients and that after a couple of ProMujer loans its clients qualify with other lenders—as witnessed by the fact that so many of its clients have multiple loans. Its main targeting strategy is setting an upper bound on loans of $1,000. If ProMujer narrows its market to those clients who cannot borrow from other lenders, however, it becomes harder for it to achieve financial viability.

The pressure on methodologies just described is a general feature of increasing competition in microfinance. Although it is difficult for microfinance institutions, this type of competition brings benefits to clients, just as it should, making services faster, higher quality, and lower priced. During the late 1990s, Bolivian microfinance interest rates dropped and clients began paying attention to small differences in interest rates from one lender to the next. Throughout the system lenders strove to turn loans around faster, aiming for turn-around measured in hours rather than days. (Recall that in the early 1980s loan turn-around was generally measured in weeks or even months.) The microfinance institutions are scrutinizing every aspect of their methodologies and introducing new products, looking for ways to make themselves more attractive to clients.

Unquestionably, most microfinance clients benefit from the advent of competition. More people have access—virtually anyone in a city or town who wants a loan and has an enterprise (or a salary). Clients now know that they are in the driver's seat. They can choose whom they deal with, and they can demand favorable terms. BancoSol's Juan Domingo Fabbri says, "The new (microfinance) banks were schools for clients to learn, and once they learned, they began to seek better options." These benefits for the majority of clients are, or should be, the main story about the arrival of competition. However, the good news for most is tempered by questions on two fronts: over-indebtedness and mission drift (discussed in chapter 7).

Unhealthy Competition: Over-lending

Poaching clients from other institutions through the offer of larger loans has proven to be an extremely successful marketing technique in Bolivia, as elsewhere. And it has been shown repeatedly that clients are not good judges of their own debt capacity. Apparently, credit is like good food: when seated at the table in front of a feast, many people eat too much and regret it later. Perhaps more experienced borrowers than Bolivian microentrepreneurs can learn to exercise restraint, but the fact that over-borrowing has happened in many societies (and is, for example, a chronic problem in the United States) suggests a common trait of human nature. The truly unfortunate dynamic is that if over-lenders are successful at luring clients away from more responsible lenders, the responsible lenders are virtually forced to follow suit. The pressure to lend more to keep good clients is nearly as irresistible as the client's desire to borrow more. Worse, if clients begin using one loan to pay off another, the game becomes, as Elizabeth Naba of FIE says, "Who collects first?" In short, the sector as a whole starts to become one big Ponzi scheme. Although the microlenders feared what was happening, they could not escape the syndrome without assistance. In such a situation only a central body, like the Superintendency of Banks, can stop the spiral, with regulations like those it put in place in 1999.

Meanwhile, the borrowers' revolt demonstrates how thin the line is between microfinance, which has always aimed to help people, and consumer lending, a purely profit-seeking activity. Hermann Krützfeldt described what it felt like to be inside BancoSol when demonstrators were hurling garbage at the building. The staff walked from window to window in shock and disbelief. "We're here to help these people!" they exclaimed. "How can they turn against us?" Clearly, the microfinance lenders of Bolivia now face the task of polishing a somewhat tarnished public image by helping to define the parameters of responsible lending. What really makes microfinance lenders better for customers? As microfinance becomes more commercial in more countries, this task will rise higher on the microfinance agenda. It has already been a focal point for microfinance institutions in South Africa, where a separate regulatory body oversees consumer protection in microfinance and a professional microfinance association issued a code of conduct to distinguish its members from unscrupulous lenders.

REFLECTIONS

The events of 1999 represent a coming of age for microfinance in Bolivia. As Alfredo Otero says, if the microfinance institutions survive this crisis, microfinance will have become a mature industry. It will have demonstrated genuine sustainability. In some ways the experiences of this difficult period have been good for the microlenders. Former Superintendent Trigo says that it has taught them humility. Earlier, he argues, the microlenders had a "triumphalist" air. They thought they were the best, invulnerable. Now they recognize that survival requires continual learning and change. From now on, the Bolivian microfinance industry will progress on its own, fueled by competition.

Nevertheless, as with any coming of age, this is a nostalgic moment. When it began in the mid-1980s, microfinance had a revolutionary mystique. The staff of Prodem, FIE, and other microlenders lived and breathed to change society. They were proud to be the first to give credit to people long scorned and marginalized. They showed Bolivia that their clients were worthy of trust and capable of acting responsibly to contribute to the nation's development. They believed that their methodology helped clients transform their lives. This was the gospel according to Pancho Otero, and it propelled the Bolivian microfinance institutions to major accomplishments throughout their first decade.

Today, however, what was revolutionary has become ordinary. The mystique of trust and responsibility is being replaced by the modern marketing concept of service quality. Although it may have a friendly face, it is not genuinely personal, as consumers in developed countries well know. In Bolivia today, although the loan itself is just as valuable to clients as ever, it no longer carries a subtext of empowerment. Clients have already become more included members of society. They accept the empowerment that access to credit represents without recognizing it as anything out of the ordinary.

But for some of the activists who saw microcredit as a weapon of social change, the commercialized microfinance arena is too antiseptic. Having achieved their mission, they are left wondering what to do next. Some who were motivated by revolutionary fervor lose interest when they see that their work really involves the rigorous but mundane tasks of retail banking. Fernando Romero observes, "BancoSol was once a shining star, but now it is just a small bank making small loans." For microfinance activists, the time in which urban microenterprise credit represented a transforming social force has passed, and it is time to seek another frontier.

The transition from revolutionary movement to competitive industry is a natural and, for clients generally, positive development. The competitive drive toward better service and new markets is combined in Bolivia with the rededication of socially motivated players to new frontiers. The next chapter explores some of the new frontiers to which Bolivian microfinance institutions are turning, each motivated by its own unique mixture of competitive spirit and social mission.

NOTES

1. Jeffrey Poyo and Robin Young, "Commercialization of Microfinance: The Cases of Banco Económico and Fondo Financiero Privado FA$$IL," Microenterprise Best Practices Project (Bethesda, Md.: Development Alternatives, Inc., 1999), 3.
2. Poyo and Young, "Commercialization," 43.
3. Poyo and Young, "Commercialization," 37.
4. Elisabeth Rhyne and Robert Peck Christen, "Microfinance Enters the Marketplace" (Washington, D.C.: United States Agency for International Development, 1999), 13.
5. Müller and Associates, "Evaluación del Sistema Financiero Nacional," *Informe Confidencial* (La Paz), no. 115 (Mar–Apr 1998), 13.
6. Superintendency of Banks, Circular 282 (La Paz, January 4, 1999).
7. The sources for all the data in this section are published figures of Asofin and Finrural, the trade associations for microfinance institutions.

CHAPTER SEVEN

REASSESSING THE MISSION: A SEARCH FOR NEW FRONTIERS

IN LIGHT OF COMPETITIVE CONDITIONS, many institutions involved in Bolivian microfinance have started to reassess their strategies. As the new century begins, prime customers—successful urban market vendors and manufacturers—can easily obtain short-term business credit from any of several institutions, but new frontiers lie beyond urban microenterprise credit, particularly among the half of Bolivians who live in rural areas and remain very poorly served. There are also frontiers among small enterprises and in new services, principally deposit and payment services, but also housing and other term loans, leasing, and nonfinancial business development. This chapter considers the two main thrusts at the frontier: rural finance and savings. It concludes with a look at how donors and government are reassessing their roles. But first we examine an important question behind the push for new frontiers: In the commercialized, competitive microfinance industry, who will serve the poor?

THE NEW MICROFINANCE INDUSTRY AND THE POOR

The early innovators in Bolivian microfinance usually expressed their aims in terms of enterprise development rather than poverty alleviation. However, they included poverty within their mission, recognizing that most of the informal-sector clients they targeted were poor. The early microfinance institutions were not preoccupied with differentiating between degrees of poverty; all their clients were obviously needy and obviously unwelcome in banks. With the entry of poverty-focused microcredit programs like ProMujer and Crecer, and influenced by the drumbeat from MicroCredit Summit and other advocacy groups, the poverty question became explicit. More recently it has become even sharper because the population of the excluded has shrunk dramatically with the success of microcredit. Those concerned with poverty today want to distinguish between the moderately poor, who now have access to credit, and the severely poor, who still do not.

Microfinance services can (and sometimes do) reach the severely poor in Bolivia through a variety of sources. The transformed microlenders (BancoSol and others) and the new commercial entrants serve some very poor clients as part of the general mix of their predominately moderately poor clientele. Poverty-focused microfinance institutions like ProMujer and Crecer specialize in clients at the lower level. A variety of institutions offer savings services or other risk-related products that are increasingly acknowledged as more relevant to the very poor than credit.[1] Finally, as microfinance extends into rural areas, where the vast majority of families fall below the poverty line, more of the very poor will be included. We will examine each of these paths to serving to the poor.

Will Commercial Microfinance Institutions Drift Upmarket?

Carmen Velasco of ProMujer and other poverty-focused lenders note that the newly commercialized microlenders never served the extremely poor, a view corroborated by the financial economists of Ohio State University. Their analysis of 1995 data revealed that the clients of the larger microfinance lenders were mainly just below and just above the poverty line. At BancoSol, 78 percent of clients clustered just below or just above the poverty line. Most of the remaining 22 percent were not poor. At FIE and Caja Los Andes, most clients were above the line (80 percent and 74 percent, respectively). Only 2 or 3 percent of the clients at any of these institutions were in the bottom categories, labeled indigent or poorest.[2] Of the institutions Ohio State studied, only the rural lenders Prodem and Sartawi served primarily people below the poverty line. Although the urban lenders do not serve many of the poorest, the sheer number of their clients gives them a fairly important downward reach below the line.

One of the concerns arising from increased competition and commercial entry is that these institutions will gradually move upward, abandoning the clients below the line.

This question has nagged at microfinance institutions since shortly after BancoSol began operations, well before competition heated up. In 1992, for example, BancoSol's average loan balance was US$250. By 1995 this figure had doubled, and by the end of 1998 it had reached $908.[3] When they first noticed this trend, the managers of BancoSol argued about its cause. Everyone recognized that growing average loan sizes were inherent in the BancoSol methodology, and even an integral part of the philosophy of *juntos crecemos*. As client enterprises grew and as clients proved their trustworthiness as good repayers, long-term customers would receive larger loans. As more and more long-term customers stayed with BancoSol, its average loan size inevitably would rise.

But it was hard for BancoSol managers to tell whether the actual increase came mainly from this kind of desirable growth or from a worrisome move away from the traditional client base. Some managers thought the drive to make BancoSol profitable was changing behavior throughout the bank. As regional manager German Sanchéz noted, when loan officers know that larger loans are more profitable, they are naturally tempted to pursue larger clients, especially when trying to meet portfolio and income targets. Pancho Otero recalls the initial wariness about loan size creep: "There's no problem making larger loans to more successful clients, even individual loans. The difficulty is to stay excited about the smaller clients. We were scared of what might happen if we made larger loans inside BancoSol."

BancoSol first began to investigate the upward trend in loan sizes in 1994. Acción staff member Jean Steege pulled the portfolio apart, looking at loans in separate cohorts. Her study concluded that most of the growth was coming from repeat clients and not mission drift. Ohio State University, in a study of BancoSol and four other leading microfinance lenders, concurred: "There is no evidence of drift from the organizations' mission of lending to the poor, even though the average size of loan has grown as their portfolios have matured." In fact, the study found that Caja Los Andes was actually moving downmarket during this period as it opened its doors increasingly to market vendors.[4]

Steege's research also examined the relationship between loan size and profitability by identifying the break-even loan size for BancoSol. This number, which BancoSol guards closely, quantified what staff at all microfinance institutions had known intuitively: small loans lost money and were cross-subsidized by larger loans. For clients who start small and grow, the overall client relationship is profitable, but for clients whose loan sizes stay small—or who leave the bank after a first or second loan—it is not. During the precompetitive years this observation did not pose a problem. Rather, it underscored the importance of turning every customer into a repeat customer, a core principle throughout all service industries.

However, with competition the arithmetic of break-even loan sizes grew harsher. First, the new commercial entrants, both consumer lenders and others, entered the market at the upper end, presumably at loan sizes near or above their own break-even sizes. They are unlikely to cross-subsidize even temporarily. Second, if clients begin jumping from lender to lender, they might abandon a particular institution just when they reach the break-even point.

Finally, the stringent documentation requirements the Superintendency imposed in response to competition raise costs, driving up the magic break-even point. When these requirements involve more formal collateral, they may disqualify some lower-end clients.

If the purely commercial lenders take over a major share of the top end of the microfinance market, they leave the mission-driven organizations with some unpleasant choices. In order to remain competitive, mission-driven organizations may have to reduce cross-subsidization so as to offer the upper-end clients better terms. Alternatively, they may be left with a client group whose loans are too small to be a basis for profitable operation, as may be the case for ProMujer.[5] Perhaps much of this dilemma could be solved simply, through differential pricing to boost the smallest loans above the break-even threshold. Differential pricing is already in place in FIE and some other organizations.

BancoSol has decided to enter a more upscale market, but senior managers argue that this involves the addition of new markets, not subtraction from their original focus. Michael Chu, Chairman of BancoSol's board, puts it this way: "BancoSol is not mission-driven, it is segment-driven. Just as McDonalds is not likely to start serving *haute cuisine*, BancoSol is not likely to move away from the segment of the market it serves best." Moreover, intense competition gives institutions a great incentive to seek new, less saturated market niches. Some observers believe that this force will lead to innovations that make smaller loans profitable.

The poverty-focused lenders like ProMujer face a starker choice than BancoSol. ProMujer has decided to remain with its original focus but finds that this choice may threaten its ability to keep its larger clients and become financially viable. By choosing to remain a poverty-focused NGO, ProMujer is actually making a strategic move to retain access to the donor funding that is increasingly aimed at the very poor.

To return to our initial question about who will serve the very poor, we see that the large urban microlenders are not involved deeply at the moment. The poverty-focused institutions like ProMujer are sticking with their low-end client group, but at some cost to their financial viability. For the future, gains for the very poor are likely to come from the move of microfinance into rural areas and from their development of specially tailored savings services.

TO THE ALTIPLANO AND BEYOND

In Bolivia, to speak of the poor is to speak of rural areas. Despite decades of urban migration, nearly half of Bolivia's people still live in rural areas, and the vast majority are poor by any standard—94 percent of households by one measure.[6] Thus, it is no surprise that of the institutions Ohio State studied, only the rural lenders, Prodem and Sartawi, had client bases largely of people below the poverty line (81 percent and 76 percent respectively) with 15 to 17 percent of clients classified as indigent.[7]

Microfinance lenders in Bolivia hesitated to enter rural areas for a number of daunting reasons, starting with the sheer poverty of the people, which would require small loan sizes. Added to this was the high cost of reaching clients, due to their dispersed settlement at the ends of notoriously bad roads or donkey paths. Low income and high cost is already a fearful formula, but the riskiness of agriculture also had to be factored in. Because agricultural risk tends to affect everyone in a given area at the same time, it is particularly hard for financial institutions, especially small, undiversified ones, to protect against. Finally, the history of failed agricultural lending in Bolivia, through state development banks and rural revolving funds, provided an object lesson in what might happen to anyone foolhardy enough to try to lend in rural areas.

Despite these barriers, a few devoted organizations had been working in rural areas throughout the late 1980s and early 1990s, including Sartawi, Fades, and ANED. Although these groups developed a deep knowledge of the rural economy, they did not succeed in developing a formula for profitability or large-scale outreach. Some remained burdened with old formulas from revolving loan fund days, such as lending in kind for crop inputs or charging interest rates far lower than costs. It was only when Prodem began to move into rural areas, after its spin-off of BancoSol, that serious strides were made toward perfecting a rural business model for microfinance.

With the urban solidarity group lending methodologies as a base, Prodem set out to make adaptations that would overcome each of the problems unique to rural areas. As Prodem's executive director, Eduardo Bazoberry, put it, "We knew that if we wanted to succeed in rural areas, we would have to come up with three things: a methodology, a structure, and a means of control."

Rural Lending Methodology

Prodem began the search for a rural methodology with the main economic unit of the rural economy—the family. In the cities Prodem/BancoSol's methodology had recognized close connections between enterprises and families but had generally based lending decisions on the individual entrepreneur and her enterprise. But in rural areas the perspective had to shift. The rural family is highly exposed to risk, especially agricultural risk. Prodem staff were delighted to find that the families of Bolivia's altiplano dealt with this risk in the same way a lender would—by diversifying.

Nearly every rural family had at least two or three and often as many as six discrete economic activities in its portfolio. If one counts different crops, the figure might climb even higher. The families of the altiplano grew potatoes and quinoa; raised cattle, goats, and chickens; made cheese; spent part of their year in La Paz as laborers; performed in bands; fished; rented their land and their houses; made artisan products; and traded goods between urban and rural areas. These various activities formed a series of steps out of poverty. According to Edgar Zurita of Fades, a poor family might diversify first by raising goats and chickens. Commerce was a middle strategy, while the upper end included dairy, carpentry, sawmills, and agricultural machinery. The unique geography of the altiplano, with its varying elevations, also allowed farmers to spread risk by obtaining land in several different agroclimatic areas.

History had shown that crop loans alone could not be the foundation for a financial institution, but in the diversified rural family Prodem found a more stable base that included agricultural activities among others. In order to address this economic unit, Prodem made a few critical adjustments to the urban solidarity group methodology. It taught its loan officers how to construct a cashflow statement for a client's family, taking into account the seasonal patterns of investment and income. The loan officer used this cashflow pattern to determine how big a loan the client could afford and to work out a repayment schedule that allowed for ups and downs of income. Clients would have to pay something each period, but the amount would vary with each client's own income pattern, a practice it called differential quotas. Caja Los Andes developed a similar approach, adapting it from IPC's successful program in El Salvador, Financiera Calpia.

Prodem also developed a large database on agricultural products. If a client said he had planted one hectare of potatoes near the lake, Prodem's database would project the likely physical yield, income, and profits from that activity. This data base, though expensive to keep current, further assisted Prodem in evaluating client ability to repay. Prodem loan officers gradually became experts on local agriculture.

Fortunately, Prodem tested its adapted methodology on a group of clients whose culture was, if anything, even more supportive of high loan repayment than that of the urban microenterprises. Here in the rural area, the Aymara value of fulfilling obligations still finds traditional expression.

This kind of tradition takes place every week at traditional cattle markets. As the trading begins to close, people stand in small groups dotted around the marketplace to witness the formalities of each sale. All eyes focus intently as the buyer and seller deliberately count out the money. After the money has changed hands, everyone joins in drinking a bottle of wine. The buyer pours a first splash ceremonially onto the ground, as an offering to the *Pachamama*, the earth mother. With this ceremony the transaction is sealed before the community and the greater powers. Prodem did not attempt to mimic such traditions, but it was acutely aware of the cultural values they embodied, recognizing their benefit for the solidarity group methodology.

In fact, Prodem's overall rural strategy is based on diversification of risk at multiple levels: the client's own diversification, Prodem's selection of different types of clients, diversification of localized risk through national coverage, and provision of a range of products with diverse risk profiles, such as money transfers in addition to credit.

Rural Branch Structure and Controls

Prodem still had to overcome the barrier of rural logistics. Although people in rural areas live far from one another, they come together regularly on market days. Each town in an area holds a market on a specific day of the week. Traveling traders circulate among these markets, while local residents might only attend the closest one. Prodem adapted its own opening times and places to fit this rotation, ensuring that all its disbursement and repayment transactions would take place in a given town on that town's market day. This simple strategy helped Prodem achieve higher volumes of clients at each location, but it alone was not enough.

Prodem also had to streamline its branch structure. Each branch would have just three loan officers who would share all the office tasks, eliminating the need for a branch manager and teller. This pared-down branch structure brought costs into balance with potential income, but because it dispensed with standard control systems, it left Prodem somewhat vulnerable. Normal banking controls require that the staff member originating a transaction and the one recording it operate separately. The three-person branch could not always fulfill this requirement, so Prodem compensated by stepping up regular supervision visits and surprise internal audits. When it became an FFP, Prodem had to bring its procedures in line with regulatory norms.

With its new system and ample donor backing, Prodem had the basis for dramatic expansion throughout Bolivia. It now has 50 outlets across the country, more than any other financial institution, and it envisions 20 additional outlets. Prodem is the only institution with a nationwide presence in rural areas. It is sitting in an enviable competitive position as the push out from the cities begins.

Despite the rural expansion of Prodem, Caja Los Andes, Sartawi, Fades, and Crecer, the rural push has yet to achieve high coverage beyond the larger secondary towns. Government officials like FONDESIF's José Martinez cite the statistic that of the 312 municipalities in Bolivia, 273, or 70 percent, have no banking services at all. Government and the donors have decided to change this. Parliament is working on a law that would get credit out to the unserved towns. The Swiss and German aid agencies are supporting a program to auction subsidies for establishing banking services in municipalities. This program features some elements of good design—as an auction it incorporates some market mechanisms and it sidesteps local government's potential for mismanagement. Nevertheless, it is unlikely to have much impact if it involves government pushing financial institutions into markets they consider unprofitable.

Sartawi's Jorg Tipisman Nogales describes some of the challenges of the remote areas. He says that 13,000 families live in the district of Batallas, where Sartawi works near Lake Titicaca. Yet, he points out, the area is half the size of France. Moreover, much of that territory is mountainous—the *suni*, *puni*, and *cordillera*—and the main economic activity is raising llamas. Tipisman estimates that only 5,000 of the 13,000 families in the district are accessible. He says that Sartawi simply cannot work with people who lack access to roads and markets. Similar kinds of problems would face anyone trying to offer banking service in a very different climatic area, the *beni*, part of the Amazon basin covered with dense jungle. Nevertheless, between the major towns now served and the impossible-to-reach hinterlands, a lot of rural territory and people remain, centered in the provinces of La Paz, Cochabamba, and Santa Cruz.

Government does have a role in supporting the move out, admits former Superintendent of Banks Jacques Trigo, but he says that as regulators they cannot force it. Rather, the Superintendency seeks a dialogue about possibilities for regulatory flexibility in rural areas. Simple regulations seem to pose major stumbling blocks, such as the requirements that bank offices be open a minimum number of hours, six days a week, and the requirement that each financial institution submit a closing report to the Superintendency every day (a precaution against illegal forms of hiding money). Rural lenders would like to open offices in remote areas only one or two days per week, or to operate from mobile locations. They cannot send daily reports from branches located where there are no telephones. Although the Superintendency staff wants to solve these kinds of problems, the microfinance institutions complain about slow progress.

Microfinance Tackles the Rural Finance Agenda

Rural finance, a development field that predated microfinance, had been languishing for twenty years, following the discrediting of its original methods, especially government development banks and subsidized agricultural credit, by Ohio State University and other financial-sector analysts. It had become a backwater as attention turned to the emerging microfinance field. In Bolivia, as elsewhere, the baton passed to microfinance institutions to take up the neglected rural agenda. But the rural agenda is broader than microenterprise credit. Because of the near absence of banking services from rural areas, the rural finance agenda includes the whole gamut of financial services. It is not yet clear whether the microfinance institutions will be able to tackle it.

Fades had been working on rural challenges since the mid-1980s, learning some hard lessons in the process. Fades saw groups as the way to solve the scale and density challenges inherent in rural finance. It worked with peasant associations of all sorts—groups of bean producers, users of joint irrigation systems, and residents of a local community. It lent for community-based projects like bridges, potable water, and electricity. But few associations knew how to manage money. Sometimes they proved to be phantom associations, put together just to qualify for the loan. Lack of success in this kind of lending convinced Fades that it could not finance community development. That was properly a role for municipal governments.

Today Fades continues to work with producer associations but focuses on lending for production and marketing. Executive Director Edgar Zurita believes supported lending to associations can have greater development impact than microcredit, because it helps groups overcome barriers that they could not overcome individually. For example, Fades created an emergency-loan fund to help grape producers in Tarijas rehabilitate their plants after a flood, and it offers technical assistance to associations to solve technical problems, like how to rid cocoa beans of bad-tasting impurities. Although the association strategy may be a good way to work on such issues, even Fades admits that it is not yet clear that association loans are a successful financial product. Other organizations, such as Agrocapital and FDC, are focusing on the middle level of agriculture/agribusiness activity, where loan sizes are in the low thousands of dollars, a stratum of producers believed to be an important growth sector. Their outreach remains small, however.

Prodem's concept of rural finance is strictly financial, but it is nonetheless set in a development framework. Eduardo Bazoberry is fond of quoting economic guru Jeffrey Sachs, who said that Bolivia would never really progress economically until it found a way to integrate the rural areas into the national economy. In Bazoberry's view, this is exactly what Prodem FFP will be about.

Bazoberry sees financial services as part of rural infrastructure. The crucial function of rural roads and telephones is to link rural producers to larger markets in cities and abroad. Financial services, especially money transfers (payments) and deposits, are a next step in building such links. In Bolivia today, dairy producers on the altiplano must travel to La Paz to receive payments for their products, and it is not unusual for rural teachers to take a day off each month to travel to the city to collect their pay. Thus, the market for payment services may be very large, and it certainly spans all rural residents, not just the traditional clients of microfinance. Prodem has begun offering international money transfers through Western Union. The process should work in reverse as well, pulling the city out to the country. Bazoberry observes that formal-sector businesses may consider the presence of banking services as a prerequisite to locating in a smaller town. As part of its rural development strategy, Prodem has opened branches in urban centers, asserting that these branches are necessary to complete the links. Through these branches, the relatives of a farmer could make deposits in town that the farmer withdraws in the country. Urban microlenders are more cynical about Prodem's motives, viewing the urban branches as an attempt to invade their markets.

The final element on the rural finance agenda is savings. A negligible portion of all financial-system deposits now originate in rural areas. However, the savings challenge is not just limited to rural areas. It is a frontier for microfinance at large.

ATTENTION FINALLY TURNS TOWARD SAVINGS

The savings side of microfinance has not kept pace with the credit side, and nowhere is this more evident than in Bolivia. Bolivia has nurtured important innovations in credit, in institution-building, and in the regulatory framework for microfinance. But it has made few, if any, contributions to the state of the art of microsavings. And yet, it is widely acknowledged that savings services can be just as important to clients, especially the very poor, and that savings in financial institutions contribute to economic growth. It may even be possible that if Bolivian microfinance had emphasized savings as a financial tool for its clients earlier on, the problem of over-indebtedness would not have become so severe when economic crisis hit.

Reasons—or excuses—for the neglect of savings abound. Most of them center on the belief that the poor can't save or don't want to save in banks. This myth was shattered in Indonesia by the runaway success of a few simple savings products designed for the low-income market and offered by Indonesia's Bank Rakyat Indonesia. Although many Bolivians involved with microfinance knew about BRI, they believed that Bolivia's culture and history created different attitudes and behavior. It won't happen here, they agreed.

Indeed, some comments from microcredit clients seem to back up their perception. Older microentrepreneurs still recall the days of high and hyper inflation. In those days they survived by burrowing beneath the money economy. A shopkeeper in Mineros described how she kept her assets in tradable goods. She traveled between the Departments of Santa Cruz and Cochabamba, each time carrying goods from one place to sell in another. Money in the pocket had a short half-life, and money in the bank was as good as gone. Today, despite fifteen years of monetary stability (though only a few years since major bank failures), she continues to think she would be a fool to keep money in the bank. She keeps her life savings in the form of cattle on her husband's farm. "After all," she says, as though stating the obvious, "cattle multiply."

This woman was already a grandmother, and she remembered the early 1980s. However, even a young farmer with a three-year-old daughter expressed the same views. He puts all his extra money into investments so that his wealth will grow faster. The surplus from his machinery-repair business is plowed into agricultural land, and vice versa. Among urbanites, investment priorities may differ, but interest in financial savings does not appear to be dramatically greater. BancoSol customers in Santa Cruz described putting their surpluses into home improvements if not their businesses.

Fernando Archondo, a Bolivian with family ties to the *hacienda* system, offers an explanation that goes back even farther than hyperinflation and bank failures. He recalls that before the agrarian reform, when the rural poor were essentially sharecroppers for haciendas, the landlords supplied the inputs for farming. People did not and probably could not plan for next year's planting, and so, he hypothesizes, a tradition of savings did not develop.

Pancho Otero believes that even if money is stable and the banks are safe, it is a rational decision for microenterprises, especially traders, to keep their surpluses working. The returns available on trading are so fast and large that it makes sense to keep as much working capital circulating as possible. His words echo those of a Bolivian market woman, Sofía Velasquez, who explained how she managed her "capital" in an interview with anthropologists Hans and Judith-Maria Buechler: "I never let my little capital that my mother had given me die. I always kept it invested in produce."[8]

Marguerite Robinson, one of the main architects of BRI's savings programs and an optimist about the potential for the poor to save, disagrees with this view of Bolivian savings behavior. She and a team from BancoSol conducted over 200 detailed interviews with clients. Those interviews convinced her that nearly everyone was engaging in some form of savings and that clients would welcome the opportunity to save in a trusted financial institution. "I did not find anything different on demand for savings in Bolivia from what I found in Indonesia or India or China," she recalls. The difficulty of identifying potential savings demand is that if banking services are not part of their routine, clients often cannot describe their savings behavior in terms bankers easily recognize.

Bolivian microfinance institutions did not ignore savings entirely. As NGOs it was illegal for them to capture deposits, but most institutions had ersatz savings—compulsory savings—where clients had to keep on deposit a certain percentage of the loan principal they received. The NGOs developed forced savings in part because they wanted to "teach" clients to save. The village bank programs (ProMujer and Crecer) took this idea a step farther. They used forced savings to create an "internal account" for each village bank, which the village bank collectively would decide how to use. A member in a pinch could ask her colleagues for a loan from the internal account, typically a short-term loan with a very high interest rate. Thus, village banks created a mechanism for amassing savings, but only offered access to that savings in the form of an expensive loan. Still, the internal account was a significant step beyond the original solidarity group programs, which allowed withdrawal of savings only when a client left the program. But forced deposits are better understood as a version of a more formal banking device, the compensating balance, used as partial loan security and as a way to increase a lender's effective income. Because of its perceived role in stabilizing lending, Pancho Otero commented, "We knew forced savings was a bad idea, but we were afraid to abandon it." Despite his qualms, Prodem abolished compulsory savings before the creation of BancoSol.

With plenty of donor money around and legal prohibitions on NGOs collecting savings, there was at first not much reason to go beyond forced savings. Not until Prodem's demands for capital first began to outstrip the supply from donors did a microfinance institution begin to consider voluntary savings deposits as a potentially important aspect of its business. This was one of several reasons for the creation of BancoSol. As the first microfinance NGO to become a licensed financial institution, BancoSol was also the first to develop savings products aimed at low-income people. After a systematic process of market research, product design, and pilot testing, BancoSol came up with a package of products including a simple passbook savings account and a time-deposit account.

When it came to the supply side—delivering the services—BancoSol discovered that savings were more expensive and more difficult than expected. Otero reflects, "We busted our brains trying to do savings. It's hard to do savings and credit at the same time. Staff can't learn both at once. One requires you to trust the client, while the other requires the client to trust you." Adding savings required some fundamental adjustments in staffing and in streamlined design at the branch level for moving credit quickly. It also required new computer systems, designed to give clients immediate information on the status of their accounts. Problems popped up when BancoSol began a too rapid rollout of the new savings products. When computers didn't work, clients were left to stand in long queues wondering whether BancoSol was really a good place to put their money. BancoSol ultimately solved its delivery problems, but at the cost of a persistent perception of savings as expensive and hard to implement.

At present, only about 30 percent of BancoSol's portfolio comes from its savings deposits, while at BRI savings are over twice the size of the loan portfolio. Nevertheless, this figure is higher than other Bolivian microfinance institutions. Fassil's Alfredo Otero says that his clients do not save much, only about 10 percent of Fassil's asset base. Caja Los Andes has savings products but does not promote them, and has raised a negligible portion of its assets that way. Its executive director, Pedro Arriola, looks at savings as an expensive undertaking that is unlikely to become an important source of funds, although he says Caja Los Andes may offer it strictly as a service.

Marguerite Robinson observes that the lack of belief in the demand side of savings may obscure the more fundamental problem on the supply side. "I think it's the supply side issues that are the real stumbling block. Savings is expensive in the early years, and you really have to put in substantial funds and scarce high-level management resources if you want to do it effectively. And if you don't believe it's going to work, you're unlikely to invest that heavily."

One of the reasons for poor savings records among the microfinance lenders has been the popular reputation of the cooperatives and the mutuals (specialized in housing finance) as the places to save. Particularly in Santa Cruz, the cooperatives and mutuals attracted most of the deposits of low-income and middle-class people who wanted to save. By 1998 the mutuals and cooperatives held about 14 percent of all deposits in Bolivia's financial system, while the microfinance lenders (microfinance FFPs and BancoSol) held only 2 percent.

The coops and mutuals gave loans on the basis of a client's savings history. They emphasized saving for long-term goals. The mutuals, in particular, tied savings to eligibility for housing loans. People would save for years in the hopes of one day qualifying for a subsidized housing loan, although only a small percentage ever got such loans. BancoSol market researchers noticed that customers of the coops would leave savings in their accounts for a long time, while BancoSol customers tended to use their accounts more like checking accounts, to manage their funds—even though the basic savings account offered was virtually identical at both institutions.

This difference in behavior reflected the fact that people save for different purposes, including liquidity management, long-term investment, and protection against risk. Products could aim specifically at one of these purposes. Sofía

Velasquez, the anthropologists' market vendor who liked to keep her capital working all the time, suffered devastating setbacks, for instance, when the masses of pork she was selling spoiled or when a thief took her money on the way home from the market. Suddenly she had no capital. She commented, "Business is climbing a soapy washboard. One eventually loses one's footing and falls."[9] Apparently, her risk-protection mechanisms were social rather than financial, because after such losses she rebuilt her capital with gifts or loans from relatives and friends. She could have used savings or some type of insurance to reduce her risk, but instead, when microcredit came along, she used loans from BancoSol and Caja Los Andes to rebuild after a loss, taking the place of friends and relations. She even commented that BancoSol and Caja Los Andes were "my husband."[10]

In fact, many of the challenges of attracting savings had a cultural dimension—from the status of holding wealth as cattle, to the reliance on family networks, to the pervasive lack of trust in banks. Perhaps if an institution responded effectively to these cultural values, it would see the savings tumbling in. In the late 1990s a surge of interest in savings sparked a new round of market research to try to understand better what might unlock the secret of demand.

Some researchers examined the *pasanaku*, a form of rotating savings and credit association (ROSCA). In some *pasanakus* members give a predetermined amount of money (*yapa*) each week to a *pasanaquero*, who at the end of the cycle collects a *yapa* as payment. John Owens of USAID began working with FIE to develop a savings product that would mimic the *pasanaku*. People would agree to deposit a fixed *yapa* each week, and FIE would be the *pasanaquero*. Owens had assisted Workers Bank in Jamaica to develop a very similar product, with excellent results. FIE staff traveled to Jamaica to see how it worked.

Several other pilot savings programs were also in the planning stages by the end of 1999, with German funding. Edgar Zurita of Fades was eager to move if he could get a waiver from the Superintendency to offer savings as a test. Zurita had quietly offered a savings product when he was running Sartawi, based on saving for some long-term goal of the client's choosing: perhaps a cow or a bicycle. In the six months before the Superintendency of Banks found out and told Sartawi to stop, it had raised enough money to make Zurita a believer in savings demand.

The new savings initiatives are more focused on providing savings as a service to customers than as a way for the financial institution to raise funds. Even if clients are enthusiastic about the products, they are so narrowly targeted that they may not result in high volumes of deposits and are likely to be costly to obtain. Thus, while they may be smart about connecting to clients, they may still fail to convince institutions to rely on savings as a core source of funds. At this writing it was too early to tell whether a breakthrough might be on the horizon.

GOVERNMENT AND DONORS REASSESS

The commercialization of microfinance in Bolivia is cause for one other set of reassessments. Government and donors must reevaluate their roles in the new setting. Microfinance has become a competitive business, and large portions of the market are saturated. The major players operate on commercial principles and are licensed and supervised by one of the best superintendencies in the region.

In this setting one would expect that government would have limited its role to supervision, and that donors would be packing up to move on to other things. Not so! Riding the microfinance wave, government has launched a major new microenterprise/microfinance initiative, and donors are supplying millions of dollars.

Throughout most of the period when microfinance was developing in Bolivia, the Bolivian government was not heavily involved. At first this followed naturally from the ideology of the MNR administrations, which focused on getting government out of the business of running enterprises, including bankrupt state development banks. The leaders saw government's hand in finance as limited to establishing the framework, and while several of their leaders were closely linked to Prodem, they believed that such experiments should proceed on their own. Moreover, at this time, microfinance was little known and informal enterprises still seen mainly as a problem. There were no obvious political gains from supporting microfinance.

By the late 1990s, however, things had changed. Microfinance was a visible Bolivian success story, and the government wanted to share in that success. At the same time, the ADN government was not quite as firmly dedicated as MNR to liberal economic principles and was therefore open to a more activist role. The microenterprise initiative it has launched has three main branches. First, for the licensed microfinance institutions, able to borrow on commercial terms, NAFIBO, a government financial intermediary, channels lines of donor credit. NAFIBO's original purpose was to support formal sector small and medium enterprises, but most of the lines of credit donors offered Bolivia focused on microfinance, so, by default, NAFIBO became a second-tier microfinance lender. For organizations still needing grant funding, the government asked a second government entity to change its stripes. FONDESIF's original job was the workout of failed banks after the banking crisis of the early and mid-1990s.

With that task over, it was an available structure to coopt into the entirely different role of promoting microfinance. FONDESIF has developed a program to get microfinance out to the rural areas and is involved in the pilot rural and savings initiatives. The third branch of the program involves nonfinancial assistance to microenterprises through the high-visibility step of establishing a vice-minister for microenterprise in the Ministry of Labor.

These initiatives all sound quite laudable. It is necessary to dig a little deeper to separate their positive and negative aspects. NAFIBO is the least controversial of the three, though it may have the most money. NAFIBO is a vehicle for the preferred instrument of many donors—the line of credit. It manages lines from the InterAmerican Development Bank, the German Kreditanstalt fur Wiederaufbau, the Spanish government, and others, in amounts averaging about $10 million each. It is not the only such wholesale lender operating in Bolivia. Funda-Pro, capitalized by funds left after a completed USAID project, offers much the same product to a slightly broader array of institutions. According to Miguel Hoyos, Funda-Pro's executive director, this kind of quasi-commercial financing has played an important role in supporting the transition of microfinance institutions including FIE, Caja Los Andes, and Prodem. Lines of credit supplied the funds those organizations needed when they started growing rapidly, but before they gained substantial access to local capital markets. Now that the FFPs have matured, however, such funding allows them to postpone becoming genuinely independent of donors through capital markets, and it reduces their incentives to raise funds from savings. If an FFP can get $5 million at one go from NAFIBO, why should it take the trouble to offer attractive savings services? Why should it make the extra effort to convince the capital markets of its creditworthiness? There is even an example of evolution in reverse, as fully commercial Fassil seeks lines of credit from NAFIBO to reduce its cost of funds to the level enjoyed by the programs of donor origin. Lines of credit should now be playing a diminishing role in Bolivia, so as not to postpone the further development of the microfinance field.

FONDESIF offers below-market funding and specialized technical assistance to organizations that have not yet become licensed and supervised. A large share of that funding supports the efforts mentioned above to get banking services to unserved municipalities and to carry out pilot savings schemes. The most controversial aspect of the program is its requirement that all donor funding for microfinance must be channeled through FONDESIF and must therefore fit within government's microfinance strategy. The FONDESIF program overall, and especially this latter provision, represent the first time the government has made a concerted attempt to control the microfinance agenda.

Many of the microfinance institutions resent what they consider inappropriate government interference, and note a tendency in some of FONDESIF's programs to direct the industry in ways that do not make market sense.

The vice-minister for microenterprise is trying to construct a program to help move microenterprises forward through market linkages, subcontracting between micros and big businesses, and the like. Although this program addresses crucial needs in the microenterprise sector, the vice-ministry is groping for effective means—and turning to models tried elsewhere without great success. The program's more significant value may be in the recognition it gives the microenterprise sector. However, friends of microenterprise are skeptical. Roberto Casanovas of Idepro is not sure the ADN government is serious about microenterprise. He sees a lot of propaganda, but little action, and views the location of the vice-minister for microenterprise within the Ministry of Labor as a signal that government still considers the sector from a political and social rather than economic perspective.

Undoubtedly government's newfound interest in microfinance is bringing the sector closer to the mainstream. Government has created a task force on microenterprise with representatives from the major government bodies, microfinance institutions, and various advocacy groups. This group has already been important in pushing through some key policy changes that had languished without the critical momentum to get passed. One of these, the inclusion of non-regulated microfinance institutions in the Superintendency's credit bureau, will have the dual effect of improving the overall effectiveness of the credit bureau and improving the reporting and financial-management standards of the NGOs (in order to qualify). The other measure is the creation of a new law allowing movable property to be registered as legal collateral, with streamlined judicial procedures in cases of default. Through this new provision, the standard practice of the individual microfinance lenders—use of household goods and machinery as collateral—has achieved legal status. Several years before, the World Bank had identified the collateral problem as an important constraint to the expansion of credit services for the larger microenterprises and small to medium enterprises, but action was slow until the task force began.[11] With the new collateral law the microfinance industry has institutionalized its two main ways of securing loans (the Superintendency had already defined solidarity guarantees as an acceptable form of loan security). More generally, the placement of the task force inside government's policy-making apparatus is ensuring that government will be far less likely in the future to make decisions as if the informal sector were a negligible part of the economy. As an example, for better or worse (depending on whether one agrees with the plan), provisions addressing microfinance are an integral part of the government's year 2000 economic-recovery program.

Much of the government's involvement in microfinance is backed by plentiful donor money available for the sector. Donors with microfinance mandates are looking for ways to move big money, observes GTZ advisor Marike Wiedmeier, and Bolivia offers them an irresistible opportunity, with its large, mature institutions that operate under the watch of a competent bank Superintendency, reducing risk to the donor. The combination of large institutions and reliable oversight has attracted a list of active donors, including the InterAmerican Development Bank, Andean Development Corporation, the German organizations GTZ and KFW, Swiss Development Corporation, the European Union, Belgium, Spain, USAID, and Canada.

The donors justify their microfinance programs with several arguments. They point out that the nature of their funding is appropriate to the type of institution receiving it. Commercial organizations receive loans or equity on commercial terms, with subsidies reserved for the weaker, still developing organizations. Moreover, donors are aiming most of the heavy subsidies toward rural areas, where many people agree they are needed. And it is true that donors in Bolivia generally avoid the biggest mistakes donors are prone to make in microfinance—like supporting programs with below-market interest rates or poor delinquency control—largely because best practices are widely understood and observed in Bolivia.

Nevertheless, some people associated with commercial lenders are vehement in their critique. Michael Chu of BancoSol says, "It's unconscionable for donors to continue pumping money into an industry capable of earning a 30 percent return on equity." Fernando Romero of Prodem calls the IDB's millions destructive, because the money will go to the weaker institutions, allowing them to compete more easily with organizations operating commercially. Since BancoSol, Prodem, and other now-commercial microfinance programs drank deeply at the subsidy well when they started, it may be somewhat disingenuous for them to claim that the water should be off limits to others. Nevertheless, once an industry shows profitability and intense competition, as in Bolivia's urban microenterprise sector, subsidies once justified as infant industry support may cross the line to become unfair competition. The continued availability of funds from second-tier lenders has clearly slowed the pace of microfinance entry into savings mobilization and private capital markets.

There are signs of recognition within at least the Ministry of Finance and the IDB that it may be time to slow the flow. The IDB provided most of its microenterprise funds in 1999 and 2000 for nonfinancial assistance rather than credit. Even so, it seems likely that the temptation to be associated with success and the real need to push the rural frontiers are likely to keep donors to Bolivia involved in microfinance for a good many years.

NOTES

1. See, for example, publications of the MicroSave Africa project.
2. Claudio González-Vega et al., "A Primer on Bolivian Experiences in Microfinance: An Ohio State Perspective" (Columbus, Ohio: Rural Finance Program, Ohio State University, no date), 26. This study is based on a poverty-assessment methodology measuring the presence or absence of basic services (e.g., water, sanitation, electricity, housing quality). It probably classifies a higher proportion of rural dwellers as poor than would a more conventional assessment based on incomes. Readers unfamiliar with poverty definitions should recognize that poverty lines in developing countries reflect a far lower standard of living than poverty definitions in developed economies. By developed-country standards, most microcredit clients above the Bolivian poverty line would still be considered poor.
3. González-Vega et al., "Primer," 23; Banco Solidaria, "Memoria 1998" (La Paz, 1999), 112.
4. González-Vega et al., "Primer," 22.
5. A parallel situation faced the Federal Housing Administration (FHA) in the United States, after its hugely successful introduction of home-mortgage insurance, which was profitable for FHA and became a commercially offered product. Once the private sector had moved in, FHA began searching for a new mission. It aimed programs at smaller population groups who still lacked access to mortgages, including very-low-income people, minorities, and the handicapped. With this set of projects, FHA lost money. FHA's first mortgage insurance product had been a genuine financial innovation, launching a new way to manage risk and create value, but the second set of projects did not form a viable business base.
6. Frits Wils, ed., *Non-Governmental Organizations and Their Networks in Bolivia* (The Netherlands: Gemeenschappelijk Overleg Medefinanciering, 1995), 7.
7. González-Vega et al., "Primer," 26.
8. Hans Buechler and Judith-Maria Buechler, *The World of Sofía Velasquez: The Autobiography of a Bolivian Market Vendor* (New York: Columbia University Press, 1996), 20.
9. Buechler and Buechler, *World of Sofía*, 102.
10. Buechler and Buechler, *World of Sofía*, 112.
11. World Bank, *How Legal Restrictions on Collateral Limit Access to Credit in Bolivia*, Report No. 13873-BO (Washington, D.C.: World Bank, 1994).

CHAPTER EIGHT

YES, BUT IS IT DEVELOPMENT?

THE CREATION OF BOLIVIA'S microfinance industry fulfilled a dream that had eluded development financiers for years. It is a true development success story (though a still-evolving one). The founders of microfinance in Bolivia wanted to build a more inclusive society, starting with access to that most basic commodity, money. Today their vision has become a reality in the cities and is advancing into the countryside. Commercialization has brought microfinance farther into the mainstream financial system than expected. However, behind the genuine accomplishments lurks a persistent question. What difference has it made? Is there a discernible impact on people's lives and the country's development? Was it worth the effort—and the cost? Although these questions resist a definitive answer, this chapter examines the evidence and viewpoints of various participants and offers the author's own conclusions. The chapter examines the impact of microfinance at three levels: the national economy, individual clients, and the social/political level.

MICROFINANCE AND THE ECONOMY

Bolivia's Basic Development Problem

In Bolivia the coverage of microfinance is so great that it is finally possible to consider the impact of microfinance at the broadest level, that of Bolivia's economic development challenges. After fifteen years it is possible to look back and see some distinct patterns emerging.

To review where Bolivia stood when microfinance started, we recall from chapter 2 that these origins coincided with a new era in Bolivia of stable democracy and liberal economic policies. In the mid-1980s reformers ardently hoped that the combination of economic and political stability would bring Bolivia the new sources of economic growth the country desperately sought. The reformers had conquered inflation and launched a program of restructuring the Bolivian economy away from state capitalism and toward the liberal economic program. During the next decade and a half, the years this book covers, the Bolivian government was remarkably consistent in holding to the chosen path. Throughout, Bolivia was the darling of liberal macroeconomists. It followed textbook macroeconomic policies, privatized major segments of the economy, and improved the framework for private sector investment. It did nearly everything the World Bank asked, with one of the best-performing soft-loan portfolios in the world.[1] Some would say that this period provides a good test of the liberal paradigm. Did it solve Bolivia's basic economic development problems?

After the 1985 crisis Bolivia's economy took several years to recover, but during the 1990s it grew consistently, at an average of 4.2 percent per year, until the recession of 1999/2000 brought growth to a standstill. The 1990s were better for Bolivians than any other recent decade. Nevertheless, as the recession showed, Bolivia continues to struggle with its central challenge, to build a diverse economic base not overly dependent on the El Dorados beneath its feet.

Bolivia's exemplary macroeconomic performance has not produced the levels of economic growth that the architects of its economic policies and the electorate who supported them had hoped for. The country still lags on almost any measure of development or quality of life—per capita income ($1,000), infant mortality (67 per 100,000), life expectancy (62 years), and percentage of the population in poverty (67 percent).[2] Given Bolivia's population growth, the 4.2 percent GDP growth rate sustained through most of the 1990s meant that incomes per person rose only 2 percent each year. A simple but sobering calculation shows that at that rate it will take Bolivia forty-three years to catch up to the economic level that its poorest immediate neighbor, Peru, enjoys today—and of course by then, Peru will have moved far beyond. In order to reduce the catch-up time to within a generation, Bolivia's economy would have grow between 6 and 7 percent every year.[3]

These calculations surface time and again in the discourse of Bolivia's economists and policy makers. The thought of facing two more generations of Bolivia as a backward nation seems to hit them like a body blow. How, they ask, can we lift this country onto a faster growth path? And, how can we make sure growth permeates all levels of society?

here are several visions, some competing, some complementary. One idea, the current government promotes, is that Bolivia is set to become an economic hub for the Southern Cone. Amparo Ballivian and Jorge Crespo, ministers in the ADN government, make the pitch that at the beginning of the twenty-first century Bolivia's geographic location has become an advantage. Intra-continental trade is expanding quickly, and as it does, Bolivia is positioned to become a hub for communications, transport, and energy. Given that Bolivia's landlocked location and impassible mountains have always been viewed as major liabilities, some observers have trouble taking this vision seriously.

Another approach, shared by government and the World Bank, reckons that Bolivia has laid the foundations for faster growth but suggests that it needs to continue deepening institutional reforms to win the trust of private investors. Apparently, it takes more than fifteen years of good macroeconomics to overcome the damage to Bolivia's reputation done by previous nationalizations and economic and political crises. Bolivia has not shed the perception that corruption still flourishes behind the scenes. Investors look for improvements in the legal and judicial systems, investor protections, and the like. Ballivian, formerly in charge of attracting foreign investment, predicts a surge in investment, as investors become fully convinced that Bolivia will work within the rule of law. In fact, as former Superintendent of Banks Jacques Trigo notes, Bolivia does attract substantial foreign direct investment, but most of this money goes into mega-projects, like hydrocarbon exports to Brazil, that have few spillover effects into the broader economy.

A third perspective focuses on export development. Crespo observes that Bolivia's internal market is very small, with only two million people having any significant purchasing power. Thus, Bolivia must penetrate the much larger markets around its borders. For this reason the government promotes nontraditional agricultural exports—cotton, soybeans, cotton, and horticulture. Business gurus Michael Fairbanks and Stace Lindsay agree that Bolivia's future depends on exports. However, in their book *Plowing the Sea* they argue that Bolivia is trapped in low-value-added, commodity-based exporting, which will fail to pull the country out of poverty. They advocate an export strategy based on product differentiation. Bolivian exporters must find market niches where their special products can maintain a competitive edge.

The problem with all these visions of economic development is that no one really seems to believe in them. When Bolivian analysts lay out their visions they use words like *hopefully* and *maybe* rather than confident, assertive language. The pronouncements of government officials have an unconvincing ring, while outside observers are openly skeptical. Although everyone would like to see Bolivia ratchet up to 7 percent growth, few expect it. And this is why, after fifteen years, the fight to divide the pie is creeping back into Bolivian politics.

The shortcomings of Bolivia's development strategies became abundantly clear during the recession of 1999/2000, which triggered the crisis in microfinance that chapter 6 described. The major cause of the recession was a general economic crisis in South America, which started with devaluation and economic contraction in Brazil and then spread to Argentina and other neighbors. These events reduced demand and worsened the terms of trade for Bolivia's exports. Prices for Bolivia's main agricultural commodities (soy, cotton, and sugar) hit bottom and the harvest was poor. The economy even suffered from the successful eradication of much of the country's illegal coca production. These events reinforced the point that Bolivia's ability to determine her own economic growth path remains limited; Bolivia is still highly vulnerable to external events.

These observations provide the context for considering the economic role of microcredit. Despite the government's highly visible microenterprise program, few government policy makers consider microcredit or its informal-sector clients central to Bolivia's economic-growth puzzle. Mario Riquena of the Ministry of Finance observes that even though microfinance covers a large share of its potential market, the amount of funds involved remains a small fraction of the total financial system. Even if microfinance caused its clients to grow very fast, he says, it is too small a portion of the economy to make a difference.

Crespo, a cabinet minister who is also a director of Caja Los Andes, says that government views microfinance mainly as a poverty tool rather than part of economic development. Jorge Rodriguez, the head of the government's wholesale lender to microfinance institutions, NAFIBO, would prefer to focus on small and medium enterprise. "People are overselling microfinance, claiming that the poor are going to become entrepreneurs and stop being poor."

Yet neither are microfinance and microenterprise at the core of efforts to address poverty. Both government ministers and the World Bank staff members who advise them view poverty alleviation through the lens of public expenditures in health, education, water and roads, long-term investments that furnish prerequisites for growth. It is not entirely unfair to say that this strategy still views the poor mainly as recipients of assistance and services.

The Views of the Visionaries

There are, however, a few visionaries who believe that the informal sector can be a force for generating economic growth and that microfinance is an important tool to help them. Among them are Pancho Otero and former president Gonzalo Sanchéz de Lozada. Both men vehemently insist on treating the poor as agents of economic development. Sanchéz de Lozada says, "It's conceited to say that microcredit is just a salve. You have to be careful with those attitudes. The undertows of economic activity are a lot stronger than you can see on the surface. You can't underestimate what people will do with their resources. We now see that it is people who make a country rich."

The sway of the conventional wisdom is so strong that both men feel compelled to apologize for their views. Otero acknowledges that his views are on the fringe but does not want to be classified as "loony," while Sanchéz de Lozada admits that his notions may be a bit romantic. Neither of these men are idle dreamers. Both have accomplished more than most of the armchair critics, and these personal accomplishments have convinced them of the power of individual action.

Nobel Laureate Amartya Sen articulates the same view in a broad way in his book *Development as Freedom*, which calls increases in freedom both the "primary end" and "principal means" of development.[4] From Sen's perspective, developments that give people a wider range of choices and capabilities are intrinsically good because freedom is in itself highly valued. Access to finance would bring such intrinsic benefits by enhancing a person's ability to construct her own life. This thought echoes Otero's observation of the boost to self-esteem that comes when clients are given trust and responsibility through loans. Equally important, Sen values access to finance as a means, because it enables people to use their capacities as economic actors more fully. In this view microfinance would contribute to prosperity.

In fact, there is strong evidence that the people of Bolivia's informal sector spent much of the 1990s doing just that—developing their full capacities as economic actors—and in so doing, helping create economic progress. Nevertheless, the tenuous connection of microenterprises to the mainstream economy left these people suffering disproportionately in the recession.

Dynamism in the Informal Sector

In chapter 2 we described the dual roles of the informal sector: a cushioning role as an occupation of last resort during economic stress, and a progressive role as a source of employment and productivity growth. During the mid-1980s, when microfinance began, the cushioning role predominated, as reflected in the flood of women becoming market vendors and the shrinking role of small manufacturing enterprises in the "semi-entrepreneurial" sector.

Today the picture has changed dramatically. The number of microenterprises has continued to grow, due mainly to continuing migration into the cities. Between 1989 and 1995, the total number of microenterprises in the three axis cities grew from just under 300,000 to just over 400,000, in line with earlier demographic trends.[5]

However, the pattern of growth within the informal sector has changed. During the six years from 1989 to 1995 the number of semi-entrepreneurial businesses more than doubled, while the number of smaller family enterprises (including one-person vendors) only increased 20 percent. In the important manufacturing sector the number of semi-entrepreneurial businesses nearly quadrupled, from 7,300 to 28,000. The remarkable surge in the semi-enterprise sector also appears in employment figures. In 1989 this group of enterprises employed only 14 percent of the labor force, but by 1995 it employed 22 percent, while the shares of all the other sectors (corporate, public, and family) either shrank or stayed the same. Another way to look at this phenomenon is to observe, as CEDLA has, that the informal sector, particularly the semi-entrepreneurial portion of it, generated 90 percent of all new jobs in Bolivia between 1992 and 1995.[6]

At the same time these businesses were becoming more advanced and productive. The proportion of enterprises using electric rather than manual tools and machinery jumped from about one-third to about two-thirds, and the proportion purchasing new rather than used equipment rose even more.

Microfinance institutions saw the same trends, as demand for loans of $3,000 and above soared throughout the middle and late 1990s. Nearly every loan officer brags about clients who have been part of this dynamic growth process. BancoSol in Santa Cruz shows off the *empanada* maker who is now selling from three of her own kiosks, competing face to face with McDonalds, and the baker whose business has grown steadily every year, now employing 14 people. There are many others like these. The brightest spot is represented by the BancoSol client in La Paz, mentioned in chapter 1, with half a million dollars worth of knitting machinery jammed into his house, selling his sweaters in Paraguay. Managers at FIE and Fassil also report clients selling clothing across the border to Argentina, Paraguay, and Brazil. Fassil's Claudia Ordoñez guesses that about 10 percent of her Santa Cruz-based clients are involved in exporting. CEDLA, which keeps statistics on the informal sector, agrees that its most dynamic area is the manufacture and export of clothing.

These numbers and observations signal a tremendous dynamism among Bolivian microenterprises during the first half of the 1990s, helped in part by economic stability. They lead to the conclusion that throughout this period the informal sector made an important contribution to Bolivia's economic development. The sector moved far beyond its safety-net function, adding a strong growth function. In at least one specific market, textiles, microenterprises contributed to the dominant paradigm of export-led economic growth. Although the causal link is impossible to prove, there is a clear correlation between the strong performance of the informal sector and growing access to credit through microfinance institutions.

Limitations of the Informal Sector

Although little doubt remains that the informal sector has been a source of growth in Bolivia, the question remains whether the sector can assist in future economic rejuvenation. In the view of economist Horst Grebe and a variety of other observers, the informal sector's inherent limitations prevent it from playing a leading role. One limitation is what might politely be called its uncertain legal status. This limitation proved overwhelming for informal exporters and importers during the recession of 1999/2000. Among exporters, Bolivia's informal-sector textile producers saw their markets in Brazil vanish overnight with its currency devaluation, and then saw every other neighboring country close trading borders or put up non-tariff barriers to protect producers in their own weakened economies. Microfinance programs reported that hundreds of their exporting clients were struggling or had closed.

Given the dynamic potential of the microenterprise sector as exporters, particularly in textiles and garments, it would seem that the Bolivian government would make every effort to support the sector. But policy makers argue that as long as these exporters are putting false brand labels on their clothes and selling on the gray market, the Bolivian government cannot represent their interests in trade negotiations. It cannot ask Argentina to remove its barriers to under-the-table trade.

Representatives of the producers do not think the government has really tried. Mauricio Vasquez, director of ADEPI, a national association of small producers on the borderline between informal and formal, is dismissive of government's actions. Yes, in some respects more informal businesses are becoming formal—paying license fees and registering as employers. Microfinance has given them access to financial services. However, Vasquez says, it is nearly impossible for them to comply with export requirements. The process is opaque, costly, and time consuming. An inexperienced exporter can spend weeks or months simply trying to figure out with whom to speak, what papers to obtain, and what fees to pay. Although Bolivia offers incentives to exporters, these largely bypass the informal producers.

The picture on the import side is equally difficult. The microenterprise trading sector grew up around contraband. Many of their (otherwise ordinary) wares were imported into the country without proper import duties. The informal economy depended on this small-time smuggling as a way of life. From a policy perspective, this type of activity meant some loss in government revenues but generated a great deal of employment. In the recession of 1999/

2000 these traders were hit especially hard, because of customs reforms. As part of the International Monetary Fund/World Bank program, Bolivia established the customs authority as a semi-autonomous body. The intent and effect has been to depoliticize and clean up the image of customs. The flow of contraband has become a trickle. One observer noted, "Before the reforms, the authorities just seized the contraband. Now they throw you in jail." Microfinance program officers see the crackdown on contraband affecting an enormous number of their market vendors' clients, even though most of the clients are not themselves involved in the importing of contraband.

The serious effects of these trade policies on microenterprises meant that the informal sector suffered as much or more than other parts of the economy during the recession. Although the country stood to benefit in jobs and overall economic stability from assisting its informal sector producers and traders, government policy makers failed to address the contradictions between their pursuit of a more formal trading regime and the realities of the informal enterprises.

In the view of many of the people who study microenterprise development, government red tape is not the only, or even the most important limitation keeping the informal sector from becoming, as Bolivians say, a "protagonist" in national development. Roberto Casanovas, executive director of Idepro, sees the sector as a base but not a future source of development. As a long-time observer of the field, he sees that outside the clothing sector there is little real change in the nature of the enterprises or their products, too few of the productivity improvements that build higher living standards. Economist Grebe says that the sector will not develop spontaneously (that is, through access to finance alone) because of qualitative differences between informal and formal enterprises. For example, few informals can leap from a family-based mode of operation, in which the proprietor handles all aspects of the business, to a corporate mode, in which business management and production are separate. Grebe sees this kind of change requiring generations, as the educated sons and daughters of microentrepreneurs bring formal skills into their businesses.

Seeing such limitations, some participants in microfinance are frustrated. Hermann Larrazábal of CEDLA lays part of the blame for the sufferings of the informal sector during the 1999/2000 recession on microfinance, which, he says, "multiplied the sector without transforming it." Casanovas says, "You can't expect major changes from tiny, short term loans." Edgar Zurita of Fades gives the example of a dairy farmer. Microfinance can assist a farm family to buy cows, which will provide income for several years, but it cannot finance the creation of the dairy. Without a dairy, the farmer has nowhere to sell the milk.

The qualitative constraints motivate organizations like FIE, Idepro, and

CEDLA, who have always been more interested in microenterprise development than microfinance per se, to find business-development tools to help microenterprises make leaps in technology, management, and market access. They hope to build cultures within microenterprises that allow them to operate more successfully in a formal milieu. They acknowledge, however, that the tools they have inherited for this task are not very effective. They want to reinvent business-development services, much as microfinance reinvented financial services. Although they have ideas, they cannot yet point to major breakthroughs.

Fernando Romero is hoping for just such a breakthrough in the latest incarnation of Prodem, the new Prodem Foundation. After spinning off Prodem FFP, the Foundation will tackle the problem of the middle-level business in rural areas by developing such businesses itself. Its first venture involves llama-wool processing. Prodem will bring in processing technology and expertise and develop market links, while training highlands llama owners to upgrade the quality of the wool they sell. These llama producers are among the poorest and most remote of Bolivians. The aim is to create a wool-processing enterprise linked to larger markets that will be owned jointly by Prodem and llama producers. As an NGO, Prodem will provide start-up subsidies, but just as with microfinance, it expects eventually to become profitable. Prodem hopes to replicate this model, if it succeeds, for other rural products and services. Initiatives such as these illustrate the growing conviction among many people involved with Bolivian microfinance that the full potential for impact of microfinance depends on transformations in the economic environment of the clients, an area of work most microfinance institutions ignore or avoid.

MEASURING THE IMPACT OF MICROFINANCE

Observing a correlation at the macro level between informal-sector progress and access to microfinance is not enough for many observers. They want to see exactly how microfinance affects individuals. Among the participants in the microfinance debate, we find four very different ways of assessing the individual impact of microfinance. Each one tells a different story to a different audience.

Everyday Experience

The first, widely applied by the staff of microfinance institutions, is the "gleam in the eye." The staff of Bolivian microfinance institutions have been so engrossed in their work that they have invested little in systematically examining the impact of their services on clients. They find the proof that keeps them going every time they see their clients progressing and hear them talk about how access to credit has changed their lives. Most front-line staff are so convinced by their everyday contact with clients that they find the idea of trying to prove the impact of microfinance rather superfluous. Unfortunately, the "gleam in the eye" method is insufficient for most policy makers and funding-agency staff cooped up in offices.

Statistical Analysis

The second approach uses statistical techniques to deduce impact. The program-evaluation profession places a daunting standard of proof on such impact evaluations, drawn from the techniques used in scientific studies. The ideal is the double-blind study, as used in medicine to assess the efficacy of a new treatment. Applying these concepts to financial services means that measurement of client status must take place at two points in time (before borrowing and after borrowing) and must be compared to people who, although similar in every other respect to the client group, did not receive services.

This kind of measurement is very difficult, in part because of the diffuse and indirect nature of the way financial services work. Loans don't create economic opportunities; they enable people to make better use of the opportunities they have. If a client's business grows, it's hard to attribute that to the loan rather than to an increase in foot traffic in the area, or a decision to work more hours in the business, or any number of other possible factors. Moreover, if you go looking for impact along a certain dimension, such as growth of business sales, you may find that like quicksilver, the impact has eluded your grasp. Perhaps the client used the loan for home improvement, to invest in another business, or to pay for a medical emergency. But statistical studies usually measure a few specific dimensions, missing the richness of the actual experience. A study of Crecer by Freedom from Hunger illustrates this problem. Because FFH's mission is to improve nutrition, it looks for impact in the size and weight of the children of participants. This is like measuring the value of a road by counting only the people who travel to one of many destinations. The study failed to find a statistically significant impact of microfinance on children's body weight.

Control groups in theory correct for the attribution problem by comparing people exposed to the same set of conditions and possible choices. However, control-group design is tricky, and skeptics hover like vultures to pounce on any weakness. It is nearly impossible in real life to construct a control group free from the possibility that its members differ in some systematic way from the clients who received loans.

Ironically, the very success of microfinance will make it increasingly difficult to use statistical techniques. Since virtually everyone in Bolivia's urban informal sector now has access to microcredit, it is no longer possible to assess the difference between those with and those without access. From now on, it will be possible only to distinguish between those who choose to borrow and those who don't, who probably aren't directly comparable, or between those who borrow from one institution rather than another, where the comparison is not very enlightening.

Facing this mine field, microfinance institutions often see impact evaluation as a no-win prospect. One can spend hundreds of thousands of dollars to do the research in as scientific way as possible, and the results will still be picked over by skeptics. Moreover, the results will probably tell the institution exactly what its loan officers already knew by gut feeling. For the most part the microfinance institutions in Bolivia have ignored this kind of evaluation, though this choice carries a cost in terms of the credibility of microfinance in academic and policy-making circles.

Qualitative Studies

A third, qualitative, approach to assessing impact provides a richer source of information, helping to build a picture of how clients use microloans. This qualitative approach is close to market research and focuses on understanding how clients perceive and use services rather than on measuring changes. Documenting use, evaluators argue, reveals the pathways along which causality works. Thus, although impact may not be statistically proven, qualitative evidence convinces by appeal to common sense.

Qualitative research, coupled with some quantitative work, has helped build a picture of the way microfinance fits into the lives of its clients. The following discussion is based on five studies that use a combination of statistical and qualitative methods, two from 1993, one from 1998, and two from 1999. A study of BancoSol and cooperatives found that clients who had been borrowing for several years, especially in manufacturing, had significantly increased their number of employees.[7] The second study, of BancoSol alone, confirmed employment growth among the upper tier of clients, especially in textiles. This study also found productivity improvements among garment producers through new technologies.[8] These findings paint much the same picture as the sector-wide CEDLA data, but they bring that picture closer to microfinance.

They also offer a small glimpse into how microcredit affects these businesses. Nearly all the retail businesses reported that the main effect was a price advantage vis-à-vis suppliers. Without a loan, they purchased inventory using supplier credit or in small amounts, generally at exorbitant implicit interest rates. With the loan, they could buy more and pay cash on substantially improved terms. Manufacturing businesses reported the main effect in terms of machinery purchases, using a combination of credit and their own savings.[9]

More recently, those who examine the impact of microfinance have shifted emphasis from enterprise and employment toward poverty alleviation and quality of life. They recognized that the basic economic unit of the informal sector is a household with several income sources and that, in fact, microfinance supports the whole unit, not just a specific enterprise.

One study, by economist Paul Mosley, offers a comprehensive look at the impact of microfinance on the household and enterprise.[10] Although his survey is based on very small samples, the design involves reasonably well-constructed control groups and comparisons across time. Mosley is confident enough to assert that microfinance makes a "considerable contribution to the reduction of poverty" and to claim that the poverty reduction he observes is "a consequence of microfinance."[11] He finds significant increases in incomes and assets—both family and enterprise—for microfinance clients relative to their non-borrowing counterparts. Unlike some others who examine effects on poverty, Mosley suggests that large loans have at least as much poverty impact as smaller loans because of their greater employment effects. He even goes so far as to calculate the cost of moving a person out of poverty through microfinance: lower than that of other social expenditures, except for the very poorest group.

The great value of Mosley's work, however, is the story it tells about the way clients use microfinance to cope with risk, echoing Sofía Velasquez's observation that business is like trying to climb a "soapy washboard." This work is related to a broader set of hypotheses that USAID's AIMS project has been developing and testing about how clients use microfinance to protect against risk.

Most microfinance clients are quite vulnerable to risks. For Bolivia's informal entrepreneurs the biggest risk is that they or their family members will get sick, costing them not only expensive medical bills, but also lost income-earning time. Two other risks also loom very large: vulnerability to crime and market changes (for example, competition). The range of other risks includes political problems, such as strikes or disputes with local authorities, family problems, business mistakes, and for farmers, the perennial risks of weather and disease.

Participation in a microfinance program, especially a group-based program, offers a significant degree of risk protection. The worst thing that can happen in a crisis is that the family loses or sells its productive assets, which reduces income-earning ability even after the crisis is over. Clients who have access to microfinance loans know that they will be able to get credit to start over if this happens. More important, they may be able to call on group members or on their savings to avoid having to sell assets. This is why, as AIMS researcher Monique Cohen discovered, ProMujer clients struggle to maintain their access to ProMujer's credit and their standing with the group.[12] Analysts of the behavior of poor people have found that when people are highly exposed to risk they pursue safe though low-return activities, and spread their sources of income among a diversified portfolio of activities. If microfinance helps people protect themselves somewhat, they may become confident enough to invest in riskier but more profitable activities. Mosley finds that the insurance functions of microfinance are more important for the poorer clients who have fewer—and worse—risk protection strategies available to them, though he stresses that the very poorest rung are not and should not be borrowers. For the poorest, he says, credit is more likely to act as a snake to hasten their path down (through over-indebtedness) than the ladder it is for most clients.

Cohen observes that as clients move up a path toward prosperity, their priorities include both investments in what we commonly think of as productive uses and others usually classified as consumption, particularly better nutrition, home improvement, and education. She points out that these consumption investments also increase the household's economic productivity. Houses, for example, often double as inventory storage locations, workshops, or sources of rent.

Debates over the value of microfinance often turn into shouting matches between those who think microfinance should focus on economic growth (and therefore larger loans) and those whose concern is poverty alleviation (and therefore smaller loans). The work of Cohen and Mosley in describing how clients use microfinance illustrates the fallacies in this dichotomy. Poverty impact may be just as great from the employment effect of large loans as from the income effect of small ones. Moreover, gains associated with poverty alleviation lay the groundwork for investments in greater productivity. On the other hand, business investments, commonly associated with economic growth, are essential for a permanent rise from poverty. As people move forward, they gradually shift emphasis from protection toward productivity. Market vendor Sofía Velasquez knew that all along.

The Market Test

Finally, the fourth way of assessing the impact of microfinance on its clients is the market test. This test is also the simplest, most unequivocal, and cheapest test available. It is based on the observation that if clients are willing to pay for a service, they must find that service worthwhile. This market test is mercifully free of methodological pitfalls. It treats microfinance like any other business product: if it is a good product, people will buy it and value it as much or more than the price they pay. This is Economics 101. And in fact, Bolivian microfinance customers have voted with their purses over and over again. There can hardly be more convincing proof that microfinance is making a difference. Calmeadow's Martin Connell notes, "The fact that so much of the potential market has taken advantage of this new supply of capital is a ringing endorsement of its value."

THE SOCIAL AND POLITICAL STATUS OF THE INFORMAL SECTOR

In reflecting on what microfinance has contributed to Bolivia's development, a central theme is the changing social and political position of the informal sector. Chapter 2 described Bolivia's core social and political challenge, to integrate the poor more fully into the life of Bolivian society, which remains split between the European-descended elites and the lower-status groups of mixed or indigenous heritage. Such divides take generations to overcome. Nevertheless, change occurs from decade to decade, and it's possible to see some progress since the mid-1980s when our story began. The influence of microfinance is discernible, from the treatment of microenterprises by local authorities, to the attitudes of some elites.

At the very local level, the informal sector is gradually establishing greater legitimacy, mainly through interactions with municipal authorities over market space and license taxes. In every market the vendors organize themselves into associations or syndicates that manage relations with the authorities and sometimes organize services like security or garbage collection. There are many small associations. Vendors inside a market create a separate association from the vendors just outside along the street. Vegetable vendors may have a separate association from clothing vendors a few paces away. The associations identify themselves by baseball caps (the men) or aprons (the women) bearing the association's color and insignia.

In Santa Cruz the informal sector has gained a seat at the table, even if it does not always get what it wants. In 1998 the city of Santa Cruz shut down some large markets in the city center that were clogging the streets, citing health and sanitation concerns. But, unlike what might have happened in an earlier time, the associations negotiated alternate space and government contributions to spacious new market sites with improvements. At La Mutualista, one of the new markets, the associations organized the construction of new structures themselves. The quality of the market stalls, with tiled floors and walls and steel pull-down night grates, reflects the aspirations of the association's members. La Mutualista lacks the customer base the vendors had in their old locations, but vendors express pride that they no longer have to sell under a blue tarp or walk on a mud floor. As evidence that the microenterprise sector has gained recognition, according to BancoSol loan officers, representatives of the microenterprise sector now sit on important economic development committees for the city.

In La Paz, syndicates of the informal sector and the municipal authorities have become cozy—perhaps too cozy. A street demonstration that took place in March 1999 is a case in point. On this day the members of each syndicate marched in orderly rows through the streets of La Paz behind huge, gold-lettered banners proclaiming each association's name. In La Paz, demonstrations of one kind or another happen nearly every day, but this one was distinguished by its size and organization. The line of marchers continued into the thousands and possibly tens of thousands of microentrepreneurs, many of them women in traditional dress, causing gridlock throughout the city for hours. The march ended at the plaza in front of the La Paz city hall, where the mayor welcomed the demonstrators. Association leaders and municipal officeholders made speeches. The purpose of this less-than-spontaneous show of civic action was to "thank" the mayor for reducing the license fee for vending-stall locations. This incident illustrates that, at least at some level, the politicians have discovered the advantages of cultivating informal-sector support, particularly in an election year.

This kind of local recognition and participation in the political process is not directly tied to microfinance. In fact, for the most part microfinance institutions avoid the politics of informal-sector associations. On the day of the La Paz demonstration, for example, Caja Los Andes pulled down the shutters of its office on the parade route and remained closed. This was not a display of solidarity but a precaution against possible street disturbances. At various times several microfinance organizations have tried to work through associations to connect to clients, for example offering a loan product accessible through an association. Fassil and the cooperatives offered this kind of loan to finance new market stalls at La Mutualista in Santa Cruz. FIE and Idepro, the most politically active of the microfinance programs, once offered special association-strengthening programs to help the associations lobby more effectively and provide their members with other services.

According to Roberto Casanovas of Idepro, however, microfinance programs have not succeeded in working through or with associations. Casanovas found that most associations are interested in little beyond preserving their own extremely localized territory. Juan Domingo Fabbri of BancoSol's market-research team learned through focus groups that most of the bank's clients had little trust in the syndicates. Clients do not want associations to mediate their loans, because they suspect that leaders will use their position to get free credit or otherwise siphon value away from the members. According to Domingo Fabbri's research, clients trusted microfinance lenders more than their own associations.

Relations between the microfinance programs and informal-sector union organizers allied with politicians reached a low with the debtors' association protests against repayment of microfinance and consumer loans. These protests reflect a vast difference in political outlook between microlenders and association organizers. Despite the cool relations, however, there may be an important underlying link. "Who gave the informal sector in Bolivia its voice?" asks Martin Connell. "I believe that the sector came to life *because* microfinance institutions gave people credit, and with credit came empowerment and an awakened political interest in what could help them further their own interests."

At the national level the informal sector still struggles to emerge as an important force. Casanovas and CEDLA's Larrazábal attribute its weakness to the high degree of fragmentation among the associations. The inability of associations inside and outside the same market to join forces illustrates just how fractious these organizations tend to be. Some federations of associations do exist, both citywide and a few nationwide, but these are weak, in part because of internal disputes. The associations have lobbied for microenterprises to have a simplified process for paying value-added tax, but they have not succeeded in changing policy. Some of the strongest leaders are attempting to link with other sectors to help revive the union movement. One political party, CONDEPA, springs in large part from indigenous rural society and informals. It shares in the governing ADN coalition, with a CONDEPA leader as minister of agriculture. Yet this party is also plagued by internal problems that prevent it from becoming an effective force. Casanovas sees glimmers that the political participation of the informal sector is becoming slightly more adept as younger leaders with more education emerge.

Meanwhile, the most important leaders in the country continue to come from the traditional elite. They seek the votes of informals and rural people by emphasizing their commitment to solving the poverty problem, but the basic mode is still "helping" the poor rather than including them as an integral part of the body politic. A significant step forward occurred in 1997, when, for the first time, legislative elections were geographically based: people elected candidates from their own districts rather than at large from a party slate. This change has important potential for changing the composition of the legislature. Fernando Romero comments that the country will not break through politically until there is a *cholo* leader. He makes an analogy between Bolivian elites and British rule over Hong Kong, and laughs that the Hong Kong governors have not yet left Bolivia, though perhaps they can now see that their lease is not permanent.

At the national level the effects of microfinance appear through changes in attitudes—both the attitudes of the informals themselves and attitudes of elites toward them. CEDLA's Larrazábal believes that the informal sector generally, and microfinance in particular, have helped make the country more governable, providing a cushion against social unrest. Microfinance clients have a greater stake in the system. This has been important in allowing the liberal economic experiment that began in 1985 to continue as long as it has. Pilar Ramírez agrees that without the outlet of the informal sector, people would have taken to the streets long before. Tacit acceptance of the economic experiment eroded quickly during the 1999/2000 recession. In April 2000, protests over water prices grew violent enough to cause several deaths and prompted the government to declare a state of emergency. Other protests followed throughout the year over a range of similar issues. Perhaps if microfinance had not been weakened by the over-indebtedness crisis and if government had been more careful about the effect of its customs reforms on the informal sector, popular patience would have held out a bit longer. Microfinance has also been an outlet for former activists. Ramírez notes, "You don't hear the radical voices anymore. They're off doing microfinance."

Certainly, microfinance has contributed to a changing perception of microenterprises as real businesspeople. Stories circulate about the bad treatment banks traditionally gave informals. A decade ago, microfinance practitioners agree, most of their clients would have been afraid to enter a bank, but today, as BancoSol's Domingo Fabbri says, "They will put on their best clothes and walk into Banco Boliviano Americano." Domingo Fabbri's market surveys have shown that clients today have very different perceptions about their acceptance at banks. Microfinance clients today are much more knowledgeable about banking practices than they were a decade ago and adopt a generally more commercial, businesslike outlook.

An important dimension of the changing image of the informal sector concerns the ability of people in the sector to pay for the services they receive. Horst Grebe comments that people now understand that informals are able to pay their loans back, but that this perception needs to be extended to other spheres of economic life. Monica Velasco believes it already has penetrated the world of social services. She sees that in all types of social services, including health care, organizations have embraced the principle of payment for services, and she attributes that change largely to the precedent microfinance programs have set.

Such changes in attitude underlie the two most important reforms undertaken during the Sanchéz de Lozada administration, Popular Participation and the joint-capitalization/pension-reform program. Popular Participation is a program to involve people at the local level, particularly in rural areas, in decisions about development activities in their communities. It sets up consultative processes through which communities develop plans for spending public funds destined for their municipalities. The links between Popular Participation and microfinance are indirect. Sanchéz de Lozada explains that his involvement with Prodem and BancoSol convinced him of the competence of the poor to manage their own affairs.

The connection of microfinance to the pension-reform program is more explicit. Sanchéz de Lozada carried out a privatization of large state-owned enterprises, which he called capitalization because the mechanisms involved bringing new private capital into the enterprises while retaining minority government ownership. Proceeds from capitalization formed the basis for a new private pension fund system. The state shares in privatized companies were used to set up BonoSol, a life annuity system for all Bolivians over 65 managed by private pension fund managers. The name BonoSol (Solidarity Bonus), reflects the link in the planners' minds to microfinance. Every year the system would pay around $250 to every older person in the country. Management of the $1.7 billion in the BonoSol fund assets was the carrot to attract fund managers into Bolivia to establish a new private pension system in place of the rapidly failing state social-security system.

For Sanchéz de Lozada, the idea behind BonoSol was very similar to that of microfinance: "The underlying philosophy of this government is that people can make better decisions about investing their money than the state, that you can do a lot more with poverty if you give people the power to decide how to spend."[13] Most political opponents of Sanchéz de Lozada disliked BonoSol intensely. Economist and former cabinet minister Herbert Müller stated, "Using the collective capitalization fund for something that does not target basic problems such as poverty or infrastructure is an unforgivable crime. You could build a major road every year. . . . And you could still put $50 million a year into targeted anti-poverty programs for health and education."[14] This argument parallels the argument (discussed above) that discounts the informal sector as an engine of development, stemming from a basic mistrust of what Sanchéz de Lozada called "the undertows of economic activity."

The ADN government modified BonoSol and dropped the name, but the new private pension fund system remains. And at this point, another evidence of microfinance's influence emerges. One of the two winners of the government's auction to become private pension fund managers was AFP Futuro, a company formed by the microfinance NGO Fades in a consortium with other

NGOs and experienced foreign pension-management companies. AFP Futuro is a sister company to EcoFuturo, the microfinance FFP Fades and the other NGOs created. A number of the managers in AFP Futuro are among the activists-turned-microfinanciers who helped build Bolivian microfinance. Among them, BancoSol's first human-resources manager, Manuel Cuevas, seeks to create the same kind of corporate culture at AFP Futuro that existed at BancoSol. Cuevas hopes that AFP Futuro will spread lessons from microfinance into a new segment of the financial sector by becoming an organization with a positive corporate culture that follows its mission to provide access to high quality financial services to ordinary Bolivians.

CONCLUSION

The accumulation of evidence suggests to this author that microfinance is assisting the informal sector in Bolivia to become a significant contributor to economic growth and poverty alleviation. Certainly, the informal sector was far more dynamic during the 1990s than anyone expected, making strides in scale, productivity, and sophistication. Tapping the undertows of the economy may not offer a magic formula for growth, but in Bolivia it is clearly part of any solution. The broader society now faces the need to respond to this awakening force, pulling it into the mainstream. Important steps to allow the sector to develop fully include improving export policies, resolving the treatment of informal importing, extending more small- and medium-scale finance, allowing easier formalization of enterprises, and furthering the integration of the sector into Bolivia's political life.

If Bolivian institutions can accomplish such steps, they will find that the people and enterprises of the informal sector hold an important part of the answer to the country's basic development challenge. Microfinance will have contributed directly to unleash the potential of the informal sector. It will also have helped change the way society regards microentrepreneurs, preparing the mainstream to respond more effectively to the opportunity the informal sector offers for Bolivia's future.

NOTES

1. World Bank, "Memorandum of the President of the International Development Association and the International Finance Corporation to the Executive Directors on a Country Assistance Strategy of the World Bank Group for the Republic of Bolivia," Report No. 17890-BO (Washington, D.C.: World Bank, 1998), i.
2. World Bank website www.worldbank.org data, updated September 1999.

3. Mario Riquena Pinto and Pedro Parada Balderrama, "Desempleo y Pobreza: El Rol de la Microempresa," in Viceministerio de Microempresa and Fundación para la Producción, *Microempresa vs. Pobreza: un desafío imposible?* (La Paz: Government of Bolivia, 1998), 127.

4. Amartya Sen, *Development as Freedom* (New York: Alfred A. Knopf, 1999), xii.

5. The figures in this and the next two paragraphs compare data presented in two CEDLA publications, Silvia Escóbar de Pabón, *Crisis, Política Economica y Dinámica de los Sectores Semiempresarial y Familiar: La Paz—Cochabamba—Santa Cruz, 1985–1989* (La Paz: Centro de Estudios Para el Desarrollo Laboral y Agrario, 1990) and Hernando Larrazábal Córdova, "La Microempresa ante los Desafíos del Desarrollo," in Viceministerio de Microempresa y Fundación para la Producción, *Microempresa vs. Pobreza.*

6. Larrazábal Córdova, "La Microempresa," 65. The data compares 1989 to 1995, a time when microfinance grew from a negligible scale to coverage of a significant share of the market. Unfortunately, in subsequent surveys Bolivia's statistical office dropped several categories for collecting data, making it impossible to examine changes within the informal sector after 1995. Hopefully, the statistical office will provide within-sector data in future survey research.

7. Anne Beasley and Fernando Mollinedo, "Results of a Nationwide Survey of Micro and Small Entrepreneurs Who Have Been Receiving Credit," unpublished (Washington, D.C.: USAID, February 1993).

8. Paul Mosley, "Metamorphosis from NGO to Commercial Bank: The Case of BancoSol in Bolivia," in *Finance Against Poverty*, ed. David Hulme and Paul Mosley, (London: Routledge, 1996), 2:17–20.

9. Beasley and Mollinedo, "Results."

10. Paul Mosley, "Microfinance and Poverty: Bolivia Case Study" (Washington, D.C.: Management Systems International, May 1999). Background paper for the World Development Report 2000/01, AIMS paper.

11. Mosley, "Microfinance and Poverty," 3 and 17.

12. Monique Cohen, "Bolivia: Loan Use by ProMujer Clients," unpublished (Washington, D.C.: USAID, July 1999), 2.

13. Richard Bauer and Sally Bowen, *The Bolivian Formula: From State Capitalism to Capitalisation* (Chile: McGraw-Hill/Interamericana de Chile, Ltda., 1997), 30.

14. Bauer and Bowen, *Bolivian Formula*, 30.

CHAPTER NINE

WHAT WE HAVE LEARNED

THE BOLIVIAN MICROFINANCE story offers a mother lode of experience relevant to microfinance and development beyond Bolivia's borders. In this chapter we attempt to mine that lode, to isolate silver nuggets that embody broader lessons. The Bolivian experience blends here with the author's own observations of international microfinance during the past ten years.

At the start of this book we introduced fundamental issues surrounding the evolution of microfinance and its contribution to economic and social development. The rest of the book has examined how those issues manifest themselves in Bolivia. This chapter distills the original issues into five questions, each highlighting choices that policy makers confront when making decisions about microfinance. With the important exception of savings, where Bolivian experience has little to offer, these five questions are among the most urgent confronting microfinance.

QUESTION 1.
HOW DO YOU MAKE A GREAT
MICROFINANCE INSTITUTION?

The microfinance field has set itself the challenge of meeting the financial needs of the world's enormous low-income population. The Microcredit Summit, a lobbying group on microfinance, wants services delivered to 100 million people by 2005, of whom it estimates 13.8 million received services by the year 2000. Nearly everyone in the field acknowledges that one of the most critical constraints to reaching the whole market is the shortage of competent institutions delivering microfinance.

The birth and maturation of Prodem and BancoSol illustrate how to create an outstanding microfinance institution. The achievements of Prodem in both its incarnations, and of BancoSol, have amply rewarded the efforts of their founders and contributed enormously to the development of microfinance, both in Bolivia and internationally. Several other Bolivian microfinance institutions, such as Caja Los Andes, FIE, and ProMujer, are also robust, important cases of institutional development.

Few institutions rank in the same league with the Bolivian institutions.[1] Why have these institutions succeeded when thousands of other programs fail basic challenges like controlling loan delinquency and covering costs? Why aren't there more good institutions? The challenge can be expressed even more pointedly: With the examples of the Bolivian organizations plain for all to see, *what excuse can there possibly be for creating an unsuccessful microfinance institution?* Whether they work with international organizations or indigenous initiatives, the promoters of microfinance today ought to operate with a deep grasp of how to create highly successful institutions.[2]

Although several Bolivian institutions offer lessons in institutional development, we will consider this question through a specific lens: the experience of Acción International in launching Prodem. Every new microfinance program requires an initiating force—some person or entity who owns the idea and pushes it toward reality. In Prodem's case this was Acción. Every donor, international promoter of microfinance, and local institution should consider whether its own strategy effectively combines the three key ingredients that Acción assembled: committed governance, dynamic management, and technical know-how.

Committed Governance

Through its own board of directors Acción successfully "pitched" a detailed concept of microfinance based on its technical experience to high-level contacts in the Bolivian business community. It assembled the best potential board members it could find, and in an unusual move it demanded a real commitment from them: personal financial contributions to the start-up budget. Thus, from the start Prodem's governance contained knowledgeable, influential, and highly committed people. Acción has repeatedly succeeded with this strategy. The truly surprising thing is that the other international microfinance promoters so rarely follow its example.

Some international organizations promoting microfinance simply ignore governance until too late, starting lending operations without creating an institution. Perhaps they are more interested in the immediate delivery of services than in the creation of an institution or are simply responding to a donor's offer of money. When they prepare to withdraw several years later, they wake up to find that they lack the relationships necessary to build an institution. They hunt for potential board members, but the time to create local ownership would have been much earlier. Even if they identify good candidates, the candidates lack commitment to the institution which, after all, was created by someone else. This scenario is distressingly common. In fact, as described in chapter 4, Crecer was in this predicament in 1999, having operated for more than five years as a project rather than an institution.

Other microfinance promoters seem afraid to build strong local governance, fearing loss of control. Acción's roots in the American business community with ties to Latin America gave it entree to top Bolivian business leaders. Other international organizations target different segments, not all of whom have the combination of business sense, commitment to mission, and influence that backers of microfinance need. They choose board members they feel comfortable with but who lack the vision and stature needed to lead a pathbreaking organization. Subsequently, the promoters are either reluctant to relinquish control, recognizing the weakness of the board they have created, or they leave behind a troubled or mediocre organization. These scenarios also abound.

A third approach international organizations use involves support to existing organizations that already have a governance structure. This approach is attractive in principle, and a number of strong microfinance programs have followed this model, though not in Bolivia. This model often fails, however, either because of differences in the vision or because the international organization is not close enough to the institution to influence it deeply. International microfinance organizations increasingly seek equity shares in such institutions as a means to establish ongoing links.

Management

For the second key ingredient, management, Acción hired the most dynamic executive director it could find, Pancho Otero, a Bolivian with relevant experience and a personality suited for leadership. Prodem hired all other senior staff directly, and they were an outstanding team. This staff was dedicated enough to go into the markets themselves and learn how to make loans from the start. The team developed a vibrant corporate culture. Prodem became more than just their job. It was their cause. Moreover, Prodem and Acción gave Otero the right combination of responsibility to make decisions, accountability for results, and technical support.

Many of the most respected microfinance institutions started with a dynamic leader—a Pancho Otero, a Mohammad Yunus (Grameen Bank,

Bangladesh), or a Shafique Chowdrey (Association for Social Advancement, Bangladesh). Certainly, truly charismatic, entrepreneurial leaders are scarce in any country, but Bolivia, a small and poor country with a weak education system, produced several outstanding microfinance leaders. Perhaps Bolivia's human endowment was unusual, but it seems more likely that for a variety of historical reasons discussed in chapters 4 and 5, microfinance attracted some of Bolivia's best and brightest.

Few microfinance programs around the world make a special effort to attract the best and the brightest. They hire on the basis of credentials rather than personal characteristics. The ex-accountants and mid-level bank officers often hired to run microfinance programs rarely have had a chance to develop leadership qualities inside their previous institutions. Mistakes continue after hiring, as Peter Kooi, technical advisor to Acleda (a rapidly growing microfinance institution in Cambodia), notes: most donor-backed projects treat these essential managers like employees, rather than supporting them to become leaders. Pancho Otero emphasizes that genuine leaders express moral authority. When managers are treated as employees who are told what to do, their moral leadership is less likely to surface. Perhaps if microfinance programs thought more carefully about what highly talented people are looking for—probably a genuine combination of trust and responsibility—they could craft strategies for attracting and nurturing them.

The problem is compounded in countries with a shortage of well-qualified local candidates. In such countries microfinance programs usually place an expatriate in the executive spot. This can be a good strategy if the organization identifies and builds up a local candidate from the start. K-REP in Kenya began this way in 1983. By 1988 the expatriate went home, leaving a highly competent Kenyan director, Kimanthi Mutua, who has gone on to create K-REP Bank. For every story of this kind, however, there are two, three, or more where the international promoters cannot extricate the expatriate because they have neglected to nurture strong successors.

Technical Know-How

Much of the third core ingredient, know-how, came initially from Acción itself. Acción trained Prodem staff in the solidarity group methodology, and it designed management information systems. Acción maintained quality control in the initial phase by employing Otero directly and by frequent visits to the project. It monitored Prodem's performance regularly.

Know-how and monitoring would seem to be such obvious requirements that no promoter would leave them out. What a surprise to find that they are still frequently omitted or vastly underestimated. No one would start a microfinance program in Bolivia today without first obtaining expert senior staff with long microfinance experience. In countries whose microfinance industries are just beginning, know-how must be sought internationally. Unfortunately, recourse to international experts often upsets North-South sensitivities.

Programs that lack know-how seem to regard microfinance as something anyone can do. Microfinance is not rocket science, but it does involve a body of knowledge beyond common sense. It is an emerging profession that combines financial management and banking operations skills with knowledge of the informal-sector market and specially adapted techniques for serving that market. The pioneers of microfinance had to figure these things out for themselves, but now that they are known, new programs can build on their experience—and must if they are to be competitive.

Local initiatives lacking international partners are especially prone to struggle along without adequate technical support, often as a matter of pride. In Bolivia, FIE, Fades, and others never had international partners. They developed their own technical competence through hard trial and error and observation of organizations like BancoSol and Caja Los Andes. They succeeded, but without partners their roads have been rugged. Even so, these organizations have been well connected to the world of microfinance, actively learning from international experience. The key lesson here is that know-how is not a matter of North vs. South, but of efficient transfer of knowledge. Because of their exposure to multiple countries, international organizations are in a good position to spread skills. The best ones do this increasingly through South-South exchanges.

Surprisingly, however, some international promoters fail to provide sufficient know-how. Several well-known international organizations based their start-up strategies on board development, leaving to the board most of the operational decisions (for example, methodology). They limit provision of technical expertise, either because they do not have it, or as an ideological preference in favor of local decision-making. This strategy condemns their partners to reinvent wheels that are already turning elsewhere and to falter in competing with entrants having access to international know-how.

Other international organizations underestimate the amount of technical support needed to launch an organization. In Prodem's first year Acción made six technical-assistance visits to Bolivia and sent Prodem staff on an equal number of observations to other countries, in addition to having a full-time staff member as executive director. In contrast, international organizations commonly start projects by assigning one international advisor to a location, giving her a budget and some loan capital, and then ignoring her until progress reports are due to donors. This low-cost option may seem attractive to donors, but it does not create winning organizations. Even the most talented executive cannot build an organization alone.

Why do so many organizations start up with one or more of these three key ingredients—governance, management, and know-how—missing or present only inadequately?[3] Many donors and promoters of microfinance follow a community-development paradigm, which places supreme value on local decision-making and regards the involvement of international experts as at best a necessary evil. A business paradigm is more pragmatic. Business investors make sure a new company has a solid group of people behind it and access to high-quality technical skills. Investors expect to stay involved in oversight and possibly decision-making as long as their money is invested. Decisions about governance and technical support depend on who is best qualified and best placed to make them. A pure business perspective may not be appropriate for donor-funded microfinance start-ups (unless microfinance is already dominated by private actors) because such start-ups do legitimately aim to create local decision-making and implementation capacity. Bolivian experience has been instrumental in demonstrating how to blend community development goals with a more businesslike approach.

QUESTION 2.
HOW DO YOU CREATE A THRIVING
MICROFINANCE INDUSTRY?

Although microfinance insiders often talk about "the industry," microfinance is not yet really an industry in most countries, but rather a field within the development profession. It only makes sense to speak of an industry in a country like Bolivia, where microfinance is a set of products offered in the marketplace by a mix of competing providers whose livelihood is derived mainly from their customers. Bolivian microfinance became an industry when its leading institutions achieved profitability, drawing in new funding and competition. Similar breakthroughs are needed in every country where microfinance seeks to become a real industry.

Answering the question, Why did it happen in Bolivia?, is like ticking off every box on a checklist for assessing whether a country setting is conducive for microfinance.[4] The first several items on that checklist involve economic conditions. When microfinance began, Bolivia had achieved political and economic stability after a long period of chaos. It had tamed inflation. Government had stepped back from active provision of directed credit and had freed interest rates. The growth of microfinance in Bolivia during a time when the government was pursuing liberal economic policies attests to the proposition that has recently gained currency in development circles: development aid works when good policies are in place.[5]

Continuing with the checklist, the explosion of the urban informal sector created huge and urgent demand for credit among customers crowded into small areas. These customers already had a strong cultural tradition of honoring obligations. And, finally, Bolivia had a cadre of people willing and able to build competent institutions. So Bolivia had it all: conditions, customers, and the raw material for institution-building.

This checklist, though simple and perhaps obvious, does help explain why microfinance has or has not emerged in various countries. For example, until recently, Brazil had virtually no microfinance industry because of its inability to shake off inflation. Argentina has been slower than some other Latin American countries both because the demand is lower and because of inappropriate economic policies. In Mozambique, microfinance began to develop when its war ended and government put good macroeconomic policies in place, but growth is constrained by Mozambique's serious shortage of educated people to staff new institutions. Uganda, with a deeper pool of people to draw on, developed a vibrant microfinance industry in a very short time.

These general observations about preconditions are already well known throughout the world of microfinance. Bolivia's example offers several additional lessons.

Microfinance thrived in Bolivia because it tapped into forces that were driving the country forward: the motivation of big business to become more socially responsible; the desire of militant activists to leave their protests behind and start building; a perception that microfinance was both a revolutionary cause and an affirmation of the market system; and the dynamism of the urban informal markets themselves. The vitality of these forces helps explain why microfinance didn't so much grow as take off.

The presence of this energy in Bolivia should not dissuade other countries with different dynamics from pursuing microfinance. Rather, it suggests that, in every country, promoters of microfinance should connect to local progressive forces. In Bangladesh, for example, microfinance sprang from the movement that created massive, powerful social NGOs with strong philosophies about women and poverty. In every country microfinance will have a unique national character.

In Bolivia part of that national character is the commercial orientation of microfinance. From an early stage in Bolivia it was sensible to think that one day private capital would substitute for donor capital. There were money and capital markets to tap, and reaching such markets required achievement of commercial-level operations. The presence of such opportunities in a modernizing financial sector is driving microfinance throughout Latin America. In countries with weaker financial systems, particularly outside Latin America, the path toward integration with the financial system—or even the reasons to do so—remains unclear. Bangladeshi microfinance institutions have become parallel financial systems rather than integrating into the sickly mainstream system. In Uganda the shocking number of bank failures prompts microfinance NGOs to wonder why they should be barred from accepting deposits; after all, they must be at least as safe as the banks.

If one is convinced, as is the author, that the long-run future of microfinance lies in becoming part of a permanent financial system, the example of Bolivia (and its counter-examples) demonstrate that microfinance should be considered in the context of overall financial-sector reform. It is not an afterthought in the overall financial-sector development picture. A modernizing financial sector is a prerequisite for the transformation of microfinance into a real industry, and microfinance may contribute in turn to the strengthening of the financial sector.

Such considerations do not indicate, however, that government should direct the path of microfinance. Bolivia shows that microfinance evolves happily with little direct government support. Government's main contribution to the industry was to stay out of the way by closing state banks and avoiding directives. The Superintendency of Banks did not regulate microfinance during the formative period, and once the first microfinance institutions had matured enough to knock on the superintendent's doors, he applied regulations flexibly. Once convinced that BancoSol could manage solidarity group loans safely, he licensed it, even though the bank was permanently out of compliance on several regulatory points. Only gradually, and with a great deal of consultation, did the Superintendency seek to solidify an understanding of microfinance into specific regulations. This process is still going on today. In contrast, banking authorities in many countries seek to define regulations for microfinance institutions in advance of their development, thus risking choking off potentially crucial innovations and adaptations.[6]

Quite a different lesson from Bolivia concerns the influence of highly successful institutions in speeding the growth of a country's microfinance industry. The early success of Prodem and then BancoSol helped create a virtuous circle of learning and higher achievement among Bolivian microfinance institutions. Anyone could see and imitate the strong institutions, which also served as training grounds for the new microfinance professionals. When one institution achieved higher financial performance, the bar rose for all institutions. Some of the worst ideas disappeared, as good practice vanquished bad practice simply by succeeding. By the mid-1990s, all the significant programs charged full-cost interest rates. The definitions of financial viability tightened over time, and the subsidized programs either changed or died out.

In fact, as chapter 4 described, methodologies converged around three basic models: individual, solidarity group, and village banking. Convergence is also seen in other countries that have a strong leading microfinance institution; until recently, nearly all the Bangladeshi programs were Grameen Bank variations and most East African programs used K-REP's adaptation of Grameen. Recently, microfinance observers like Micro-Save Africa have pointed out one cost of such convergence—a limited array of services serving a specific population stratum.[7] In Bangladesh, microfinance institutions ignore the male half of the population, while in Bolivia, they ignore the savings half of finance.

However, this observation does not diminish the great value successful institutions have in spreading know-how like brushfire. CGAP's Richard Rosenberg, among others, has long promoted the view that creating one excellent institution is far more important than creating several moderately successful institutions because of the spontaneous spread effect a great institution will have. He learned this lesson in Bolivia.

QUESTION 3.
IS THE BOLIVIA MODEL OF NGO TRANSFORMATION RELEVANT AROUND THE WORLD?

The example set by Bolivian NGOs becoming licensed financial institutions has become a kind of standard to which many microfinance institutions aspire, or toward which donors push them. Most observers no longer consider the NGO form as a natural endpoint in the development of a microfinance institution. NGOs cannot accept savings from the public, nor can they reliably escape dependence on donor sources of funds. With these limitations in mind, transformation has become almost a presumption, and organizations wishing to remain NGOs find themselves on the defensive.

Yet, the number of NGOs actually following the path of BancoSol and the FFPs is still fairly small. The MicroFinance Network, a club of some of the best-performing microfinance institutions around the world, started in 1993 as a group of organizations contemplating following BancoSol's example. Several of the best-known transformations have involved its members: K-REP Bank in Kenya, Mibanco in Peru, BancoAdemi in the Dominican Republic, ACEP in Senegal, and Acleda in Cambodia. But outside this group, the number of transformations remains small. If transformation is such an important step in sustainable microfinance, why have so few organizations taken it?

The Bolivia Model of transformation is a beautiful concept. At its core is an approach to solving the problem of ownership—a mix of owners and a linked governance structure that, as Gabriel Schor of IPC says, simulate the "ideal capitalist." The ideal capitalist upholds the mission of microfinance toward the poor while vigilantly watching the bottom line. The Bolivia Model balances owners from several sources. Although each institution varies, the four key elements of the structure are the same: the originating NGO (to uphold the mission), local private investors (some motivated by public recognition, others by returns), public-sector investors such as multilateral investment banks (substantial investment and prestige), and international technical partners like Acción and IPC (mission and know-how). A fifth element, employee ownership, has emerged more recently. BancoSol has gone farther than the others in opening itself to genuinely private, profit-motivated investors, while the other institutions have held control in a smaller group.

There is no perfect solution to ownership of financial institutions, as the Bolivian institutions well know. These models all have vulnerabilities. The model stops short of full privatization in the sense of freedom from all public sources of funds and ownership. But the mix in Bolivia contains enough accountability to satisfy bank regulators and capital markets and enough altruism to secure the focus on microfinance. Much of the credit for the Bolivia Model comes from the combination of patience and high standards of the Superintendency of Banks. The ownership blend originated in part from the Superintendency's views on the attributes of accountable owners.

The Bolivia Model also provides an excellent solution for the original NGO. It can tackle new challenges, benefiting from its ownership of the financial institution but keeping operations separate. The example of Prodem's rural outreach after the BancoSol spin-off shows how valuable the NGO's second life can be.

Despite its attractive features, this model has not been as widely applied outside Bolivia as one might expect. Some reasons for this are not especially encouraging. Many NGOs fear the loss of control that comes with dispersed ownership. Proposals featuring majority NGO ownership may get past banking authorities in some countries, especially if the NGO aspires to a limited institutional form, taking deposits from a localized clientele. However, majority ownership by an NGO does not solve the original ownership problem; it just disguises it. An NGO-dominated ownership structure is unlikely to win the new organization a place in money or capital markets, though it may qualify it for lines of credit or discount facilities. For example, CARD in the Philippines has chosen to retain ownership in the hands of clients and the NGO. Its ownership dynamics will be entirely different from the corporate model Bolivian institutions represent.[8] Its structure is unlikely to lead to real independence from donors.

Another problem has been lack of profitability. Until a microfinance institution can reliably break even without donor subsidies, its capital will continually erode, and a responsible regulatory agency will not grant it a license. Surprisingly, a number of NGOs attempt to transform well before profitability is in sight, and a few regulators don't seem to mind positive bottom lines propped up by ongoing donor assistance. In these cases the transformation is one of form but not reality.

Most organizations will transform just as much or as little as necessary to achieve their objectives. Often that objective is rather limited. Several transforming NGOs in Peru just want to gain access to public-sector lines of credit. Elsewhere, they want to get licenses to operate as limited types of institutions such as credit unions or rural banks. The Bolivian NGOs wanted access to licenses and lines of credit, but they also wanted to become full-fledged members of the financial system so that they could raise funds from commercial sources on a leveraged basis. This objective requires higher levels of accountability and performance. Gaining complete independence from donors has not usually been a central objective, as the Bolivian organizations attest. Only BancoSol wanted to attract private equity capital on a genuine investment basis.

To summarize, the Bolivia Model of NGO transformation sets a rigorous path for other microfinance institutions to follow in its insistence on mixed ownership, commercial standards, and profitable operations. If more transformations met this standard there would be more microfinance institutions gaining genuine independence from donors and integration into the financial system. However, many transformations will probably fall short of this standard, either because their objectives are more limited or because the local authorities are less rigorous.

One encouraging reason the Bolivia Model has not been applied more often is that the promoters of microfinance are finding easier paths to the desired end. They start new institutions as financial institutions (for example, Banco Solidario in Ecuador), or they assist existing banks to launch microfinance operations (for example, Centenary Bank in Uganda). In bypassing the NGO form, they bypass many of the travails involved in the often tortuous process of transformation. Over the next decade these direct models are likely to supplant NGO transformation. These direct paths exist today, however, only because pioneering organizations, including the NGOs in Bolivia, showed that microfinance institutions could operate commercially.

A question remains open regarding the long-run viability of transformation into specialized finance companies, such as Bolivia's FFPs. These institutions suffered during the 1999 microfinance crisis, prompting some observers, including Prodem's Eduardo Bazoberry and former Superintendent Jacques Trigo to comment on their vulnerability relative to more diversified commercial banks. The pressures facing such specialized institutions are discussed in the next section, on competition.

QUESTION 4.
HOW WILL COMPETITION AND COMMERCIAL
ENTRY CHANGE MICROFINANCE?

A major portion of the international microfinance community has long advocated the integration of microfinance into the mainstream financial system, looking toward a day of spontaneous commercial entry. Until recently, one could only speculate about what microfinance would be like in such conditions, but in Bolivia today, and increasingly across Latin America, speculation gives way to reality.

Bolivia's experience confirms that the future of microfinance lies in the mainstream financial sector. The advantages of providing services through a formal financial institution are so strong that once the industry in Bolivia crossed this line, with BancoSol and Caja Los Andes, there was no turning back. By mid-1999, NGOs (excluding NGOs about to become FFPs) accounted for only 16 percent of all microfinance loans in Bolivia and 8 percent of the total microfinance portfolio. In the rest of Latin America this trend is advancing, but not as fast as in Bolivia: 26 percent of the funds and 47 percent of the clients remain with NGOs.[9]

Around the world new donor-sponsored microfinance initiatives increasingly start with existing financial institutions, from the Commercial Bank of Zimbabwe to the Banco do Nordeste in Brazil. Often these initiatives build on the branch structure, technology, and access to funds of the sponsoring bank to reach a large scale more quickly than is possible with a new NGO.[10] At the same time, the private sector has begun entering the microfinance market on a profit-driven basis with or without benefit of subsidies. In Bolivia, as in Peru, Chile, Colombia, and elsewhere, this entry takes many forms. It includes direct copying of microfinance methodologies (for example, Fassil), adaptation of some of the ideas from microfinance within a more mainstream approach (Banco Económico), and the offer of products that overlap substantially with the microfinance market (the consumer lenders). This trend is advancing rapidly around the world. For example, in Mozambique, a country seemingly unripe for a commercial approach, a leading private bank has, with

IPC, launched a commercial microfinance venture.

Involvement by commercial institutions allows rapid expansion of coverage and reduction of external subsidies. If Bolivia is any indication, competition will bring the clients of microfinance good news in terms of lower prices, quicker and easier service, and a variety of new products. It will bring greater value to an increasingly large number of customers. These are the very goals the founders of microfinance sought. In this way, competition is the culmination of their quest. This major victory should not be forgotten as the microfinance field struggles with the challenges commercialization poses.

The Bolivian experience presents an early laboratory for examining these challenges, starting with the behavior of commercial entrants. Private lenders are not concerned to define themselves within microfinance's traditional borders. This is both a source of creative ideas and a potential threat to those who want to protect microfinance from change. Some joke nervously that microcredit may finally reduce to a few lines about microenterprise on a bank loan application form. In Bolivia, much of the rest of South America, and South Africa, the biggest competition comes from consumer lenders. The Bolivian consumer-finance story involves enormous blundering by private lenders who did not realize how little they knew about their market, and whose mistakes cost themselves and others dearly. Yet, if the market opportunity is real, private entrants will come back smarter. Diversified financial institutions like banks have resources to enter a market in a big way very quickly, possibly including the ability to price out weaker competitors. Finally, the private sector is likely to aim at the upper end of the microfinance market. Although the evidence that commercialization brings upward drift is mixed,[11] the possibility that it will leave the poor behind is a major preoccupation within microfinance circles. Taken together, these changes mean that microfinance institutions have lost much of their control over their industry.

Among institutions, competition is bringing severe pressure on rigid or inconvenient methodologies. Evidence shows individual lending driving out group lending. In Bolivia the ratio of individual to group loans has grown ever since Caja Los Andes and FIE began making significant market inroads. In December 1997, individual loans made up 41 percent of the aggregate group and individual microfinance portfolio. One and a half years later (June 1999), they accounted for 50 percent of the portfolio.[12] Today that figure would certainly be higher. Christen observes the same trend in Chile and Paraguay.[13]

A shift toward individual lending entails more traditional forms of collateral and more formal documentation. Desire to maintain a good credit rating will keep repayments up, but this will not bind customers to any one lender. Lenders will seek other ways to attract valuable repeat clients. These changes strike at the original foundations on which microcredit grew. As the basis for lending changes and as consumers become more demanding, microfinance institutions will become vulnerable to sudden changes in client behavior. In Bolivia this has included both desertion and over-indebtedness.

Bolivia's over-indebtedness crisis illustrates a dangerous dynamic inherent in competitive retail lending. Similar dynamics are turning up in places as diverse as Bangladesh and South Africa. While credit may be a wonderful tool, too much credit is dangerous for borrower and lender alike. Fernando Romero worries about addicting clients to credit. So do observers of microfinance in Bangladesh, where in some districts market penetration ratios are over 50 percent and clients have a choice of up to five lenders. The over-indebtedness crisis unfolding in these districts parallels Bolivia's: clients taking on too much debt as delinquency rises through the system.[14]

A tenet of microfinance is that loan sizes must match repayment capacity. But when offering larger loans becomes a marketing advantage, even the most principled lender is tempted to push beyond prudent limits. The market dynamics associated with overlending require a collective response, supported by regulatory standards. The problem of multiple loans requires top-quality credit bureaus, while the problem of excessive loan sizes requires industry-wide lending norms. In every country where microfinance is growing, credit-bureau development should be high on the agenda, even if commercialization is some years away, as it takes time to perfect such systems.

As commercialization and competition grow, microfinance lenders must face an extremely uncomfortable fact: their product does not look very different to the client from the product of lenders they consider unscrupulous. This observation is particularly awkward for microlenders whose zeal grew from criticizing banks. In Bolivia the consumer lenders provided loans with similar terms (size range, duration, interest rate), with a similar quick turn-around (a few days), and with similar rhetoric about the benefits to the client (growth and prosperity). As the debtors' protest shows, the clients barely distinguished between the altruistic microlenders and the *desleal* (disloyal) consumer lenders.

This client reaction should provoke microfinance practitioners to serious rethinking along two lines. First, what *does* distinguish lending that is good for the client from destructive lending? Second, if the private sector contains unscrupulous elements, how should the microfinance industry position itself? These are questions microfinance practitioners will need to work on during the next few years. The Bolivian experience suggests a few directions.

It shows that the principal public-image issues for microfinance are high interest rates and the consequences of default—age-old concerns about moneylending. It is ironic that the Bolivian debtors associations played the interest rate card, despite the facts that rates had never before been at issue between microlenders and their clients (and still weren't in most cases), and that rates were declining under competition. Money-lending also has a bad reputation in part because it is associated with leading people into the debt addiction Fernando Romero bemoans. One reason microfinance has been so zealous in maintaining low delinquency is to ensure that its borrowers can handle their debt. A few defaults are necessary to create object lessons, but not the 7 to 10 percent of clients the consumer lenders considered routine. Bolivia's consumer lenders tolerated a level of default that the microlenders considered unconscionable because of its toll in broken families, and because other borrowers had to pay for those failures. Microfinance needs to define clearly what lending practices are good for clients, recognizing that the human weakness for fast cash may make a purely market-based solution less than ideal.

Microlenders in South Africa made some early attempts to meet public-image concerns. In South Africa consumer lenders to low-income salaried workers charged very high interest rates and used somewhat coercive measures to secure repayment. Public anger toward these lenders affected the image of the microlenders. To distance themselves from practices the public dislikes, the Microfinance Alliance, an association of microlenders, put forward a code of conduct stating norms of good practice. Predictably, the consumer lenders countered with an association and code of conduct of their own. Clearly, the burden is on the microfinance profession to define and promote good, ethical practice in an effective way.

The commercialization of microfinance raises an interesting analogy to organic farming. Both microfinance and organic farming started as revolutionary movements radically critical of mainstream practices. They gradually developed their own techniques to a level that attracted commercial operators. In organic farming some large food processing and supermarket corporations have started organic divisions. All the companies appropriate the rhetoric of purity that surrounds organic products. The involvement of commercial players has sparked intense controversy within the organic movement. An organic industry analyst put the dilemma this way: "Is this about getting better food grown in an environmental way to the most people possible, or is it about creating an alternative food system that is small, local and sensitive to issues like social justice?"[15] Substitute "finance" for "food" and "poverty" for "social justice," and the voice could come from microcredit.

Microfinance advocates for poverty alleviation and empowerment profoundly distrust the private sector. They fear, with some reason, that the private sector will take up the vehicle but not the values. Once commercialization begins, however, the bare truth appears to be that utopian microfinance institutions—like organic farms—cannot isolate themselves. Like it or not, the future of microfinance requires engagement with the mainstream. The prudent course is to work with the private entrants to ensure that they adopt the values and practices of greatest importance to microfinance.

QUESTION 5.
WHAT MESSAGES DOES MICROFINANCE HOLD FOR DEVELOPMENT THINKING?

Development policy makers—in donor agencies, international NGOs, and national governments—often regard microfinance as outside the main focus of their concern, sometimes even dismissing it as a fad. Yet over the course of its evolution, microfinance has developed several important messages that are penetrating development thought in three areas—development finance, attitudes about the poor, and concepts of development assistance.

Development Finance

The early experimenters in microfinance in Bolivia and elsewhere did not set out to transform the whole development finance field. Now, however, development finance as a field has all but disappeared, leaving microfinance to take up the baton.

Microfinance emerged into a vacuum created by the failure of the old models of development finance. Finance gurus had convinced governments everywhere to curtail directed credit as part of financial-sector liberalization programs.[16] However, the gurus had nothing to suggest regarding the low end of the economy. In Bolivia the state-owned development banks had closed, taking with them most small-business lending and rural finance. The cooperatives looked moribund, buried under governance problems. The proponents of financial-sector liberalization succeeded in changing the concept of development finance into financial-sector development, a much more viable approach for the long run, but they left it up to the private sector to choose which clients to serve. This notion, though based on sound economic principles, left an enormous unfulfilled agenda.

When microfinance first appeared, development thinkers largely disregarded it, partly because it served a clientele those same thinkers also disregarded. If they worried at all about how to finance underserved groups, they worried about small enterprise and agriculture—regarded as more productive than the informal sector. For example, not until the mid-1990s do World Bank reports on Bolivia mention microfinance. Why would a small movement working with clients most policy makers dismissed emerge as a leading voice in development finance? It happened because microfinance approached finance in two novel ways, both in harmony with the dominant financial-sector liberalization movement.

First, microfinance focused on building lending businesses that could sustain themselves. The early promoters of microfinance in Bolivia (and in selected other countries) saw that credit programs were just gap fillers that did not create permanent change. They knew that the subsidized credit approach went bankrupt because it neglected the needs of financial institutions to operate profitably. Microfinance embraced lessons coming from the advocates of financial-sector liberalization; for example, pricing products for full cost recovery and removing government from the credit delivery process. Throughout the 1990s, much of the learning within microfinance involved incorporating the techniques of financial-institution management into microfinance institutions. To the surprise of most development-finance gurus, institutions learning their lessons well succeeded in becoming sustainable.

Second, microfinance saw finance as a process of technical innovation driven by the needs of the customer. This observation was something nearly everyone else missed. Microfinance began as the application of a few innovative techniques for lending to the poor, adapted from the milieu of the clients. Prodem staff went into markets and talked to vendors about their businesses, and they adjusted their products to fit. The private financial sector constantly generates client-driven innovation, but somehow that idea had not penetrated development finance, whose economists tended to think of the financial sector in static terms. The products offered through most development-finance efforts had been mainly "dumbed-down" versions of commercial products. Even the cooperatives, although they got it right on savings, offered traditional loan products not well suited for microenterprises. With an understanding of how the informal sector worked, microfinance institutions created a market based on a clientele not reachable through traditional banking technology.

The application of these two principles, financial viability and finance as client-based innovation, enabled the microfinance institutions to reach scale and sustainability. And success in scale and sustainability gave microfinance its voice in development finance.

Since the collapse of the old development finance, microfinance has been nearly the only force trying to fill the empty agenda. Few advances have been made, for example, in the areas of agricultural credit or small-business finance. Throughout its first decade, however, microfinance stuck pretty close to its corner; in Bolivia this was urban microenterprise credit. In recent years, as it has gained maturity and in the continuing absence of other players, microfinance has begun to tackle more. In chapter 7 we discussed its attempts to address rural finance, savings, and small business. Bolivia offers some evidence of success on the rural front, with Prodem and Caja Los Andes basing rural lending on the diversified economic portfolios of rural households, and with Prodem layering diversification throughout its institutional structure. The ultimate success of microfinance at tackling the remaining development-finance agenda depends on innovation. Its systematic search for innovation is much more likely to lead to breakthroughs than the old approach, which assumed stasis. Nevertheless, innovations do not appear on command, and they seem to come most often from the ground up. No one can say whether or when microfinance will help close the remaining gaps in the financial sectors of developing countries.

The important point is that as policy makers seek progress on the unfinished development-finance agenda, they remember the lessons of microfinance concerning product innovation and institutional viability. A retreat from these advances constantly threatens. The old quick fixes, like bribing banks with lines of credit and guarantees to offer inherently unprofitable products, continue to tempt those with an urgent desire to get credit to their preferred sector. But the old model did not work then, and, for the same reasons, will not work now. The only basis for real progress is the creation through innovation of products and institutions that can sustain themselves.

A final note on microfinance in the financial sector: experience in Bolivia confirms that all financial institutions remain fragile and vulnerable. The mechanisms available for protection against the risks inherent in finance are still imperfect. Even the best-designed and -managed financial institution can, and probably will at some time, stumble.

The Role of the Poor in Development

Microfinance in Bolivia presents an image of the poor and the informal sector as economic actors. This image is relevant for conceptualizing approaches to poverty. The poor participate actively in their betterment. They are not passive recipients of assistance, not simply refugees from a failed formal sector, but economic actors out to improve the quality of their lives, and as such, they are potential contributors to economic growth.

Going farther, the Bolivian approach to microfinance placed the poor into a business context, with individuals as customers and the sector as a market. This latter perspective has a very specific corollary: the poor can and will pay for services designed to meet their needs. The double principle (paying for services and designing appropriate services) has direct application in areas like health, training, housing, municipal services, and any other area where the poor receive services. Microfinance is not the only development movement to have increasing respect for the capabilities of the poor, but it has gone farther than other fields in placing the relationship between the poor person and the service provider on a businesslike footing.

This businesslike approach is directly counter to another prevailing model for uplifting the poor: collective action and protest. Microfinance sees the basis for progress as the individual operating within a network of facilitating institutions. Different from more militant views, Pancho Otero's vision of empowerment is the self-esteem created through work. Microcredit contributes by facilitating the client's ability to work.

The microfinance approach also differs from more mainstream approaches to poverty alleviation that talk in terms of government delivery of social and other services. The World Bank's *World Development Report* for 1990, on poverty, for example, espoused delivery of health, education, and physical infrastructure as the main weapons against poverty. Ten years later the *World Development Report* revisited poverty, and this time its views echoed the model microfinance illustrates. In 2000, the *Report* framed the poverty debate in terms of facilitating the ability of the poor to pursue progress by giving them tools and access to the institutions, including the financial sector, that provide opportunities in society. The mechanisms for this include greater political participation and the restructuring of dominant institutions to serve the poor. Microfinance has been one of several movements during the 1990s that have led mainstream thinkers like the authors of the report to an understanding of the poor as active economic agents.

In Bolivia the fight to recognize the informal sector as a potentially progressive economic force is still an uphill battle, hampered by the limitations of the informals themselves, particularly in education and organization. Microfinance in Bolivia has helped raise the profile of this sector. The ADN government's task force on microenterprises represents the first time in the country that the problems facing microenterprises are addressed through dialogue among government, the private sector, and advocacy groups. This task force has potential to make progress on major constraints to the sector, such as import and export policies. It would never have been formed without the prominence microfinance brought to the sector.

Development Assistance

Finally, Bolivia's microfinance experience provides some generally applicable lessons about donors and development assistance. As noted, it illustrates the proposition that aid works best in a good policy environment. Beyond that, it shows a particular model of development assistance in which development aid helps create structures that become institutions within the national economy.

This concept is very different from much of what development assistance has been about (getting roads and schools built, delivering condoms and vaccinations). Its theme is building a long-run future, rather than reacting to the shortcomings of the present. This model uses subsidies but treats them as start-up investments, expecting institutions to stand on their own over time. Importantly, in Bolivia's case the primary initiative came from the implementers, while donors took a more supportive role and urged the field to higher achievements. Government facilitated by allowing the implementers free rein.

When the task at hand involves institutional development, the experience of Bolivian microfinance is highly instructive. It shows that the art of development assistance consists of catalyzing the exchange of ideas and nurturing leadership within a framework of high and rising standards.

NOTES

1. For example, the database of the *MicroBanking Bulletin* No. 4 (February 2000) includes 60 fully sustainable microfinance institutions internationally that are generally compatible in performance with the five leading Bolivian institutions. This database is believed to include most sustainable programs.
2. International promoters of microfinance that have appeared in this book include Acción, IPC, Freedom from Hunger, Calmeadow, World Council of Credit Unions, and Finca. Others not discussed here include Women's World Banking, Opportunity International, Save the Children, CARE, Catholic Relief Services, Des Jardins, Socodevi, Food for the Hungry, Mennonite Economic Development Association, Volunteers in Technical Assistance, and ACDI/VOCA, to name some larger North American organizations.
3. Although this discussion focuses on creating strong microfinance organizations, it does not address the question of sustaining and growing such organizations, beyond pointing out that organizations possessed of strong governance, management, and technical expertise have the crucial elements for continued success. Development of microfinance institutions is the subject of much how-to literature, such as Robert Peck Christen, *Banking Services for the Poor: Managing for Financial Success* (Somerville, Mass.: Acción International, 1997); Joanna Ledgerwood, *Microfinance Handbook: An Institutional and Financial Perspective*, Sustainable Banking with the Poor (Washington, D.C.: World Bank, 1999); and Elisabeth Rhyne and Linda Rotblatt, *What Makes Them Tick? Exploring the Anatomy of Major Microfinance Institutions* (Cambridge, Mass.: Acción International, 1994).
4. See, for example, Ledgerwood, *Microfinance Handbook*, chap. 1.
5. See World Bank, *Assessing Aid: What Works, What Doesn't and Why* (New York: Oxford University Press, 1998).
6. For more on this perspective about regulation, see Robert Peck Christen and

Richard Rosenberg, "The Rush to Regulate: Legal Frameworks for Microfinance" (Washington, D.C.: Consultative Group to Assist the Poorest, 2000).

7. See David Hulme, "Client Exits (Dropouts) from East African Micro-Finance Institutions" (Kampala: Micro-Save Africa, 1999).

8. Anita Campion and Victoria White, *Institutional Metamorphosis: Transformation of Microfinance NGOs into Regulated Financial Institutions*, Occasional Paper No. 4 (Washington, D.C.: MicroFinance Network, 1999), 79.

9. Robert Peck Christen, "Commercialization and Mission Drift: The Transformation of Microfinance in Latin America," draft (Washington, D.C.: Consultative Group to Assist the Poorest, 2000), 4.

10. For a fuller discussion of these issues, see Elisabeth Rhyne and Robert Peck Christen, "Microfinance Enters the Marketplace" (Washington, D.C.: United States Agency for International Development, 1999).

11. Christen, "Commercialization."

12. Author's calculation, based on Asofin, Cipame and Finrural, *Microfinanzas: Boletin Financiero* (July 1998 and June 1999).

13. Christen, "Commercialization," 14.

14. Graham A. N. Wright, Robert Christen, and Imran Matin, "ASA's Culture, Competition and Choice: Introducing Savings Services into a MicroCredit Institution," draft (Kampala: Micro-Save Africa, 2000), section 6.7.

15. *New York Times*, April 9, 2000, BU 10.

16. For example, the World Bank's *World Development Report 1989* on financial-sector development and subsequent policy paper, known as the Levy Report, were extraordinarily influential in changing development institution behavior.

BIBLIOGRAPHY

History, Economy, and Politics of Bolivia

Bauer, Richard, and Sally Bowen. *The Bolivian Formula: From State Capitalism to Capitalisation.* Chile: McGraw-Hill/Interamericana de Chile, Ltda., 1997.

Buechler, Hans, and Judith-Maria Buechler. *The World of Sofía Velasquez: The Autobiography of a Bolivian Market Vendor.* New York: Columbia University Press, 1996.

Grebe Lopez, Horst. "The Private Sector and Democratisation." Unpublished paper. La Paz, 1998.

Instituto Nacional de Estadísticas de Bolívia. Website: www.ine.gov.bo.

Klein, Herbert S. *Bolivia: The Evolution of a Multi-Ethnic Society.* Second Edition. New York: Oxford University Press, 1992.

Mitchell, Christopher. *The Legacy of Populism in Bolivia: From the MNR to Military Rule.* New York: Praeger Publishers, 1977.

Müller and Associates. "Bolívia: Hacia el siglo XXI: Opportunidades para el crecimiento." *Informe Confidencial.* No. 112. La Paz, September 1997.

Müller and Associates. "Evaluacion del Sistema Financiero Nacional." *Informe Confidencial.* No. 115. La Paz, March-April 1998.

Sachs, Jeffrey, and Juan Antonio Morales. *Bolivia: 1952-1986.* International Center for Economic Growth. San Francisco: Institute for Contemporary Studies Press, 1988.

Superintendencia de Bancos y Entidades Financieras. *Boletin Informativo.* No. 124. La Paz: December 1998. Subsequent supplements from website: www.superbancos-bo.org.

Wils, Frits, ed. *Non-Governmental Organizations and Their Networks in Bolivia.* The Netherlands: Gemeenschappelijk Overleg Medefinanciering, 1995.

World Bank. *Bolivia: Poverty, Equity, and Income: Selected Policies for Expanding Earning Opportunities for the Poor.* Report No. 15272-BO. 2 volumes. Washington, D.C.: World Bank, February 1996.

World Bank. *Bolivia Poverty Report*. Report No. 8643-BO. Washington, D.C.: World Bank, 1990.

World Bank. *Economic Memorandum on Bolivia*. Report No. 5680-BO. Washington, D.C.: World Bank, 1985.

World Bank. "Memorandum of the President of the International Development Association and the International Finance Corporation to the Executive Directors on a Country Assistance Strategy of the World Bank Group for the Republic of Bolivia." Report No. 17890-BO. Washington, D.C.: World Bank, May 1998.

Microfinance and Microenterprise in Bolivia

Asofin, Cipame, and Finrural. *Microfinanzas: Boletin Financiero*. Various years.

Beasley, Anne, and Fernando Mollinedo. "Results of a Nationwide Survey of Micro and Small Entrepreneurs Who Have Been Receiving Credit." Unpublished paper. Washington, D.C.: USAID, February 1993.

Berthoud, Olivier, and Walter Milligan. *Sector Informal Urbano y Crédito: Bolivia 1995*. La Paz: CEDLA and COTESU-NOGUB, 1995.

Casanovas Sainz, Roberto, and Silvia Escobar de Pabón. *Los Trabajadores por Cuenta Propia in La Paz: Funcionamiento de las Unidades Económicas, Situación Laboral e Ingresos*. La Paz: Centro de Estudios Para el Desarrollo Laboral y Agrario (CEDLA), 1988.

Escobar de Pabón, Silvia. *Crisis, Política Económica y Dinámica de los Sectores Semiempresarial y Familiar: La Paz—Cochabamba—Santa Cruz, 1985-1989*. La Paz: Centro de Estudios Para el Desarrollo Laboral y Agrario (CEDLA), 1990.

Funda-Pro. "Annual Report 1997." La Paz, 1998.

Funda-Pro. *El desarrollo de las microfinanzas en Bolivia*. Serie Crédito No. 2. La Paz, 1998.

Funda-Pro. *El problema de las guarantias en el crédito para la pequena y la microempresa en Bolivia*. Serie Crédito No. 1. La Paz, 1997.

González-Vega, Claudio, Richard L. Meyer, Sergio Navajas, Jorge Rodriguez Meza, Mark Schreiner, and Guillermo F. Monje. "Bolivia's Microfinance Market Niches: Clientele Profiles." Columbus, Ohio: Rural Finance Program, Ohio State University, June 1996.

González-Vega, Claudio, Mark Schreiner, Sergio Navajas, Jorge Rodriguez Meza, and Richard L. Meyer. "A Primer on Bolivian Experiences in Microfinance: An Ohio State Perspective." Columbus, Ohio: Rural Finance Program, Ohio State University, no date.

Government of Bolivia. "Proyecto de Decreto Supremo, para reglamentar aspectos normativos de la Ley de Propriedad y Crédito Popular, en los aspectos de Microcrédito y Fortalecimiento de las Entidades Financieras no Bancarias." Draft. La Paz, 1999.

Hochschwender, James. "Preliminary Analysis of Microfinance Institutions in Bolivia." Microenterprise Innovation Project, Microserve Delivery Order 3. Washington, D.C.: Chemonics, June 1997.

Jackelen, Henry, Robert Blayney, and John H. Magill. "Evaluation and Preliminary Project Design for the USAID/Bolivia Micro and Small Enterprise Development Program." Washington, D.C.: Development Alternatives, Inc., September 1987.

Lee, Nanci. "What Bolivian Micro Finance Programs Can Learn from Participants About Rural Livelihood Strategies." Master's thesis. University of Guelph, 1997.

McKnelly, Barbara. "Impact Study of Credit with Education in Bolivia." Research Paper No. 5. Davis, Calif.: Freedom from Hunger, 1998.

Ministry of Finance (FONDESIF). "Microcredit, the Pillar of Opportunities." La Paz: Government of Bolivia, 1998.

Mosley, Paul, "Microfinance and Poverty: Bolivia Case Study." Background paper for the World Development Report 2000/01, AIMS paper. Washington, D.C.: Management Systems International, May 1999.

Navajas, Sergio, and Mark Schreiner. "Apex Organizations and the Growth of Microfinance in Bolivia." CGAP-OSU Research Project on Microfinance Apex Mechanisms. Columbus, Ohio: Ohio State University, Department of Agricultural, Environmental and Development Economics, September 1998.

Navajas, Sergio, Richard L. Meyer, Claudio González-Vega, Mark Schreiner, and Jorge Rodriguez Meza. "Poverty and Microfinance in Bolivia." Economics and Sociology Occasional Paper No. 2347. Columbus, Ohio: Ohio State University, Department of Agricultural, Environmental and Development Economics, December 1996.

Olmos, Herberto. "Movilización de Ahorro en Mercados Financieros Emergentes (Resumen)." Unpublished paper. La Paz: Finrural, 1998.

Rock, Rachel. "Bolivia." In *Regulation and Supervision of Microfinance Institutions, Case Studies*, edited by Craig Churchill. Occasional Paper No. 2. Toronto: The Microfinance Network, 1997.

Rodriquez Auad, Tania. "Autosostenibilidad Financiera en Instituciones de Microfinanzas en Bolivia." Serie Crédito No. 3. La Paz: Funda-Pro, 1998.

Trigo Loubiere, Jacques. "Supervision and Regulation of Microfinance Institutions: The Bolivian Experience." In *From Margin to Mainstream: The Regulation and Supervision of Microfinance*, edited by Rachel Rock and Maria Otero. Monograph Series No. 11. Cambridge, Mass.: Acción International, January 1997.

Viceministerio de Microempresa and Fundación para la Producción. *Microempresa vs. Pobreza, un desafío imposible?* La Paz: Government of Bolivia, 1998.

Wisniwski, Sylvia. "Formas de ahorro y demanda potencial para ahorro institucionalizado en las areas rurales de Bolivia." La Paz: EDOBOL, 1995.

World Bank. *How Legal Restrictions on Collateral Limit Access to Credit in Bolivia*. Report No. 13873-BO. Washington, D.C.: World Bank, 1994.

Individual Microfinance Institutions

Banco Solidario, "Memoria 1997." La Paz, 1998.

Banco Solidario, "Memoria 1998." La Paz, 1999.

Caja Los Andes, "Memoria 1997." La Paz, 1998.

Cohen, Monique. "Bolivia: Loan Use by Pro Mujer Clients." Unpublished USAID paper. July 1999.

Drake, Deborah, and Maria Otero. *Alchemists for the Poor: NGOs as Financial Institutions*. Monograph Series No. 6. Cambridge, Mass.: Acción International, October 1992.

FADES. "Memoria 1997." La Paz, 1998.

Fidler, Peter. "Bolivia. Assessing the Performance of Banco Solidario." Sustainable Banking with the Poor. Washington, D.C.: World Bank, 1998.

FIE. "Centro de Fomento a Iniciativas Económicas." La Paz: FIE, 1995.

Frankiewicz, Cheryl. *Building Institutional Capacity: The Story of PRODEM, 1987-1999*. Toronto: Calmeadow, 2001.

Glosser, Amy. "The Creation of BancoSol in Bolivia." In *The New World of Microenterprise Finance: Building Healthy Financial Institutions for the Poor*, edited by Maria Otero and Elisabeth Rhyne. West Hartford, Conn.: Kumarian Press, 1994.

Krützfeldt S., Hermann. "Banco Solidario, S.A." In *El reto de las microfinanzas en América Latina: La visión actual*, edited by Claudio González-Vega et al. Corporación Andina de Fomento, 1997.

Mosley, Paul. "Metamorphosis from NGO to Commercial Bank: The Case of BancoSol in Bolivia." In *Finance Against Poverty*, volume 2, edited by David Hulme and Paul Mosley. London: Routledge, 1996.

Poyo, Jeffrey, and Robin Young, "Commercialization of Microfinance: The Cases of Banco Económico and Fondo Financiero Privado FA$$IL." Microenterprise Best Practices Project. Bethesda, Md.: Development Alternatives, Inc., 1999.

Prodem. "Twelve Years Promoting and Developing the Microenterprise Sector." La Paz, 1998.

Pro Mujer. "Graduating Communal Bankers: Pro Mujer's Program in Bolivia." La Paz, September 1994.

Ramírez, M. Pilar. "Fondo Financiero Privado FIE, S.A. Private Financial Fund Bolivia." In *Seminar Reader, Second Annual Seminar on New Development Finance*. Frankfurt, Ohio: Ohio State University, International Project Consult, Development Alternatives, et al., September 1998.

Rhyne, Elisabeth, and Linda Rotblatt. *What Makes Them Tick? Exploring the Anatomy of Major Microfinance Organizations*. Acción Monograph Series No. 9. Somerville, Mass.: Acción International, 1994.

Solares de Valenzuela, Mery. "Caja de Ahorro y Préstamo Los Andes." In *El reto de las microfinanzas en América Latina: La visión actual*, edited by Claudio González-Vega, Fernando Prado Guachalla, and Tomás Miller Sanabria. Caracas: Corporación Andina de Fomento, 1997.

Velasco, Carmen. Presentation on ProMujer. Unpublished. La Paz: ProMujer, 1998.

General Microfinance and Other Sources

Acción International. *Annual Report 1999*. Somerville, Mass., 2000.

Acción International and the Calmeadow Foundation. *An Operational Guide for*

Micro-Enterprise Projects. Toronto: The Calmeadow Foundation, 1988.

Berenbach, Shari, and Craig Churchill. "Regulation and Supervision of Microfinance Institutions: Experience from Latin America, Asia and Africa." Occasional Paper No. 1. Washington, D.C.: MicroFinance Network, 1997.

Berenbach, Shari, and Diego Guzman. "The Solidarity Group Experience Worldwide." In *The New World of Microenterprise Finance: Building Healthy Financial Institutions for the Poor,* edited by Maria Otero and Elisabeth Rhyne. West Hartford, Conn.: Kumarian Press, 1994.

Bosworth, Barry, Andrew Carron, and Elisabeth H. Rhyne. *The Economics of Federal Credit Programs.* Washington, D.C.: The Brookings Institution, 1986.

Campion, Anita, and Victoria White. *Institutional Metamorphosis: Transformation of Microfinance NGOs into Regulated Financial Institutions.* Occasional Paper No. 4. Washington, D.C.: MicroFinance Network, 1999.

Christen, Robert Peck. *Banking Services for the Poor: Managing for Financial Success.* Cambridge, Mass.: Acción International, 1997.

Christen, Robert Peck. "Commercialization and Mission Drift: The Transformation of Microfinance in Latin America." Unpublished draft. Washington, D.C.: Consultative Group to Assist the Poorest, May 2000.

Christen, Robert Peck, and Richard Rosenberg. "The Rush to Regulate: Legal Frameworks for Microfinance. Washington D.C.: Consultative Group to Assist the Poorest, 2000.

Churchill, Craig F. *Client-Focused Lending: The Art of Individual Lending.* Toronto: Calmeadow Foundation, 1999.

Cross, John C. Website on the informal sector: www.openair.org/cross/cross.html.

DeSoto, Hernando, *El Otro Sendero.* Buenos Aires: Sudamérica, 1987.

Dunford, Christopher. "Microfinance: A Means to What End? Sustained Pursuit of Different Objectives for Microfinance." Speech. Davis, Calif.: Freedom from Hunger, 1998.

Fairbanks, Michael, and Stace Lindsay. *Plowing the Sea: Nurturing the Hidden Sources of Growth in the Developing World.* Boston: Harvard Business School Press, 1997.

Hirschman, A. O. *Development Projects Observed.* Washington, D.C.: The Brookings Institution, 1995.

Hulme, David. "Client Exits (Dropouts) from East African Micro-Finance Institutions." Kampala: Micro-Save Africa, 1999.

Ledgerwood, Joanna. *Microfinance Handbook: An Institutional and Financial Perspective.* Sustainable Banking with the Poor. Washington, D.C.: World Bank, 1999.

Meagher, Kate. "Crisis, Informalization, and the Urban Informal Sector in Sub-Saharan Africa." *Development and Change* 26 (1995). Oxford: Institute of Social Studies: 259-84.

The Microbanking Bulletin, no. 4. Toronto: Calmeadow, 1999.

Microcredit Summit, "Empowering Women with Microcredit: 2000 Microcredit Summit Campaign Report." www.microcreditsummit.org.

Nelson, Candace, Barbara McKnelly, Kathleen Stack and Lawrence Yanovitch, "Village Banking: The State of the Practice," Washington, D.C.: SEEP, 1995.

Otero, Maria. *The Solidarity Group Concept: Its Characteristics and Significance for Urban Informal Sector Activities*, Acción Monograph Series No. 1. New York: PACT, 1986.

Otero, Maria, and Elisabeth Rhyne, eds. *The New World of Microenterprise Finance: Building Healthy Financial Institutions for the Poor.* West Hartford, Conn.: Kumarian Press, 1994.

Paxton, Julia. "A Worldwide Inventory of Microfinance Institutions." Sustainable Banking with the Poor. Washington, D.C.: World Bank, 1996.

Portes, Alejandro, Manuel Castells and Lauren A. Benton, eds. *The Informal Economy: Studies in Advanced and Less Developed Countries.* Baltimore: Johns Hopkins University Press, 1989.

Rhyne, Elisabeth, and Robert Peck Christen. "Microfinance Enters the Marketplace." Washington, D.C.: United States Agency for International Development, 1999.

Schmidt, Reinhard H., and Claus-Peter Zeitinger, "Creating Viable Financial Services for Poor Target Groups in LDCs: The Experience of NGOs." Sustainable Banking with the Poor Occasional Paper No. 8. Washington, D.C.: World Bank, 1996.

Sen, Amartya. *Development as Freedom.* New York: Alfred A. Knopf, 1999.

Steege, Jean, "The Rise and Fall of Corposol: Lessons Learned from the Challenges of Managing Growth." Bethesda, Md.: Development Alternatives Inc., 1998.

Tendler, Judith, *Ventures in the Informal Sector and How They Worked Out in Brazil,* AID Evaluation Special Study No. 12. Washington, D.C.: U.S. Agency for International Development, 1983.

World Bank. *Assessing Aid: What Works, What Doesn't and Why.* New York: Oxford University Press, 1998.

World Bank, *World Development Report 1989, Financial Systems and Development.* New York: Oxford University Press, 1989.

World Bank, *World Development Report 1990, Poverty.* New York: Oxford University Press, 1990.

World Bank, *World Development Report 2000/2001, Attacking Poverty.* New York: Oxford University Press, 2001.

Wright, Graham A. N., Robert Christen, and Imran Matin. "ASA's Culture, Competition and Choice: Introducing Savings Services into a MicroCredit Institution." Draft. Kampala: Micro-Save Africa, 2000.

INDEX

ABOUT THE AUTHOR

ELISABETH RHYNE has been involved with microfinance since witnessing early experiments while living in Kenya in the mid-1980s. She has since been one of the leading thinkers and writers on the subject, whose publications have helped move the field forward (including *The New World of Microfinance*, with Maria Otero, published by Kumarian Press). She has influenced the field directly through her ten years of leadership in the US Agency for International Development's microfinance programs, having been responsible for much of USAID's microfinance research, policy work, and financial support to practitioners. As an independent consultant, she has advised a range of microfinance institutions, international NGOs, and governments. She is currently a member of the senior management of Acción International. Dr. Rhyne has a bachelor's degree from Stanford University and a master's and Ph.D. from Harvard University's Kennedy School of Government.

Also from Kumarian Press...

Microfinance

The New World of Microenterprise Finance
Building Healthy Financial Institutions for the Poor
María Otero, Elisabeth Rhyne

Defying the Odds: Banking for the Poor
Eugene Versluysen

Conflict Resolution, Environment, Gender Studies, Global Issues, Globalization, International Development

Aiding Violence: The Development Enterprise in Rwanda
(Winner of the 1999 Herskovits Award by the African Studies Association) Peter Uvin

Bound: Living in a Globalized World
Scott Sernau

Capitalism and Justice: Envisioning Social and Economic Fairness
John Isbister

The Cuban Way: Capitalism, Communism and Confrontation
(Named 'Outstanding Academic Title' by CHOICE Magazine) Ana Julia Jatar-Hausman

Exploring the Gaps: Vital Links Between Trade, Environment and Culture
James R. Lee

New Roles and Relevance: Development NGOs and the Challenge of Change
Edited by David Lewis and Tina Wallace

Patronage or Partnership: Local Capacity Building in Humanitarian Crises
Edited by Ian Smillie for the Humanitarianism and War Project

Reconcilable Differences: Turning Points in Ethnopolitical Conflict
Edited by Sean Byrne and Cynthia L. Irvin

Transcending Neoliberalism: Community-Based Development in Latin America
Edited by Henry Veltmeyer and Anthony O'Malley

War's Offensive on Women
The Humanitarian Challenge in Bosnia, Kosovo and Afghanistan
Julie A. Mertus for the Humanitarianism and War Project

Visit Kumarian Press at **www.kpbooks.com** or
call **toll-free 800.289.2664** for a complete catalog.

KUMARIAN PRESS

Kumarian Press, located in Bloomfield, Connecticut, is dedicated to publishing and distributing books and other media that will have a positive social and economic impact on the lives of peoples living in "Third World" conditions no matter where they live.